FOOD GROWN RIGHT, IN YOUR BACKYARD

FOOD GROWN RIGHT, IN YOUR BACKYARD

A BEGINNER'S GUIDE TO GROWING CROPS AT HOME

COLIN McCRATE & BRAD HALM

CO-FOUNDERS OF
SEATTLE URBAN FARM CO.

PHOTOGRAPHY BY HILARY DAHL

SKIPSTONE

Published by Skipstone, an imprint of The Mountaineers Books
Printed in China

First printing 2012
15 14 13 12   5 4 3 2 1

Copy Editor: Barry Foy
Design: Jane Jeszeck / www.jigsawseattle.com
Illustrations © Elara Tanguy

ISBN (paperback): 978-1-59485-683-9
ISBN (ebook): 978-1-59485-684-6

Library of Congress Cataloging-in-Publication Data on file

Skipstone books may be purchased for corporate, educational,
or other promotional sales. For special discounts and information, contact our Sales Department at 800-553-4453 or
mbooks@mountaineersbooks.org.

Skipstone
1001 SW Klickitat Way
Suite 201
Seattle, Washington 98134
206.223.6303
www.skipstonebooks.org
www.mountaineersbooks.org

LIVE LIFE. MAKE RIPPLES.

In memory of Brendan and Marcus,
without whom Seattle Urban Farm Company
and this book would never have
been possible.

Contents

INTRODUCTION

We love to grow food. We think that once you learn how, you'll love it too.

Growing food isn't something that came naturally to us. We both grew up in Midwestern suburbs, with industrial cities in one direction and endless acres of corn in the other. Neither of us gave much thought to the food we ate, other than thinking that we always wanted more of it. We spent our youths like anyone else—playing sports, trying to act cool, and sitting in after-school detention.

It wasn't until college that we got acquainted with food in its natural setting. We met at Denison University while working at the Homestead, a vegetable garden located off campus and run entirely by students. After we'd spent most of our college years searching for a meaningful vision for our lives, the Homestead finally provided us with a purpose. That purpose was growing: growing long hair, growing long beards, and growing organic vegetables.

Gardening at the Homestead was a haphazard affair to say the least—we probably killed twice as many plants as we grew. But despite the many factors limiting our success (most of which we would prefer to keep off the record), in time something dawned on us: Growing food was an amazing experience. We could only imagine how amazing it would be if we actually knew what we were doing!

Once out of school (yes, we both graduated), we went our separate ways. But both of us pursued agriculture and studied under skilled professional growers. Over the years, we became immersed in farming life and learned organic crop management through hands-on experience. In 2007, we reunited to start Seattle Urban Farm Company, a business that helps people learn to grow their own food at home.

When we started the company, we had no idea whether the business would succeed. Sure, we knew how to grow vegetables, but could we help people learn to do it in their own yards? Would anyone hire us to find out? Would we have to cut our hair?

Somewhat surprisingly to us, we had great results with our first few customers. After that, word got around quickly, and the company grew faster than we could have imagined. Over time, we've expanded to work with restaurants, schools, and businesses, although the majority of our clients are still people who want to grow food at home.

Since Seattle Urban Farm Company's founding, we've guided hundreds of novice home farmers through their first growing seasons. We've learned that most people feel intimidated at the thought of growing vegetables, because they don't know where to start. Our approach is to simplify the process. Once that happens, it isn't long before our customers realize how easy and rewarding growing their own food can be.

This book walks you through that same process, helping you plan, plant, and maintain your garden in a simple, straightforward way that maximizes your chances of success from the very beginning. We're certain that if you start small, choose only a handful of your favorite crops, and spend only the amount of time that's practical for you, you will enjoy your gardening experience and produce even better results than you expected.

You don't have to study with professional growers for years, as we did, to be a successful gardener. This book distills our years of food-growing and garden-building experience into an easy-to-understand guide for new backyard farmers.

Every new gardener has a different reason for getting started. Some want a more nutritious diet, and others want to save money on grocery bills. Some are serious cooks who have discovered that fresher food tastes better, while others are suspicious of a food system that recalls large quantities of vegetables every year because of contamination. Many parents start gardening because they want their children to understand where food comes from. We also know people who see gardening as a way to build community and meet their neighbors, or who want to spend more time outdoors, or who just think gardening is fun.

Regardless of their original intention, we find that, as people become more involved in growing food, they start to embrace all of those ideas. Seeing that transformation is one of the things we really love about our job. We hope you too will experience all the benefits of gardening, and that you'll find the simple, intangible joy that can only be experienced when you "grow your own."

All of the information in this book is based on organic farming and gardening principles. Organic growers do not use chemical fertilizers, pesticides, or herbicides. Instead, they use compost and other natural amendments to build healthy soil. Organically managed gardens can grow beautiful, delicious crops and help preserve and restore our environment.

part I

GARDEN PROFILES

What Do You Want From Your Garden?

One of the first things we do with every new customer is assess their property and help them decide which areas are best suited for a garden. We've visited hundreds of homes over the years, and believe it or not, we have never seen a yard in which growing food was impossible. While some properties offer vast areas to work with and others provide only a small deck or porch, we're convinced that nearly every home has the potential for growing at least a few fruits and vegetables.

Choosing a site is only the first step, of course. Then comes deciding on the style and design of the garden, on how it will be watered, and so on. A variety of factors influences these decisions, and they vary from case to case. Once all that's figured out, the real hands-on work begins.

Following are profiles of five gardens we've built over the years (though the names of people and pets have been changed to protect the innocent). Although each is unique in its way, we've chosen these examples because they illustrate conditions we encounter again and again when people are setting up their first home gardens. Your scenario may not be exactly like any one of them, but certain elements are bound to sound familiar. Seeing how other people went about it will help you visualize your own home-gardening project.

GARDEN PROFILE 1
Mounded Raised Beds

CHOOSING THE SITE

Emily and Ben had a nearly perfect property for growing food. Their house was surrounded by sunny lawn on all sides, and there were a few small trees scattered throughout the yard, so they could put their garden almost anywhere. They were first-time gardeners, but they loved to eat vegetables on a regular basis and were excited about the idea of having extra produce for canning and freezing.

Emily and Ben wanted the garden space to be flexible, and they wanted to avoid buying extra materials if possible. There was an old overgrown ornamental garden in their side yard that was perfect for a vegetable garden because it was close to the back door and visible from the kitchen—two of the most important factors to consider when choosing a site are visibility and proximity to the house. We decided to clear this space and create a simple garden of mounded raised beds.

Emily and Ben make dinner at home several nights a week, so we decided to set up five garden beds. Each bed is 4 by 10 feet long, giving them 200 square feet of planting space, perfect for an ample supply of vegetables for fresh eating and a little extra for preserving.

BUILDING THE GARDEN

To get started, we cleared the overgrown vegetation from the site, then marked a 30- by 14-foot rectangle with stakes and flour (our version of the lines on a baseball diamond). We cleared the remaining grass and vegetation inside the rectangle to create an open patch of bare soil.

Next, we marked the corners of the beds with stakes and forked up the soil in the beds. We added a four-inch layer of compost to the beds and mixed it into the existing soil to create a healthy environment for crops (you'll read much more on that in chapter 4: Preparing Your Soil). After making a few other additions to the soil, we mulched the paths with bark mulch and set up a simple two-foot-high fence with vinyl-coated wire and metal posts to keep Emily and Ben's wily chocolate Lab from running amok in the garden.

IRRIGATION

Emily and Ben wanted to keep things simple for their first year, so they set up an oscillating sprinkler in the middle of the garden, controlled by a hose thread timer. They don't get much rain, so they set the timer to run for 25 minutes every other day.

HOW IT TURNED OUT

After their first season, Emily and Ben considered their garden a major success. Apart from planting too many beans and too few beets, they felt they had plenty of their favorite crops to eat. Now they plan to add two new beds, so that they can grow extra leeks and pie pumpkins for winter storage.

OPPOSITE TOP LEFT: Emily and Ben's garden site, before installation. OPPOSITE TOP RIGHT: Mounded raised beds, after installation. OPPOSITE BOTTOM: Mounded raised beds, after planting.

GARDEN PROFILE 2
Comb-Shaped Beds

CHOOSING THE SITE

Karen had just bought a house with a small, sunny yard. She wanted to grow some of her own food but had a busy work schedule, so she needed a garden that would take a minimal amount of time to manage. The backyard was too shady to grow food, so we decided to build the garden along the edge of the front yard.

The brick wall along the property line provided a natural edge for one side of the garden, and the narrow profile we proposed would leave some open yard space for her Adirondack chair. The garden would have about 70 square feet of planting space, just right for her needs.

BUILDING THE GARDEN

We started by outlining the perimeter of the garden with flour, curving the edge to add a little flair to the bed. After cutting out the sod, we lined the inside perimeter with landscaping rock to keep the grass from creeping back in. We chose a comb shape for the garden, to maximize the usable garden space and make it easy to reach all the plants without stepping in the beds.

After marking the paths, we forked up the soil, mixed in a layer of compost, and raked it smooth. We tested the soil and found that it was perfect for vegetables, so we put some bark mulch on the paths and called it good.

IRRIGATION

We used quarter-inch emitter tubing to irrigate Karen's garden because we were dealing with some oddly shaped beds—it is very easy to make curving lines with quarter-inch tubing. We ran the main line from a faucet on the side of the house and set the timer to run for 30 minutes, four times per week. When it's hot and dry, Karen checks on her direct-seeded crops every day and gives them additional hand watering until they emerge.

HOW IT TURNED OUT

Karen surprised even herself by declaring that she needs to plant more kale in the garden next year. She felt that having fresh vegetables right outside the front door motivated her to cook more often and to incorporate things like fresh herbs into even the simplest meals. As soon as she harvested her last crop, she was already gearing up for the next spring.

OPPOSITE TOP: Karen's yard, before installation.
OPPOSITE BOTTOM: A comb-shaped bed, after installation.

GARDEN PROFILE 3
Wood-Framed Beds

CHOOSING THE SITE

Curran was renting a home in a semiurban neighborhood, and he wanted a garden for growing greens and his kids' favorite food, potatoes. He was an avid cook, but it was his first time growing food, so he wanted a garden that would be easy to manage.

His yard space was very limited: The front yard was steeply sloped, and the backyard was partially shaded by a tree. The only sunny space was a 22-by 9-foot gravel strip along the driveway. This was clearly the best site for the garden.

BUILDING THE GARDEN

Three four- by eight-foot beds (96 square feet of planting space) would be a good size for Curran to manage and would fit perfectly on the gravel strip. But we didn't want to remove the gravel, so we decided to build cedar-framed raised beds that we could set directly on top of it. This would also make maintenance easy and keep the space looking neat and tidy.

We made the beds 16 inches deep, so the plants would have plenty of soil to grow in. We filled each one with one and one-half cubic yards of garden soil mix.

IRRIGATION

Half-inch emitter tubing works great for wood-framed raised beds, so we ran a main line from a faucet around the corner and into the beds. We put a valve on each bed, in case Curran decided to leave one bed unplanted in the future.

HOW IT TURNED OUT

Curran wanted a wide variety of crops so he could try "a little bit of a lot of things." He enjoyed having a single zucchini plant, four basil plants, a few tomatoes, and a patch of potatoes (among others). He started harvesting greens from the garden in June, and from then on always had some sort of vegetable to pick, all the way until October.

GARDEN PROFILE 4
Limited Space, Containers, and Existing Beds

CHOOSING THE SITE

Devin and Kerry lived in an older home amid a beautifully designed landscape. Their backyard was covered by a stone patio and had no usable garden space. Their front and side yards got only moderate sun and were occupied by landscaping beds filled with ornamental plants.

When looking for a garden site, we noticed that the best sun on the property was along the south side of the house. This side also had a great microclimate because it was protected by the neighbor's house and the garage. Most of the space on the south side was taken up by the driveway, but there was a small landscaping bed with only ground cover growing in it. This bed was clearly the best spot for a vegetable garden.

OPPOSITE TOP LEFT: The sunniest spot in Curran's yard was a gravel strip along the driveway. OPPOSITE TOP RIGHT: Wood-framed beds, after installation. OPPOSITE BOTTOM: Wood-framed beds, after planting. RIGHT: Devin and Kerry's garden site, before planting.

BUILDING THE GARDEN

After testing the soil to make sure it was lead free, we cleared the bed, turned in about two cups of lime, and added a four-inch layer of compost. We also set eight large ceramic containers by the house along the driveway.

IRRIGATION

Fortunately, an easily accessible faucet was mounted on the south side of the house. We set up a drip system, with drip tapes for the bed along the house, and quarter-inch emitter tubing for the pots. We set the timer to run for 15 minutes, three times

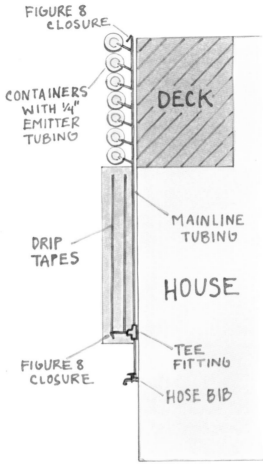

FIGURE 8 CLOSURE

CONTAINERS WITH ¼" EMITTER TUBING

DECK

DRIP TAPES

MAINLINE TUBING

HOUSE

FIGURE 8 CLOSURE

TEE FITTING

HOSE BIB

a day, to keep the containers from drying out. This sent extra water to the mounded bed, but that was actually helpful because the bed was under the eave of the house and didn't get any rain.

ABOVE: Limited-space garden, after planting.
ABOVE RIGHT: Although this garden has various elements, it was possible to set up a very simple irrigation system from the hose bib.

HOW IT TURNED OUT

Devin and Kerry were pleased with their first year's garden. It was only about 32 square feet including the containers, but it grew a surprising amount of basil, tomatoes, carrots, and salad greens. They were amazed that the plants just kept growing all summer long even after they had started fruiting, but they enjoyed pruning the plants to keep them in control. They especially liked their Sungold cherry tomatoes (one of our favorites too!).

GARDEN PROFILE 5
Container Garden on a Patio

CHOOSING THE SITE

To eliminate the need for a work commute to the local college, Noah lived in a small townhouse close to downtown. He didn't have any outdoor ground space, but he did have a patio in his backyard that was just right for a small container garden.

Noah's patio faced west, so although it was shaded in the morning, it was blazingly hot in the afternoon. That meant he needed to water his garden frequently and might not be able to grow cool-loving crops such as lettuce and spinach.

BUILDING THE GARDEN

Given the nature of Noah's property, our only option was to create a container garden. There was no water supply on the patio, so Noah decided he'd water the pots with a watering can that he filled from his kitchen sink. His flexible work schedule would allow him to run home to water on hot afternoons.

Setting up a container garden can be messy, so we laid down painter's plastic to protect the carpet while transporting the materials around the townhouse.

BELOW: Noah's backyard patio, before the containers.

IRRIGATION

Watering by hand worked well for Noah because of his attentiveness to the garden. He often needed to water two or three times a day.

ABOVE: Container garden, after planting.

HOW IT TURNED OUT

Noah doesn't have as much planting space as he'd like, but he feels he is doing the best he can with what's available. He can grow a surprising amount of food in just 10 square feet of container space. He plans to add another container next year, so he can grow rosemary for his summer barbecues. He's also thinking about buying self-watering inserts for the containers so he doesn't have to water as frequently.

part II

BUILDING A GARDEN

"Agriculture is our wisest pursuit, because it will in the end contribute
most to real wealth, good morals, and happiness."

~ Thomas Jefferson ~

We hope the garden profiles have provided a little bit of insight into the strategies we use in planning and designing a garden. In the next several chapters we will explain the process in more detail, to help you find the best site, size, and design for your own home garden. The information is arranged in the order in which it should be addressed: Find the best site, determine the right size, decide on a design and bed type, examine your soil, and then get started building!

1
CHOOSING A SITE

CHOOSING A GARDEN SITE can be a big decision, but it doesn't have to be a difficult one. This chapter looks at the key factors that should guide your quest for the ideal garden site, as well as some additional considerations you can bring into play if you have multiple sites to choose from.

If any aspects of the garden profiles seemed familiar, use that information to help you evaluate your own yard, balcony, rooftop, or broken-down pickup truck (yes, you can build a vegetable garden in a broken-down pickup truck—we've done it!).

KEY FACTORS IN GARDEN SITE SELECTION
SUNLIGHT

The first and most important thing to look for when you're deciding where to put your garden is exposure to the sun. In some parts of the country (Arizona, for example), plants actually require shade from the intense summer sun, but generally speaking you want all the sunlight you can get. Nearly every fruit and vegetable plant will benefit from getting as much sunlight as possible.

Although you can remedy almost any other problem a garden site might have (poor soil, poor drainage, lack of water), you can't change the time of sunrise and sunset. You're also likely to have difficulty getting the sun to shine someplace it doesn't shine now (envision cutting down large trees or tearing down your neighbor's house). So when you're looking for a site, keep in mind that it is *essential* that your garden receive a minimum of six hours of sunlight each day at the height of the summer.

Finding the Sun

You may already know which part of your property gets the most sun, or you may never have thought about it before. Once you start looking, you may be surprised which areas are the sunniest. To find them, take a walk around your yard with these considerations in mind:

OPPOSITE: Wood-framed beds in a sunny front yard. RIGHT: "Crops for Clunkers" on display at the Northwest Flower & Garden Show.

WINTER VS. SUMMER

Because of the high latitude of the northern United States, the arc of the sun changes dramatically there from winter to summer. The sun sits much lower in the sky during the winter, so shade extends much farther to the north, east, and west than it does in the summer. Bear this in mind if you're looking for a garden site in the winter: A spot that is shady in December may get good sun in midsummer. Also remember that deciduous trees (trees that lose their leaves in winter) will create more shade in the summer than in the winter. If, during winter, sunlight is filtering through the naked branches of large trees, remind yourself that those trees will look very different in the middle of July.

Parts of the yard may receive different amounts of sunlight in summer than in winter.

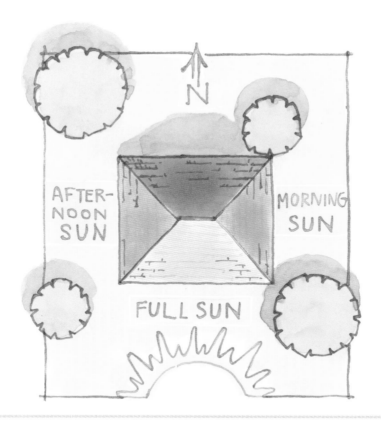

Figure out the orientation of your yard and notice how much shade is cast by tall objects in and around the yard (the house, hedges, sheds, trees in your yard and those in your neighbors' yards).

- The sunniest area may be on any side of your house—north, south, east, or west. It all depends on the house's location, the number and location of nearby trees and fences, and the location of nearby houses.
- If you want to place a garden on the north side of your house, assume that the house will cast a shadow toward the north for a distance equal to its height, and allow enough space between the house and the garden. For example, if your house has a roof 20 feet high, a garden on the north side of it should be at least 20 feet away.

- The house will not cast any shade to the south, so a garden on the south side can be placed as close to the house as you like.
- Southwest exposure is slightly better than southeast exposure, because afternoon sun is generally warmer than morning sun.

When you've found a likely spot for your garden, wait for a clear, sunny day and keep an eye on that area throughout the day. Note what time the area starts getting sun, and what time it becomes shaded. An ideal spot will get sunlight for eight hours or more at the height of the summer (the

longest day of the year being the summer solstice, on or around June 21). Any spot that receives at least six hours of sunlight is a good location for a garden. It's OK if the garden gets six hours of morning sun, or if the sunlight doesn't reach it until midday. The sunlight doesn't need to be continuous; a few hours of midday shade is not a problem, as long as the total sun exposure adds up to six hours. Keep in mind, too, that the actual number of hours of sunlight will change depending on the time of year.

ACCESS AND VISIBILITY

Set up your garden so that it is easy to get to and work in. Ideally, new vegetable beds are not only easily accessible but are visible from your house. Garden maintenance will be much easier if you happen to walk by the garden each day as part of your normal routine. Just like anything else, if your garden is out of sight, it will be out of mind.

ELBOW ROOM

It's very important to separate your garden beds from landscape beds. Although they can be adjacent, you'll find it helpful to set aside space specifically for your vegetables.

Why? Because you'll be treating your garden differently than you treat your landscaped areas. Most vegetable plants are annuals (meaning they grow from seed to harvest in a single season and die in the same season), so your vegetable garden will be replanted every year. To manage your garden properly, you'll need to start each season with a clear garden bed, so that you can add compost and organic fertilizers, and turn in your cover crops, without fear of disturbing perennial plants.

With that in mind, if you expect to plant some perennial vegetables (like asparagus, rhubarb, or artichokes) or perennial herbs (rosemary, sage,

ABOVE: Placing a garden close to your house and in sight will help you remember to check on the plants regularly. OPPOSITE TOP: Unused spaces can seem intimidating at first. OPPOSITE BOTTOM: Once cleared, a space can take on a whole new life.

oregano, etc.), plan to put them in a separate perennial garden bed, or at the extreme edges of your annual vegetable beds.

OTHER FACTORS TO CONSIDER

A simple guideline: If there's a spot on your property that receives significantly more sun than any other, that's where you want to put your garden. You can always adjust the other conditions to make it work. But if you have several very sunny spots to choose from, the following factors will help you narrow down the list.

Grade

If possible, your garden should be flat as well as sunny. A flat plot is easier to work on, and it will be subject to less soil erosion. It's certainly possible to grow crops on a sloped surface, but since you'll be loosening up the soil to set up your garden beds, a sloped site is more vulnerable to erosion over time. The beds may require some sort of retaining structures to ensure that soil doesn't wash away. If your sunniest spot also happens to be a very sloped area, consider building terraces to retain the soil.

Terraces can be very simple, with a row of rocks or a piece of wood along the low side of your garden bed. If the area is very steep, though, you

ABOVE: Make sure your deer fence is tall enough to keep out the highest-leaping animals.

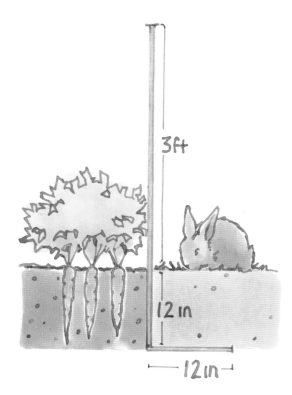

3ft

12 in

├── 12 in ──┤

may need to set up a true retaining wall. Building a retaining wall is beyond the scope of this book. Consider consulting a professional, or pick up a copy of *Walks, Walls & Patio Floors: Build with Brick, Stone, Pavers, Concrete, Tile and More,* by the editors of Sunset Books.

Access to Water

You can't count on rainfall alone to supply sufficient water to sustain a garden. Expect to do some

ABOVE: Many small animals like to dig, so a short fence is much more effective when a portion of it is buried underground.

hand watering, or to set up an irrigation system from your hose bib (outdoor faucet) to ensure that your garden gets the water it needs. The closer your garden is to your house, the easier the watering will be. However, if the best site is far from a hose bib, don't worry—it will just take a little more time and a little extra hose.

Site Clearing

You may want to consider how much work will be necessary to clear the space for your new garden. The goal is to find a space that meets the above criteria while requiring the least amount of work to transition to a workable garden. It's easier to remove sod than to remove a 10 ft. tall hedge, for instance (or a concrete driveway—more on that in the next chapter). Be prepared to make decisions about plants or other landscape features that may need relocating or removal.

Fencing

If you think you may face issues with large garden pests (possibly including your own dog!), take a few minutes to think about fencing. Consider the following:

You may need as much as an 8 ft. high fence to keep deer out of the garden. Alternatively, site the garden in an area that is already deer-proofed.

If rabbits or groundhogs are active in your yard, you may need 2–3 ft. high fencing around the garden area. The fence should also be buried at least 12 inches underground to prevent burrowing.

Very excitable or active dogs have been known to trample newly planted garden beds. Consider whether your dog is likely to frolic in the garden, and fence appropriately.

(Find more information on pests of all sizes and kinds in chapter 23: Garden Problems and Solutions.)

Soil

Soil quality is extremely important to the long-term success of a garden. However, when choosing a site, the soil's current condition is not typically a big concern; chances are, none of the soil in your yard is in good enough shape to grow vegetable crops. Don't worry, though—it can be fixed.

Most yards have similar soil throughout, so you'll probably be dealing with the same soil type in any given location. However, if you have a number of sunny sites to choose from, and one of them happens to have especially dark, loose, crumbly soil, consider that a bonus, and think of it as a good spot for a garden.

One other important consideration is the possibility of soil contamination. Soils around older homes that may have been painted with lead paint, or homes near heavy industrial sites, may be contaminated with heavy metals such as lead or arsenic. Also, treated wood manufactured before 2004 can contain arsenic, so older treated-wood structures may have contaminated nearby soils. If you're worried about potential contaminants, test your soil before deciding on a garden site. (See chapter 4: Preparing Your Soil for general information on testing, and the Resources section for information on how and where to get your testing done.)

ABOVE: A dog fence should be sturdy enough—and tall enough—to keep out excited pets.

OPPOSITE: A productive garden bed can be fit into many different spaces. This wood-framed bed was built against a rock wall.

2

DETERMINING GARDEN SIZE

IT MAY BE THAT YOU DON'T have much of a choice as to how big your garden will be; you will just fill what space you have available. On the other hand, you may have 400,000 acres of sunny real estate at your disposal. Let's figure out what overall size of garden is right for you. Start by answering the following questions:

- How many people are in your household?
- How often do you cook meals at home?
- Do you want extra vegetables to give to friends, neighbors, or food banks?
- Do you hope to put up some of your harvest as frozen or canned goods for later use?
- How much time can you realistically spend in your garden? This book is geared toward the 60-minute-per-week gardener, but maybe you want to spend a little more time than that.

The key is to build a garden small enough that it doesn't hog all your free time but is not so small that you run out of vegetables in the middle of making a BLT. On the next page are some guidelines to help you get started. Note that the numbers we give represent the amount of space actually planted in vegetables; you'll also need to set aside a little bit extra for pathways, so you create a space that is easy to work in.

GEOMETRY LESSONS

"I haven't had a math class in two decades. What the heck does '100 square feet' mean?!"

A square foot is just what it sounds like, a square of space that is 1 foot wide by 1 foot long. To figure out the square footage of a given area, multiply the length of the space by its width. For example, a garden bed 4 feet wide and 8 feet long gives you 32 square feet of gardening space.

What about irregularly shaped spaces? Don't worry about being too precise. You can get a good enough estimate of square footage by measuring an imaginary square or rectangle that roughly covers the area.

OPPOSITE: Rows of maturing crops in a mounded bed garden.

- If you will be the only person eating out of the garden on a regular basis, consider starting in the 50–70 sq. ft. range. A standard 4 × 8 garden bed is 32 sq. ft., so two 4 × 8 beds will give you 64 sq. ft. of planting space (**A**). This is a nice size for a solo beginning gardener.
- A household of two to four people who cook dinner at home several nights a week can use a garden in the 100–150 sq. ft. range. A garden with 120 sq. ft. of space might have two beds at 4 × 15 ft. (**B**) or three at 4 × 8 ft. A garden with approximately 150 sq. ft. of planting space might have three beds each at 4 × 12 ft., or five at 4 × 8 ft.
- A household of four people who love vegetables and plan to cook many dinners at home can easily make use of a garden in the 200 sq. ft. range. This size of garden might have seven

C

D

garden beds that are all 4 × 8 ft. (192 sq. ft.) (**C**), or five at 4 × 10 ft. (200 sq. ft.).

- A household of more than four people, or someone who wants to donate produce to food banks (or do a lot of preserving), might want a garden in the 300–400 sq. ft. range, such as five 4 x 20 ft. beds (**D**).

We recommend that even a vegetable-hungry household start with a 150–200 sq. ft. garden until they have a pretty good understanding of the work involved. A garden larger than that will likely get you out of the "easy-to-manage" maintenance routine and into a slightly bigger commitment.

Remember, smaller is better! You can always expand in the future.

3

DESIGNING YOUR GARDEN

SHAPES, DIMENSIONS, AND PATHWAYS

ONE OF THE EASIEST ASPECTS to get hung up on is the design and layout of the garden. We build beautiful vegetable gardens, but we don't labor over designs for months and months. We evaluate the site, come up with a design that our customer likes, and get to work, usually within a couple of days.

A garden can take any shape you can imagine. It can be a series of straight beds, it can curve and twist throughout your landscape, it can be arranged in geometric patterns like traditional English potager gardens. You can combine these styles or develop a style all your own. Remember, you aren't building a Rube Goldberg machine. If you stick to simple designs, you shouldn't have much trouble coming up with a layout that suits your aesthetic and works for your site. With that in mind, rather than launching into a lengthy discussion of landscape design, we're going to take a practical approach to the two main elements you need to consider: shape and specific dimensions.

3

OPPOSITE: Foreground to background: alyssum, lettuce, cilantro, and kohlrabi.

GARDEN BED SHAPE

Keep it simple! There's no need to get wild with the shape of your garden. Rather than a complex design, let the variety of your vegetation make the space beautiful and provide visual interest.

We find ourselves using certain garden shapes again and again, shapes that, with a little creativity, suit almost any landscape. The first is the **rectangular or square garden**. Gardens built as a series of rectangular beds (or just a single bed) create a great, traditional garden look. Crops can be planted in rows, which adds a very farmlike feature to your yard. Rectangular beds can fit into many yard spaces. If a square garden seems a little rigid, consider offsetting a few beds to create a more relaxed feel.

The **comb-shaped garden** (also called keyhole garden beds) is a design we use when we want to put the garden close to the edge of a yard (out of the way of soccer balls, lawn darts, etc.), usually when there is a fence line, wall, or other linear feature in the landscape that we can build the garden against.

Comb-shaped beds are laid out similarly to the rectangular beds mentioned above, but with an additional perpendicular bed connecting all of the primary beds along the fence line. This makes use of the extra space between the ends of the beds, which would otherwise be wasted, and creates a

nice long bed where you can plant tall crops so they'll be out of the way of the rest of the garden. The perpendicular bed is a great space in which to rotate tomato, bean, and pea crops, plant sunflowers, or trellis squash.

In some cases, the easiest and/or most appropriate thing is either to incorporate the vegetable garden into an existing landscaping bed or create a new bed along similar lines. Such beds are more likely to have curved edges and *organic* shapes ("organic" as in "not geometric"—a usage

LEFT: A comb-shaped garden bed. BELOW: After removing ornamental plants, this garden was placed in the existing curving bed.

unrelated to the underlying concepts of organic gardening)—**curving beds**.

The main thing to keep in mind, as we mentioned earlier, is that your annual crops should have their own separate space. Vegetable crops planted too close to perennial ornamental plants will be outcompeted by the perennials' large root balls. That will prevent them from absorbing enough water, nutrients, and sunlight.

GARDEN DIMENSIONS

As we discussed in the last chapter, the overall size of your garden should reflect, among other factors, the size of your household and how you plan to use your produce. Once you have arrived at a suitable size, it's time to start actually drawing lines in your yard. Following are a few simple guidelines for arranging and orienting your garden, to help you create a space that is both beautiful and easy to work in.

Bed Width

We generally recommend that a garden bed never be wider than 4 ft. If your bed is 4 ft. wide and accessible from both sides, it should be possible to reach the middle of it from either side. If this seems like too much of a stretch, consider making the bed 3½ or 3 ft. wide. If you can access the bed from only one side (if the other side is against a wall or some other barrier), reduce the width to 2 or 3 ft.

Bed Length

Garden beds can be any length, but if a bed is 30 ft. long and you want to get from one side to the other, it can be a hassle to walk all the way around the end. So, many people prefer to divide up beds into sections of 8–15 ft. Having more divisions between beds can also make it easier to plan

out your garden each season: The extra sections make it easier to keep track of what you plant in each bed.

Bed Depth/Height

A wood-framed bed can be any height you like, from a few inches to a few feet. The frame on a shorter bed functions mainly to create hard edges that delineate the beds from the pathways and ensure that the soil stays in place over time. A taller bed will hold more soil (a bonus when you are placing beds over an impermeable surface or on rocky ground) and can be nice for people who want to alleviate the stress of bending down to work close to the ground.

An unframed mounded bed should be 4–8 in. above the level of the pathways. If it's too high, the mounded soil tends to run down into the

ABOVE: An extra-long (30 ft.) wood-framed bed.

paths over time, and keeping the bed properly shaped can be a hassle. If you want to add a lot of new soil to improve your mounded beds, you can simply add extra mulch to your pathways to prevent the soil from slumping out.

PATHWAYS

Whatever type of garden you build, you'll need pathways to allow access to the various sections of your beds. A very space-efficient, experienced gardener may create paths that are only 12 or 18 in. wide, but we recommend making your garden paths at least 2 ft. wide. This will provide enough space for you to comfortably crouch down, kneel, and work in the space without encroaching on the surrounding beds. If 2 ft. seems too narrow, don't be afraid to make them even wider (3 ft. or more). In larger gardens it's nice to have at least one main pathway 3–4 ft. wide, so you can easily move wheelbarrows and other equipment through the garden.

OTHER FEATURES

If you have the room, consider putting a bench, a table, chairs, a water feature, a retired space shuttle, or some other "accent" in your garden. Don't forget, if you have something like that in mind, to leave adequate space for it in your design.

GARDEN STRUCTURE

Now that you've chosen a site and a shape for your garden, you need to decide what type of structure to use. By structure, we mean the element that keeps your garden soil in place and separates the bed from the rest of your property. Fortunately, it's not a complicated decision. You simply need to figure out what your garden location will allow you to do, and then decide how

much time, money, and effort you want to invest in constructing your garden.

There are three general structures to choose from: a mounded bed garden, a wood-framed-bed garden, and a container garden. (We deal in more depth with the third approach in chapter 6: Creating a Container Garden.)

ABOVE: A standard 12 in. high bed (foreground) and an extra-deep 24 in. high bed (background). OPPOSITE: A gravel or mulched path helps keep the walking/working areas free of mud.

We'll look at each of these types of garden and consider which is right for you. The first two options are both types of raised beds. A raised-bed garden is exactly what it sounds like: a garden in which the planting surface is higher than the level of the surrounding yard, usually by 4 to 12 inches (or even more in some wood-framed beds). You can think of containers as miniature, ready-made raised beds.

A raised bed physically separates the planting area from the walking area, so you're not compacting your soil every time you stroll through your garden, and you're not fertilizing your path every time you add compost. Raised beds also drain well and warm up quickly when the sun hits them. And a raised bed allows you to plant your crops close together, so you end up using your available space productively and efficiently.

MOUNDED BED GARDENS

A mounded bed is a garden bed that is raised slightly (4–8 in.) above the surrounding area but isn't bordered by a wooden frame. You can put a mounded bed garden in just about any spot in your yard. You create it by loosening and lifting the existing soil and adding new soil and compost to improve its structure.

Advantages of mounded beds:
- They're simple. You can easily build a few mounded raised beds in a day, and you don't have to worry about gathering up a lot of extra materials to get started.
- They're cheap. All you have to buy is soil, compost, and organic fertilizers.
- They fit easily into existing landscaping. Most ornamental landscaping beds are mounded raised beds, so if one of these exists in your ideal garden site already, all you have to do is pull out

the unwanted plants and improve the soil.
- They're easy to dress up. You can make attractive edges for mounded beds by surrounding them with stones, bricks, or any other material you may have on hand. This is especially useful for keeping garden soil from slumping into an adjacent driveway, path, or patio, and it can also slow (but not stop) the intrusion of grass into the beds.

WOOD-FRAMED GARDENS

A wood-framed garden is similar to a mounded bed garden, but it's contained in a large wooden frame (hence the name). The frame can be made of almost any type and size of lumber and can stand anywhere from a few inches to a few feet tall. Square or rectangular shapes are relatively simple to build and are the preferred structure for many home gardeners.

Advantages of wood-framed gardens:
- They're deep. The frame lets you pile a lot of new garden soil on top of the existing soil. This is a huge advantage if your yard is really rocky or the soil is so compacted that you'd otherwise have to work it with a pickaxe. You can build the beds, set them in place in your ideal location, fill them with soil, and start planting.
- They allow for clearly defined paths and planting space. With the frames in place, there's no worry about tramping on the edges of your beds.
- They're easier on your back. You can build a wood frame as high as you like, which can be a plus if you want to minimize back stress.
- They look good. Wood frames are beautiful and complement many existing landscapes well.

- They're a good way to learn some new skills: If you've always wanted to learn a little basic woodworking, a wood-framed bed is a great first project.

CONTAINER GARDENS

A container garden uses store-bought pots, troughs, old hot tubs, or any other vessel you can imagine to grow vegetables. You simply fill them up with soil and you're ready to go (though you may have to drill some drainage holes if you're using found objects).

Advantages of containers:
- They're flexible. A container can turn any space that gets enough sun into a garden. It is mobile (it can even be put on wheels!), and expansion is only a matter of adding more containers.
- They're simple. Since you provide all the soil, you don't have to worry about inheriting poor-quality soil. Just fill the container with organic potting soil, add fertilizers, and plant.
- They're less physically demanding. Growing food in containers keeps you from having to dig up subsoil or build large wooden frames.

ABOVE: A container full of arugula and baby lettuce mix.

4

PREPARING YOUR SOIL

YOU'RE PROBABLY CHAMPING at the bit to start actually building your garden. But first you need to know a little bit about soil. Hold on to your seat....

A well-managed organic vegetable soil is a beautiful, complex organism that is the product of interactions among plants, insects, bacteria, fungi, macro- and micronutrients, climatic conditions, and lots of other variables. It's incredible to ponder, but it can be a little overwhelming.

You could spend your entire life studying soil science, but that wouldn't leave you any time for playing softball or drinking mint juleps, would it? So we've decided to limit our soil discussion to a few pages to keep your brain from exploding. If you keep these basic concepts in mind, you'll have no trouble maintaining a healthy, productive vegetable garden.

Start with these two essential principles:

1. The health of your plants depends on the health of the soil. This is the main tenet of organic growing: Build healthy soil and you will have healthy plants. And what makes healthy soil? Biological diversity. Your soil is a mini-ecosystem, and it will be healthiest when there are many different insects and microorganisms to keep each other in balance.

2. Your garden soil and garden health will improve with time. When your garden is just getting started, you can add as much compost and fertilizer as you want, but it still takes time for all of the right insects and microbes to arrive and build a healthy, balanced soil system. Nature has its own timeline, and the best thing we can do is try to work within that schedule. So even though your garden will be excellent this year, it should get even better in the future, as long as you follow the guidelines below.

CREATING AND MAINTAINING HEALTHY SOIL IN YOUR GARDEN

Each growing season, the compost in your soil will be broken down into nutrients and absorbed by your crops. To keep your soil in good condition, you need to do three things:

- Add **compost** to increase the amount of organic material in the soil.
- Add **organic fertilizers** to ensure that your plants get the nutrients they need.
- Check your **soil's pH** every two or three years.

OPPOSITE: Adding compost to a mounded garden bed.

Let's look at each of these jobs in a little more detail.

Soil and compost are sold in bags or in bulk. Look for them in both forms at nurseries or hardware stores, or from landscaping companies. Bulk soil is usually cheaper than bagged soil.

A ready-made soil mix is the easiest material to work with when building a new garden. Check the contents of any given soil mix before you buy it. For growing vegetables, you're looking for something that combines loam topsoil, compost, and sand. If it also includes worm castings, peat, or other organic amendments too, that is a bonus.

Avoid soils with wood chips, bark, or sawdust mixed in; these high-carbon materials will rob nitrogen from your vegetables. Also avoid sewage sludge, which is potentially contaminated with heavy metals.

If ready-made soil mix is not available, or if you can't find a mix that includes compost, that's OK. You can always buy bulk soil or clean fill dirt and compost and mix them yourself, or add compost to a mixture that's lacking it. If soil is not available, a mix of half sand and half compost makes a great garden soil.

COMPOST

Vegetable crops are "heavy feeders"; in order to grow quickly and produce well, they need a lot of nutrients. These nutrients come from the *humus* (broken-down organic matter) in your soil. Each year, your soil loses some of its humus as the crops utilize its nutrients for growth.

Organic matter is the backbone of healthy garden soil. In fact, it is the heart and soul of true organic agriculture, more so than just the absence of synthetic fertilizers and pesticides. Organic matter forms from the breakdown of once-living things—plants and animals and soil microbes. It gives your soil a loose, crumbly structure that plants love (called *tilth*), helps the soil absorb water and hold it so plants can soak it up, and supplies nutrients that crops need to grow.

The easiest way to increase the amount of organic matter in your soil is to mix in high-quality compost. It's important to note that in a newly built garden, it can take some time for the soil organisms to turn compost into humus. This is especially true in colder climates, because the microorganisms work more slowly in cool soil. While you're waiting for the compost to break down, you will need to add extra plant food to the beds in the form of organic fertilizers, so your plants have nutrients from the very beginning.

What's the difference between compost and soil? Compost is organic matter such as plant debris, animal manure, food scraps, or leaves that have been broken down by aerobic bacteria and fungi. It makes an excellent soil amendment but should not be used on its own to grow vegetable plants.

Soil, on the other hand, is a mixture of broken-down rock particles and organic matter. *Topsoil* is the uppermost layer of soil in a natural environment; it usually has more organic matter and biological life than soil layers below it (called *subsoil*). An ideal garden soil results when compost is added to mineral-rich topsoil to increase its organic content.

Before you start planting, you'll need to add compost, soil, or both to your garden. What you add to the garden will depend on which garden structure you choose.

ORGANIC FERTILIZERS

Compost should always be your primary soil building material, but you'll use fertilizers to supplement the nutrients it supplies. (Remember: Compared with grass or typical landscaping plants, vegetables are *very* heavy feeders.)

There is a tendency among beginning gardeners to shy away from fertilizers, even organic ones. For many people, the term *fertilizer* carries the connotation of *chemical* or *dangerous*. But not all fertilizers are derived from chemicals; some come from natural sources. Organic fertilizers can safely be used around people, pets, and wildlife.

We'll discuss organic fertilizers in depth in chapter 10: Fertilizing Your Garden.

DETERMINING YOUR SOIL'S PH

The pH scale measures acidity and alkalinity. If it's not in the appropriate range, your plants may not be able to absorb all the nutrients you're providing them.

As you may remember from high school chemistry class, the pH scale ranges from 1 to 14. A substance with a pH of 7 is neutral, 1 is very acidic, and 14 is very alkaline (also called "basic"). The ideal pH range for most vegetables is 6.3 to 6.8.

There are two ways to measure your soil's pH: You can buy a test kit from your local nursery or hardware store, or you can have your soil professionally tested by a soil lab. Home pH tests give you a good baseline to start from (by the way, we've found that litmus pH tests, the ones that use the colored paper strips, are more accurate than many battery-powered electric testers), but you'll get more precise and thorough information from the professionals.

Adding a significant amount of new soil and compost will alter a garden's pH. If you're building a new garden, add your new soil and compost first, then test your sample

Testing by a Lab

Professional soil testing sounds complicated, but it's really quite simple. And once you've done it, you'll know whether you need to add lime or sulfur to your soil, and how much. You'll also know whether your soil is deficient in major nutrients and whether you need to worry about lead levels.

To make a sample to submit to a lab, collect scoops of soil from 8 or 10 different spots in your garden site, taking each one from depths between 1 and 8 in. If grass or other plants are growing on the site, clear a small opening in the vegetation for each scoop. The samples shouldn't contain any living plant matter or roots. Collect them when the soil is relatively dry, and before adding any fertilizer.

Next, thoroughly mix all the samples in a bowl or bucket. Measure out 1 cup of the mix, seal it in a plastic bag, label it according to your tester's instructions, and send it away. If the option exists,

LEFT: A few types of home pH kits.

request organic amendment recommendations. The results you receive should tell you how to apply any necessary soil amendments.

We've listed some soil-testing laboratories in this book's Resources section. Many state universities and some county or other local governments offer free or inexpensive soil testing. We particularly like the University of Massachusetts program because it is inexpensive, it gives results for major and trace nutrients, and it tests for lead.

Testing for Arsenic?

Arsenic is toxic to humans, and soil contamination can be a concern for gardens situated near current or former industrial areas (particularly those with smelters), as well as old beds bordered by chemically treated wood or near treated-wood structures such as decks or playgrounds. As mentioned in chapter 5: Creating Garden Beds, treated wood manufactured before 2004 contained arsenic, which can leach out into the soil.

Unfortunately, while most agricultural soil-testing labs test for lead and other heavy metals, they don't test for arsenic. If you're concerned about arsenic, you'll need to either purchase a home test kit (see the Resources section) or contact a local analytical lab (search online for "analytical labs" in your city or state). Local labs may have insight as to whether arsenic contamination is a problem in your area.

Testing It Yourself

If you're hankering to get planting, you don't have concerns about lead or arsenic, and you're afraid that waiting around for results from a soil lab will diminish your resolve to get started, then by all means test the soil's pH yourself. Just buy a home pH test from your local nursery, conduct the test according to the instructions, and add lime or

A QUICK NOTE ABOUT LIME

There are two types of lime you may come across at your local nursery or hardware store:

Calcitic lime (called garden lime, limestone, or agricultural lime) is derived from natural mineral deposits and comes in powdered and granulated forms. In addition to balancing soil pH, it's a good source of soil calcium. Granules may be more expensive but are easier to apply; the powdered form can be very dusty and is easily carried away by the wind.

Dolomite lime (sometimes called dolomitic lime) will make your soil more alkaline and add calcium, but it will also add a large amount of magnesium. This is an essential plant nutrient, but if your soil already has a sufficient amount, dolomitic lime can make magnesium levels too high. This can actually be harmful to your crops.

You'll want to use calcitic lime for your garden if it is available. Dolomite lime is good for adjusting pH and correcting magnesium deficiency, but otherwise it may cause problems in your soil. Avoid it unless you've professionally tested your soil and it shows a magnesium deficiency. You can't go wrong with calcitic lime.

sulfur if needed. A home test won't allow you to check for lead or assess your nutrient levels, but it will supply the information you need to adjust your soil's pH. Follow up a home pH test by adding amendments as directed below and elsewhere in this book, and plant your crops!

If Your Soil Is Too Acidic

Applying agricultural lime is the easiest way to bring acidic soil into the proper pH range (*lime* as in limestone, not the tasty green citrus fruit). To apply agricultural lime, select a rate from the PH Adjustment Table below, sprinkle it over the surface of the soil, and use a trowel or rake to mix it into the top 2 in. of soil.

If Your Soil Is Too Alkaline

If your soil is alkaline, you should apply elemental sulfur or another "organic" sulfur-based soil acidifier. To apply elemental sulfur, select the appropriate rate from the PH Adjustment Table, sprinkle it over the surface of the soil, and use a shovel, trowel, or rake to mix it into the top few inches of soil.

PH ADJUSTMENT TABLE

IF YOUR PH IS:	ADD:	EQUIVALENT:
5.0 or less	10 pounds lime per 100 square feet	2 cups per 10 square feet
5.0-6.0	5 pounds lime per 100 square feet	1 cup per 10 square feet
6.0-7.0	nothing	relax in your lawn chair
7.0- 7.5	1 pound sulfur per 100 square feet	¼ cup per 12 square feet
7.5 and above	2 pounds sulfur per 100 square feet	½ cup per 12 square feet

NOTE: 1 cup of powdered or prilled lime equals about ½ pound
        1 cup of sulfur equals about ½ pound

OPPOSITE: Mixing in lime helps adjust the pH of overly acidic soil.

5

CREATING GARDEN BEDS

NOW THAT YOU HAVE a site chosen, have a shape and structure in mind, and know a little bit about soil, it's time to get started!

PREPARING YOUR SITE

Let's take a closer look at your garden site. What's there now? Is it a patch of grass? Is it a weedy plot of soil next to an old garage? A landscaping bed filled with huge bushes? A patio? A driveway? Don't worry if it doesn't look like a place that could ever grow vegetables—you can make it work.

Through experience, we've found that almost any site can be turned into an excellent vegetable garden. Grass sod or weeds can be removed, and mounded or wood-framed beds built right on top. A landscaping bed can be cleared and planted as is, or lined with bricks or rocks. With the addition of a few pots or wood-framed beds, even a patio or driveway can become a vegetable garden.

You'll need to spend anywhere from a few minutes to a few days preparing your site before you start building your garden. The amount of prep work will depend on the type of garden you're building and the site's current condition.

SITE PREP FOR CONTAINER GARDENING

If you're gardening in containers, all you need is a level place to set up shop. If your site is on a driveway, deck, or patio, you're ready to proceed. If you're setting containers on the ground, you may want to clear away existing vegetation and lay down a layer of mulch, so you don't have to spend time weeding between your pots.

WHAT YOU'RE PREPARING FOR

Site preparation is different for each type of garden structure. If you're planning a container garden, you may not need any prep at all. But if you're planning to build mounded raised beds, you'll almost certainly have some digging to do, because you need to start with a patch of bare soil. Any grass sod, weeds, plants, sticks, rocks, patios, or small children will have to be removed or relocated. If you're building wood-framed raised beds, you can start with a patch of bare soil or you can simply build the beds on top of what's already there.

The advantages of placing the beds without clearing anything first are 1) it's fast and easy, and 2) it may let you take advantage of a sunny site where you can't easily dig downward (for example, on a paved surface or in rocky or clay soil).

On the negative side, if you build on top of a

hard surface, your plant roots will have access to limited soil—they can only send roots into the soil you've put in the bed. Digging up the ground underneath will allow roots to move more easily into the subsoil in search of nutrients and water.

CLEARING

Here's an overview of different types of yard clearing and removal.

REMOVING GRASS SOD

If you're getting ready to build a garden bed, it is best to get rid of any grass that's on the site. It is possible to set up a bed on top of sod, but we find that the grass inhibits vegetable root growth, thereby reducing the vigor of the garden. Grass is a pervasive weed that can wreak havoc on gardens. It can be very difficult to kill, and it reproduces both from seed and underground through horizontal stems called *rhizomes*.

Tall wood-framed beds or extra-deep mounded beds (at least 12 in. deep) can sit right on top of grass because the new soil will kill the sod below it. Generally, however, we remove sod beneath all garden beds. This makes leveling the ground for a wood-framed bed easier, as well as making it easier for crops to send their roots deeper.

Before you start pulling up sod, you'll want to figure out what you're going to do with it once it's removed. Because of its ability to reestablish itself,

you don't want to casually add sod to a compost pile or leave it lying around near your garden.

NOTE: Sod removal is a lot more work if the ground is wet, so try to wait for a few dry days in a row before you start working.

What You'll Need:
- Spade-tipped shovel
- Stakes (pieces of rebar or wooden sticks)
- Flour
- Wheelbarrow or trash can to move sod
- MP3 player

Optional Equipment:
- Sod fork
- Mattock or Pulaski (a tool for fighting forest fires, which combines an axe and an adze in the same head)

How to Do It:
1. With your MP3 player turned up loud, play "Eye of the Tiger" on repeat (or other preferred inspirational music, such as the "Spice World" soundtrack, Beethoven's Ninth, or "Led Zeppelin III").
2. Mark the perimeter of your bed with the stakes.
3. Sprinkle a line of flour on the ground to connect the stakes all around the perimeter of the bed.
4. Remove the stakes.
5. Using the shovel, slice the marked-off patch of sod into easily manageable pieces about 8 in. square (kind of like slicing up a sheet cake).
6. Detach each slice from the ground by working the shovel underneath it and levering it up, or by chopping it out with the mattock or Pulaski. You can now load each piece of sod into your wheelbarrow or trash can and haul it away.

OPPOSITE TOP LEFT: A wood-framed bed can be placed directly on top of sod. OPPOSITE TOP RIGHT: Use a spade shovel to slice the sod into small, manageable pieces. OPPOSITE BOTTOM: Flipped sod decomposes and adds organic matter to your soil.

REMOVING ORNAMENTAL PLANTS

One easy way to start a garden is to repurpose an existing bed filled with ornamental plants. Since, as we've already advised, you want to avoid planting your vegetables among existing ornamentals, your best option is to remove the ornamentals altogether. Unless you're attached to the existing plants, simply dig them up and get rid of them. Make sure you get most of the roots out, so they don't resprout as weeds among your vegetables.

If you want to save the ornamentals to give away or move elsewhere in your yard, follow these steps:

1. Decide where a plant is going before you dig it up! If you'll be keeping it, start preparing its new site before digging it up, including digging the hole in advance.
2. Using a spade-tipped shovel, dig up as much of the root ball as possible (don't worry if you cut through some of the roots). If the plant has a long taproot, you may have to sever it by jamming the shovel or a mattock or Pulaski under the plant. Moving the plant back and forth or tipping it to one side can help with this process.
3. Lift the plant out, and move it to the new site immediately.
4. Adjust the size of the hole to make sure the root ball will fit; it should be the same depth and a little wider than the root ball. Place the plant in the hole, water the roots, and then pack soil around the roots using your hands, your feet, or the shovel handle. Water again to soak the soil around the plant.

If you need to keep a plant out of the ground for an extended time, put it in the shade and make sure the roots stay moist.

REMOVING LARGE WEEDS AND BRUSH/RECLAIMING AN OLD GARDEN

Your chosen site may already have had a garden on it that is now overgrown with weeds, or it may be undeveloped space covered with brush. Clearing these out can seem like a daunting task, but once you jump into it, you'll realize that giving a new purpose to the site can be very satisfying.

Start by clearing the top growth. For tall grasses and slender weeds, a weed whacker will help knock things down. If you're dealing with brush, brambles, or saplings, then a pair of long-handled loppers, hand pruners, and/or a small saw are your tools of choice. You can use a tarp to haul away the plants for composting. (If the site is really overgrown, consider hiring a landscaper or a goat.)

Next, clear the soil of roots and stumps. This helps prevent weeds from regrowing in your garden. Use a Pulaski or mattock to loosen the soil initially, then dig up roots and stumps with a shovel or sod fork. Rake the soil clear of debris, and proceed with building your garden!

REMOVING LARGE AND UNWIELDY OBJECTS (TREES, DRIVEWAYS, STONE PATIOS, COLLAPSING BUILDINGS, WILLIAM HOWARD TAFT, ETC.)

Sometimes you have to do strange things to open up space for a garden. If you feel confident enough to take on the task yourself, go for it! You can learn a lot of these skills on the Internet. Otherwise, call an arborist, landscaper, or construction company for assistance.

NOTE: No matter which type of garden you're planning, the paths between your beds or containers are best cleared of vegetation and covered with mulch to keep weeds down and make for pleasant

You'll need to do something with all the grass you've dug up. Here are the three basic options:

1. **Bury It:** Bury the sod, with its roots turned up, underneath the new soil of your beds (called "flipping" the sod). This is the simplest option, but flipped sod can cause problems if you don't lay enough new soil on top of it. The grass can grow back up through shallow soil; also, your vegetables can get stressed when their roots run into the buried sod.

   If your beds are deep enough, keeping the sod in place will actually add organic matter to the subsoil in future years. We recommend sod flipping only if you're building a wood-framed bed that's at least 12 in. deep.

2. **Hide It:** If you have space somewhere out of the way in your yard (maybe a back corner near the tool shed), you can make a pile of flipped sod. It will break down in one or two years.

3. **Haul It Away:** The cleanest, though most labor-intensive, option is to transport the sod off your property. Your city or county or a local nursery or landscaping company may have composting systems or dumping areas for sod; call around to find a place that is close to you and to check prices. (How you'll get it there is up to you.) If all this sounds like more trouble than it's worth, you may want to start thinking about a wood-framed bed or containers, so you don't have to get rid of the sod in the first place.

walking. We cover the exciting world of mulching in chapter 12: Essential Garden Skills.

BUILDING A MOUNDED BED GARDEN

Building mounded raised beds is fairly simple. You just loosen the existing soil, incorporate new soil and compost, and then smooth out the tops of the beds so they are easy to plant in.

What You'll Need
- Shovel
- Hard rake
- Tape measure
- Stakes
- Flour
- Compost or a mixture of compost and soil
- Mulch (for pathways)

Optional Equipment:
- Sod fork
- Landscape edging

How to Do It
1. Start by clearing your garden site as described above.
2. If your site is surrounded by grass, the roots will perpetually want to push into your garden

and add to your weeding chores. You can slow this process by burying plastic landscape edging around the perimeter of the garden (find landscape edging at any hardware store). Dig a narrow trench around the garden's perimeter, deep enough to accommodate the edging, usually about 5 in. Place the edging in the trench, and pack soil around it to hold it in place. It helps to have two people for this task, as the edging can get squirrelly on you.

3. Use the tape measure and stakes to measure out and mark the corners of your garden beds. Draw the outline of each bed with flour.

ABOVE: Landscape edging can help slow the intrusion of grass roots. ABOVE RIGHT: Take time to loosen your subsoil as much as possible before adding new soil to your beds. RIGHT: Two mounded beds ready for planting.

4. Using a shovel or spading fork, dig down inside the bed perimeter and loosen the soil to a depth of 7–9 in. This action usually brings up random roots from whatever was previously growing in the space, so you can pull these out for disposal (composting).
5. Spread a 4 in. layer of compost or soil/compost mixture on top of the loosened soil.
6. Using a shovel or sod fork, mix the soil and compost into the top 4 or 5 in. of existing soil.

ABOVE: A row of rocks at the lower side of each bed can turn a sloping site into a series of level garden beds. RIGHT: Rocks look great, and they help keep the soil in place and out of the adjacent driveway.

CREATING A BORDER AROUND A MOUNDED BED

A border of rocks or bricks can be useful in keeping garden soil from slumping into an adjacent path or driveway. Set rocks or bricks in place after clearing your site. Some rocks will sit best on a level base, while others may require digging a shallow trench. After you set them in place, pack soil around the rocks so they do not shift. Proceed with building the bed as described in this chapter.

WHERE DO I GET ROCKS OR BRICKS?

Prices can vary considerably between rock suppliers and rock types (e.g., basalt may be cheaper than granite), so call several suppliers before choosing one. Alternatives to store-bought rocks include concrete or clay blocks or bricks from a hardware store, used rocks or bricks from your own property or from friends or neighbors, and broken pieces of concrete, often available for free from construction dump sites.

WHAT SIZE ROCKS SHOULD I USE?

If you are planning to use natural rocks, tell the rock supplier what you are doing and that you need rocks 8–12 in. in diameter. Many preformed blocks come in 12 in. or 16 in. sizes that work well for garden bed perimeters.

HOW MANY SHOULD I BUY?

Measure the perimeter of the beds you want to border. Based on that total, the rock supplier may have a formula for calculating the weight of stones you'll need. For example, a very general rule of thumb is that 1 ton of 12 in. rocks will enclose a garden with about a 40 ft. perimeter.

HOW DO I TRANSPORT THEM?

Many suppliers will deliver rocks in a dump truck, but there is usually a delivery cost. If you go this route, make sure to pick out a space for dumping the rocks before they arrive. If the spot is on a nice driveway or sensitive lawn, lay down scrap plywood to protect the surface. Alternatively, you can pick up the rocks yourself in a pickup truck. This is a little more work, but it's usually less expensive, and you can pick through the available rock to choose exactly what you want. Most pickups will carry about a ton.

HOW DO I PLACE THE ROCKS?

Here are a couple of tips to help add stability to your rock perimeter:
1. Make a stable base for the rocks by leveling the surface underneath them with a flat shovel. If you're working on a slope, angle the base slightly into the slope. If you're using bricks or preformed blocks and want to make a perfectly level wall, consider digging a 4–6 in. trench and filling it with gravel. Water the gravel in the trench, and tamp it down until it is fully compacted. It will be easier to level the bricks on a gravel base.
2. When positioning the rocks, consider which side of each rock makes the best base. Place the rock, then pull it toward you; if it rolls easily, try another side. Using a trowel, you can pack or remove soil under a rock to stabilize it.

7. Level the soil with a hard rake.
8. Add another layer of compost or soil mix to the top of the bed as needed to bring the bed to the desired height (ideally 6–8 in. above the surrounding ground).
9. Mix the new layer into the bed, and level the soil with the hard rake.
10. If you're adding lime or sulfur to correct the soil's pH, spread it on top of the bed and turn it into the soil with your shovel. Rake smooth.
11. In between your mounded beds, you will want to create a smooth, easy-to-walk-on pathway. Clear any weeds and debris from the soil between the beds and smooth the area out with your hard rake. If the soil in the path is loose from removing sod or weeds, you can walk back and forth on it a few times to compact it. Cover the paths with the mulch of your choice (we like to use bark or wood chips).

BUILDING A WOOD-FRAMED GARDEN BED

Building a wood-framed garden is a little more work than building other types, but many of our customers feel that it's worth the time and expense.

Start by deciding what type of wood to use.

CHOOSING YOUR WOOD

When it comes to wood, you want something that won't rot too quickly but won't leach anything nasty into your vegetable soil. To begin with, let's rule out treated lumber. Treated lumber is designed to resist rotting when exposed to moist soil. The treatments used today are not as toxic as they used to be, but treated wood still has the potential to leach chemicals into your garden bed. Its use is prohibited for farms producing certified organic crops, and it is best left out of the home food garden as well.

Note that if you already have beds bordered with treated lumber, they may be safe to use for food. Most leaching from treated wood happens in the first few years after installation, so most contaminants may have already left the wood and leached out of the nearby soil. Unfortunately, there is no clear research indicating how long the contamination may persist, and toxin retention can vary depending on soil type.

Treated lumber manufactured before 2004 contains arsenic, which is toxic to humans. We recommend testing for arsenic if you're considering reusing an old bed made of treated wood to be sure the soil is clean. (See the Resources section and chapter 4: Preparing Your Soil for more information on arsenic testing.)

The most commonly available untreated options are pine, fir, cedar, redwood, juniper, and composite lumber.

Pine/fir: The main advantage of pine is that it's inexpensive; the main disadvantage is that it rots relatively quickly. Pine or fir beds may start to show signs of rot after three to five years. This may not be a problem if you are looking to save money, or you think you may want to move or redesign your garden in the future.

Cedar/redwood/juniper/black locust: These woods can be quite expensive, but they are naturally rot resistant and beautiful. They should last at least twice as long as pine or fir when used outside.

Composite lumber: Composite lumber is made from a mixture of recycled plastic and wood fibers. This option is also expensive, but it has great longevity and doesn't require additional treatment. It also makes use of recycled material. Unfortunately, it's a little harder to work with than real wood: Normal wood screws won't hold composite lumber together, so you will need special screws or bolts.

Attaching hardware cloth to the bottom of a wood-framed bed.

NOTE: You can extend the life of a natural wood bed by coating it with a nontoxic wood treatment. See the Resources section for suppliers.

THE WOOD—DIMENSIONS

We like to use 2 × 6 lumber for the sides of garden frames. Stacking two or three 2 × 6 boards will give you a frame 11 or 16½ in. high (2 × 6 boards are actually 5½ in. wide instead of a full 6 in.). We've built them much taller than that and it isn't a lot of extra work, so don't be afraid to make tall beds. For corner posts, we recommend 4 × 4 post lumber, and we use a 2 × 4 for braces. Lumber commonly comes in 8 ft., 10 ft., and 12 ft. lengths.

So, let's say you've decided on a 4 ft. × 8 ft. × 11 in. bed. Here's what you'll need:

- Six 2 × 6 boards, 8 ft. long
- One 4 × 4 post, 8 ft. long
- One 2 × 4 board, 8 ft. long
- 2 pounds of 3 in. wood screws (about 90 screws)

Before heading off to the lumber store, call and ask if they cut lumber in-house. Many will cut your wood for free or a nominal fee, which will save you a lot of time. Make sure to bring your cutting list with you. For your own cutting, use a hand saw or some kind of power saw, whatever you're comfortable with.

Whether you're cutting the wood yourself or having it done at the store, here's what you should end up with:

- **Long sides:** No need to cut these. Just set aside 4 of your 2 × 6 boards.
- **Short sides:** Cut the other two 2 × 6 boards into 4 ft. pieces.
- **Corner posts:** Cut your 4 × 4 into four 11 in. pieces (you'll end up with a little scrap).
- **Braces:** Cut the 2 × 4 into one 4 ft. piece and two 11 in. pieces.

What You'll Need

You decided on the size and shape of your garden bed(s) in chapters 2 and 3, and you've made up your mind about what kind of wood to use. It's almost time for a trip to the lumber yard. But first, take a look at this list of tools you're likely to need:

- **Hand saw or power saw** (If you know how to use it, a power circular saw or power miter box will speed up the cutting process.)
- **Tape measure**
- **Pencil**
- **Speed square**

ABOVE: To get the best protection, treat the cut ends of your wood before assembling your beds.

- **Electric drill, with both drilling and screw-driving bits** (Cordless drills are great when you're outside!)
- **Paint brush or roller** (if applying a wood treatment)

Don't have tools? The tools above are relatively inexpensive to buy, but if new tools aren't in the budget, you may be able to borrow them or find them used at a salvage or pawnshop. Many hardware stores rent power tools by the hour or day.

Assembling Your Frame

1. First, if you're using a wood treatment, now is the time to apply it. This will let you coat the end cuts before any of them get butted up against other pieces.
2. Measure as shown in the diagram, and drill pilot holes for your screws.
3. Assemble the frame. Start by screwing the

short sides to the corner posts. Then stand the short sides up and screw the long sides to the posts (it helps to have an extra set of hands for this step). Screw the side braces to the long sides and the center brace to the side braces, and you're done!

ABOVE: A cordless drill comes in handy at assembly time. ABOVE RIGHT: Move your soil with whatever tool works best. We typically use a wheelbarrow or buckets.

Positioning and Filling the Frame

1. Set the frame in place. If you're placing it on level or gently sloping grass, no preparation is necessary—just put it down where you want it. If you're placing it on bare soil, use a shovel or trowel to make a level base.
2. Fill the frame with soil. If you're using a wheelbarrow, make a prop out of old bricks or scrap lumber to help you tip the soil into the bed (an old doormat will protect the lumber from getting beaten up). However, tipping out the soil can be difficult if the bed is 11 in. high, and impossible if it's taller. If necessary, shovel the soil out of the wheelbarrow and into the bed.

We discussed how to calculate the volume of your soil in chapter 4: Preparing Your Soil. The following table gives estimates based on some standard bed sizes.

SOIL VOLUME FOR STANDARD BEDS

BED SIZE	APPROXIMATE SOIL VOLUME	
	CUBIC FEET	CUBIC YARDS
4 ft. × 8 ft. × 11 in. bed	27	1
4 ft. × 8 ft. × 16½ in. bed	40½	1½
4 ft. × 10 ft. × 11 in. bed	33	1¼
4 ft. × 10 ft. × 16½ in. bed	50	1.85
3 ft. × 8 ft. × 11 in. bed	20	0.75
3 ft. × 8 ft. × 16½ in. bed	30	1.1
3 ft. × 10 ft. × 11 in. bed	25	0.9
3 ft. × 10 ft. × 16½ in. bed	37	1.4

6

CREATING A CONTAINER GARDEN

CONTAINERS ARE A GREAT WAY to grow food in small or otherwise unusable spaces. They can turn a sunny patio, deck, or even a driveway into a custom-sized, productive garden. Containers are often overlooked for vegetable production, but we're huge fans.

If container gardening is the best option for your home, don't look on it as a limitation. While not every crop is suited for container planting, many will thrive if properly tended. The key to successful container gardening is knowing what will grow best and giving your crops the resources they need.

KEYS TO HEALTHY CONTAINER GARDENING

Container gardening history is fraught with good intentions gone sour. Listed here are solutions to the most common mistakes people make when setting up container gardens.

OPPOSITE: An old wine barrel makes a great, deep container for potatoes.

SUN

As with almost any vegetable plant, you want your pots to receive as much sun as possible. People often say things like, "I get too much sun, and all my plants on the patio got fried last year!" But while it is true that some plants will get heat stressed in the middle of the summer (lettuce and other salad greens, for instance), in most cases the "fried" plant probably didn't get watered enough.

USING THE RIGHT SOIL

It is not a good idea to dig dirt out of your garden to fill your containers. Unlike an in-ground bed, a container is a closed system. It's similar to the difference between an aquarium and a pond: Both are good living environments for fish, but the aquarium needs a lot more human management to keep the fish alive!

Potting soil (formulated specifically for potted plants) is the right soil to use in a container garden. If you use normal garden soil in your containers, it won't have the insects and microorganisms necessary to properly turn and aerate it. The soil will become compacted, and there will be no space for air or water to move through the system. The plant

There are many brands of potting soil on the market. When possible, look for one that is organically certified. If you don't see a clearly labeled organic certification, there may be chemical (also called synthetic) fertilizers mixed into the soil.

Of course, some potting soils are better than others. It can be hard to tell just by looking at the bag. Make sure you read the label: Some potting soils are designed especially for indoor plants, or cacti, or outdoor plants. You want a blend suitable for outdoor vegetable growing.

Examine the ingredients listed on the bag. Good soil may have ingredients like chicken manure, kelp meal, worm castings, or organic fertilizers. Questionable soil may contain ingredients like anhydrous ammonium nitrate or phosphoric acid.

Keep in mind that even if the potting soil contains some organic fertilizers, you will want to add more when planting vegetables. Some ornamental plants do just fine without supplemental fertilization, but vegetable plants are hungry! Before making a final choice, it's always a good idea to find somebody who looks like they know what they are doing and ask them which they would recommend for container vegetable growing.

roots will then either rot from being consistently waterlogged or die from lack of air (drowning or suffocation—what kind of options are those?!).

Potting soil is typically a combination of peat, little white rocks called perlite, and a few soil amendments. Together, these three ingredients make a soil that retains water, resists compacting, and supplies the nutrients your plants need. Want to make your own potting soil? It's amazingly simple. Just mix one part compost with one part sand! You can also add one part peat or one part perlite, if available, to improve the soil structure.

CHOOSING THE RIGHT SIZE POT

Plant containers come in all sizes, and many common household items can stand in as makeshift pots. No matter what type of pot you are using for your crops, the most important factor is that the container be appropriately sized for the plant.

NOTE: Even though potting soil is sold in cubic feet, most plant pots are sold according to their volume in gallons.

ABOVE: Light rocks such as perlite or pumice help keep potting soil loose.

drainage is essential to plant health. When creating plant pots out of found objects, drill a series of holes in the bottom to allow water to drain easily. Drill a ¼ in. hole every 3–4 in. across the bottom of the container.

FERTILIZING YOUR POTS

A common reason that people have limited success with potted plants is lack of fertilizer. Since these plants are growing in a pot, they have access only to the food you provide for them. Unlike a plant that is in the ground, a potted plant cannot stretch out its roots to find additional nutrients. As we have mentioned, vegetable plants are very hungry, and if we want them to produce a bountiful harvest, we need to give them the resources they crave.

When setting up a container for vegetable plants, it is imperative that you mix balanced fertilizer into the soil. You'll also want to add supplemental organic fertilizers to the pot over the course of the season. Each time you water the pot,

Some small and short-season crops can be grown in 1 gal. pots, whereas many half season and long-season crops should be grown in 3–5 gal. pots or larger. If you have very large containers and are planning to put numerous plants in each one, determine the right number of plants based on the volume of soil they need. The individual crop profiles in part III of this book provide details about soil volume and container size.

Types of Containers

Plant pots can be made of just about anything, including plastic, wood, ceramic, or metal. Choose the material, shape, and color based on your own sense of aesthetics—as long as it's the right size for your plant, it will work just fine. Any pot made specifically for plants should have drainage holes in the bottom, but check to make sure, since proper

ABOVE: A layer of rocks, gravel, or pottery can help ensure that your pots drain properly.

In the gardening world, there is much controversy about the environmental effects of peat mining. In fact, many people have begun to discourage the use of peat. As with many other environmental topics, it can be hard to find accurate information on which to base your decision.

Peat is a natural resource that is "mined" from areas known as peat bogs. There are vast reserves of this resource, and the issues surrounding its use are not related to exhausting the resource, but to how the resource is extracted. The question is, is it being sustainably harvested? It is not always easy to tell. If you choose to buy potting soil mix that contains peat, look for brands that claim environmental stewardship in their mission statements, and reuse what soil you can after a planting.

The most commonly available alternative to peat is a coconut-based product called coir or, simply, "coconut fiber." In our opinion, the potential environmental consequences of international coconut fiber shipping, combined with the other known hazards of coconut plantations (deforestation, pollution, etc.), make this a less appealing option than organic peat-based potting soils.

some of the soil nutrients will be washed out the bottom, so they need to be replaced periodically.

How Much Fertilizer Should You Add?

A 5 gal. container (a good size in which to bring vegetable plants to maturity) will hold a little more than ½ cu. ft. of soil and should get ½ cup of balanced organic fertilizer mixed into the soil before planting. Be careful not to overfertilize the pots, as potassium salt buildup can damage plants very quickly and excess nitrogen forces them to grow too quickly, making them more susceptible to pest problems.

ABOVE: Make sure to mix fertilizers throughout the soil.

CHOOSING THE RIGHT CROPS

In Part IV: Crop Profiles, we go into detail about specific plants' adaptability to container gardening. Information is given on ease of growth in a container and any potential limitations the crop might have in that environment. Look for these three ratings:

Good: This means the plant will thrive in a container environment and should be considered when trying container gardening for the first time. *Examples: lettuce, bush beans.*

OK: An "OK" plant can perform well in a container but may be reduced in size and have a more limited harvest than if planted in the ground. *Examples: kale, summer squash.*

Not Recommended: While it may be possible to grow this plant in a container, it is very difficult and may produce a minimal harvest (or no harvest at all). *Examples: winter squash, corn.*

WATERING

Because containers hold only a relatively small amount of soil, and that soil is directly exposed to the heat of the sun, it will dry out more quickly than soil in the ground. On hot days, a container may require two to three waterings per day, whereas an in-ground garden may need only one or none at all. It is vital, when planning your container garden, that you figure out a watering system that works for you. See chapter 7: Watering and Irrigation for more on this.

Self-Watering Containers?

Self-watering containers are a good option for keeping your vegetables well watered if you aren't able to run irrigation to your container garden. They usually have a reservoir in their base that keeps the soil moist using wicks or evaporative action. You refill the reservoir every few days or so using a hose or pitcher. You can also purchase self-watering inserts for containers that don't have this feature (see the Resources section for more information).

CONTAINER PERENNIALS IN WINTER

Depending on your location, you may need to consider moving your potted perennials during the winter months. In colder regions, you will want to bring them all indoors, but if you live in a mild climate, you may be able to leave them outside all winter. If so, make sure they are in a location where they'll receive some precipitation. If they are under an eave or some other dry location, the soil can become so dry that the plant will get stressed—even during the winter.

WASH YOUR POTS!

Even if your plants don't appear to have any disease or pest problems, it is crucial to clean your containers each year before planting. Aphid eggs and other pest larvae can sit dormant in the dirt stuck to the sides of the container, just waiting to eat next year's arugula. Pretty much any disease or pest you may have had during the last season can take up residence on your pots and wreak havoc the following spring.

Washing pots is easy. First, hose or scrub them down to knock off any clumps of dirt, cobwebs, etc. Once they are free of chunky residue, soak them (in a large tub or a utility sink) in a mild solution of bleach or hydrogen peroxide (¼ cup per gal. of water). Let the pots soak in the solution for a few minutes, then let them air dry.

If you use clean pots, fill them with the right soil, choose the right crops, and keep those crops fed and watered, they will repay you in the best possible currency: food.

7

WATERING AND IRRIGATION

VEGETABLES NEED A LOT of water to grow well. Most vegetable plants are 70–95 percent water, and they need to get all that water from somewhere.

Once you've built your garden, you need a way to deliver water to your crops. In some parts of the country, rain will help you out with this task. But you can't rely solely on the weather to take care of your garden. No matter where you live, you'll want to have a way to irrigate your garden to make sure it reaches its full potential.

TOO WET, TOO DRY, AND JUST RIGHT

Think of your soil as a sponge. When a sponge dries out completely, it hardens, and it takes some effort to get it to absorb water again. On the other hand, if it's completely saturated with water and stays that way all the time, it becomes a foul-smelling mess. Your soil is very similar: If you let it dry out completely, it can be difficult to get water to soak back in, but leaving it constantly saturated raises the likelihood of disease problems and fungi.

Ideally, you'll always keep your soil moisture in the "golden range" for plant growth. This is comparable to the feel of a damp sponge after you've

wrung it out. At that stage, a handful of soil can easily be pressed into a cohesive ball; if it can't, it is too dry. Then, if that ball is dropped from waist height, it should shatter; if it doesn't, the soil is too wet. Proper garden watering means adding water to the soil until it is saturated, then letting it dry out until it reaches the low end of the golden range, then watering it again.

When it comes to watering your garden, you have three options: hand watering, watering with a sprinkler, and setting up a drip irrigation system. Each method has its advantages and disadvantages.

Vegetables grow best when they are watered deeply every few days. This encourages them to grow substantial root systems as they chase the water into the subsoil. It also allows the soil surface to dry out between waterings, which reduces disease problems.

A drip irrigation system with a timer is the best way to achieve this in a home garden. While a little more costly and time consuming to set up initially, it's well worth the effort: It saves you a huge amount of time in the long run, you can go on vacation and not worry about the garden watering, and it uses water more efficiently than a sprinkler.

Even if you install drip irrigation, your plants may need a little extra help at the beginning of their lives. Seeds and newly transplanted crops

OPPOSITE: Young kale plants growing next to a drip tape.

don't have roots that extend into the subsoil to soak up water, so they are very susceptible to drying out. If they are not located right next to the emitter in a drip irrigation system, they may not receive enough water to get them through their vulnerable early growth stages. Having a hose or sprinkler available to supply extra water to young transplants and seedlings will really help them get off to a great start. We've found that drip irrigation with a timer combined with occasional hand watering works perfectly for a small garden.

No matter which watering method you choose, we highly recommend that you develop a feel for the soil, for when it is too dry, too wet, or just right. Do the soil ball test described above a few times to get an idea of what soil feels like in the ideal moisture range. Feel your soil after hand watering and after a rainstorm. Likewise, grab a handful from a spot where it's really dry, perhaps under an eave of the house.

When you are first getting started with your garden, poke your finger in the soil each day to see what the moisture level is like an inch below the surface. Once you've gained a little experience assessing soil moisture, you'll easily be able to tell whether your chosen watering system is providing enough water, or whether you need to increase the frequency or duration of your watering.

IRRIGATION OPTIONS
OPTION 1: HAND WATERING
Hand watering is the manual use of a hose or watering can to supply water to your garden.

Advantages: Hand watering gives you a reason to inspect the garden every day (to determine whether it needs watering). These frequent visits help ensure that you are aware of all the other happenings in the garden: the arrival of new pests,

for example, or the crops' approaching readiness for harvest. Hand watering helps you really monitor your garden, plus you need to buy only a few supplies to get started.

Disadvantages: Hand watering can be very time intensive—you may end up devoting at least half of your total gardening time to this task. Even a small garden can require 20 to 30 minutes' watering every few days. Hand watering is also not the most water-efficient option, since water is likely to flow out of your hose nozzle faster than your soil and plants can absorb it. Don't forget that water is a limited resource, and it's expensive.

OPTION 2: WATERING WITH A SPRINKLER
Sprinklers can be set on a timer or operated manually. A sprinkler can be connected to an existing in-ground irrigation system or with a hose to an outdoor faucet (hose bib). If it's connected to a hose bib, you can operate it manually simply by turning the faucet on and off, or you can attach a battery-operated timer to the faucet so the sprinkler waters at a set time.

Advantages: A properly adjusted sprinkler will water the entire surface area of your garden, delivering adequate water to all of your young transplants and newly planted seeds. Sprinklers are also relatively inexpensive.

Disadvantages: Most sprinklers sold for home use are designed for watering lawns, which means they may have an unnecessarily high flow rate and can be finicky to use on a small space such as a vegetable garden. It can be difficult to deliver water only to garden beds with a sprinkler; you may end up also watering pathways and the area surrounding the garden, leading to increased weed growth. Running them too long will waste water and leach nutrients from your soil, and the large, heavy droplet size can compact the bare soil in a newly planted garden.

OPTION 3: DRIP IRRIGATION

This is our favorite. Drip irrigation is a system of narrow tubes that deliver water at a slow drip directly to the surface of the soil.

Advantages: Drip irrigation is the most time- and water-efficient way to water a garden. A properly installed drip system with a timer delivers an adequate amount of water with very little waste. Once installed, it is largely hands-off, although you will want to check the moisture level of the soil every week or so as the weather changes, to make sure you are not over- or underwatering. A simple weekly moisture check and 30 seconds' updating of your time settings will ensure proper watering all season long.

Disadvantages: A drip system requires a fair amount of time to set up and a larger initial investment in materials. But although setting it up may seem intimidating at first, it's actually a fun, straightforward project once you get started. Also note, as described above, that drip irrigation may need to be supplemented in the early stages of plant growth with some hand watering.

GETTING IT DONE
HAND WATERING

1. Attach a hose to the hose bib that is nearest to your garden. The hose should be long enough to easily reach the far side of the garden, and it should have a nozzle able to spray with a gentle shower.
2. Spray until the water just starts to pool on the surface of the soil. Water the entire garden, then return to the spot where you started and

poke your finger about an inch into the soil. If the soil is wet at that depth, you are finished. If it still feels dry an inch down, water again until it has soaked in.
3. Repeat as needed. In the spring this may mean only once a week; in the summer it may mean every day or occasionally even twice a day. If you get a rainstorm, you can take a few days off!

ABOVE: When hand watering, make sure to use a gentle shower.

Oscillating Sprinklers

An oscillating sprinkler is a good choice for a beginning gardener. They're inexpensive, and with some adjustment you can get them to water over the top of tall crops later in the season. You can vary the watering area by turning your water pressure up or down at the hose bib, and by adjusting how far the sprinkler head moves back and forth.

To get the right flow, start by watering for 15 minutes. Then use your finger to see whether the water has soaked in. If the soil's still dry an inch down, run the sprinkler longer, in 5-minute increments, continuing to test. For most gardeners, from 15 to 25 minutes, three or four times per week, is a good starting point. If you live in a hot, dry area and need more water, try watering in the morning, then again in the evening a few hours before the sun goes down. This gives the leaves time to dry off before nightfall and lessens the amount of water lost to evaporation.

Impact or Impulse Sprinklers

Impact sprinklers are generally more efficient with water than oscillating sprinklers. But they are harder to use when you need to distribute water over tall crops, and they can also be harder to adjust to cover only a small garden.

You can adjust the spray pattern on some types of impact sprinklers, and you can adjust the pressure at the hose bib to water a larger or smaller area. For a larger garden (200+ sq. ft.) with a square or circular shape, an impact sprinkler on a stand located in the center is a good choice.

Start by watering for 20 minutes, then check to see if the water has soaked in by poking your finger an inch into the soil. If it's still dry at that depth, run it longer in 5-minute increments.

WATERING WITH A SPRINKLER

When using a sprinkler, you will want to water in the morning, as early as possible. This allows the water to soak thoroughly into the soil, and the leaves of the plants to dry off, before the hottest part of the day. Watering at midday is less efficient, since you will lose more water to evaporation. And watering in the evening can promote disease in the garden, since the water sits on the leaves of your crops throughout the night.

ABOVE: An oscillating sprinkler placed in the middle of a garden patch.

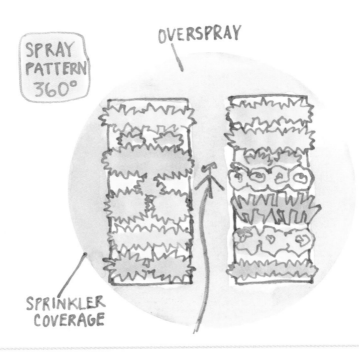

SPRAY PATTERN 360°

OVERSPRAY

SPRINKLER COVERAGE

Place your sprinkler in the center of the garden to minimize overspray.

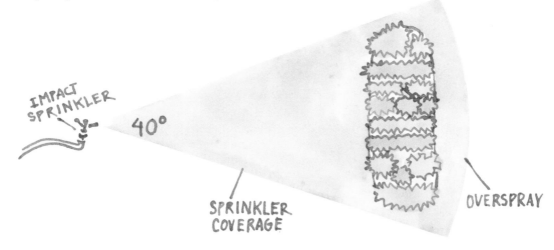

IMPACT SPRINKLER

40°

SPRINKLER COVERAGE

OVERSPRAY

You may be able to adjust the spray pattern of the sprinkler so that it only waters the area where the beds are located.

Setting Up a Sprinkler

1. Attach a hose to the hose bib that is nearest to your garden. It should be long enough to easily reach the far side of the garden. Attach the sprinkler to the hose.
2. Try setting the sprinkler in various spots, until you find a spot where its spray pattern reaches all parts of the garden. If your garden is very large or has a unique shape, you may need to move the sprinkler to a new location halfway through the watering, or even set up two separate sprinklers.
3. If you like, attach your sprinkler to a hose thread timer so you don't have to manually turn it on and off every time you water. (See the drip irrigation section below for more information on hose thread timers.)

DRIP IRRIGATION

Drip irrigation systems can get very complex, but all you need for a vegetable garden is something simple, easy, and inexpensive.

Finding and Buying Materials

Many companies sell drip irrigation kits for small gardens that include everything you need to build your system, plus instructions for putting it all together. We strongly recommend looking into these! We particularly like the Heart of the Garden Kit from Dripworks (see the Resources section).

If you want to assemble your own system, pay a visit to the irrigation section of a hardware or home improvement store, or a store that specializes in irrigation. You can also order the components you need online (see Resources).

Drip Lines

Drip lines bring water from your main line (see description below) to your crops. Choose one of the following three types of drip line based on the size and shape of your garden:

Drip tapes: If you have a square or rectangular garden, drip tapes work well. They are low in cost and super-efficient at using water, but can only be used in a straight line. These usually need to be ordered from an irrigation company.

¼-inch emitter tubing: If your garden has a curving shape, you'll probably want to use this. It is very flexible and easy to work with. It is also readily available at most hardware stores and online. Quarter-inch emitter tubing is a good substitute for drip tape in smaller square or rectangular gardens. A drawback is that you can run it only short distances from the main line, which can be a liability in long, narrow beds. It's also more expensive than drip tape.

½-inch emitter tubing: Half-inch emitter tubing is the most expensive option, but it is very versatile and durable. It can be used for both straight runs and curves and can carry water a longer distance from the main line.

For all types of drip lines, look for emitters spaced 6–9 in. apart. This will provide sufficient coverage for the entire surface area of your garden.

Drip tapes and ¼ in. emitter tubing have their own fittings that allow you to attach them to the main line. You'll need a specially made *irrigation punch* to make a hole in the main line for the fitting. Half-inch emitter tubing attaches to the main line using ½ in. couplers or tees.

OPPOSITE TOP LEFT: A visual comparison of ¼-inch tubing, drip tape, and ½ inch tubing. OPPOSITE TOP RIGHT: Rows of ½-inch emitter tubing in a raised bed. OPPOSITE BOTTOM: Each type of drip irrigation needs a special fitting to seal the end of each row. Shown here: a drip tape grip sleeve.

The ends of your drip lines will need to be sealed off to prevent water from gushing out. Each type of drip line has its own fitting to seal it. Drip tapes are sealed with a grip sleeve, a small piece of hard plastic that slips over the end of the tape to hold it closed; ¼ in. emitter tubing is sealed with a *goof plug*, a small piece of plastic that inserts into the end of the drip line; and ½ in. emitter tubing is sealed with a *hose end cap*, a fitting that slides over the end of the tube to seal it shut.

Drip lines to avoid: Avoid using black porous soaker hoses. These do not water evenly and they break down quickly.

Main Line

The main line is what brings water (via the timer, filter, and various other connections) from the hose bib to the drip lines. It's sometimes called *header tubing*, *distribution tubing*, or *feeder line*. For most home gardens, ½ in. polyethylene (poly) tubing is perfect for the task. You'll need to use *elbow* and *tee* fittings to go around sharp corners or to split the line. Use a *figure-eight fitting* to seal the end of the tube. Use an adaptor to attach the main line to the supply side of your system (the timer).

If you're buying fittings from a hardware store, you'll probably end up with compression fittings, which take some effort to connect to the poly tubing. Don't be afraid to push hard—grunting repeatedly helps get the job done! If you can find them, Easy-Loc fittings are a little bit more expensive but are much easier to use (you can order them from Dripworks—see the Resources section).

Backflow preventer: This fitting ensures that no water from the irrigation system trickles back into your home's water supply. Make sure it has hose threads, labeled FHT or MHT (not pipe threads, which are labeled FPT or MPT), on both

the inlet and outlet sides, so you can screw it right onto your hose bib.

Y-Valve: The Y-valve gives you two water outlets on one hose bib. Use one outlet for your drip system and the other for your hose.

Timer: The timer is going to save you hours of hand watering and let you go on vacation without frying your crops, so choose it wisely! You'll want a simple timer that threads onto your outdoor faucet (hose bib) and uses battery power. You can find or order one at any hardware store. We like the ones made by DIG Corp. for their ease of use, quality, and reasonable price.

Pressure regulator: The pressure regulator reduces the water pressure from your house, to make sure it isn't too strong for your drip lines. Read the label on your drip line to determine what PSI (pounds per square inch) your regulator should be rated for. It will probably be around 10 PSI for drip tapes, 10–30 PSI for ¼ in. emitter tubing, and 10–50 PSI for ½ in. emitter tubing. It should have hose thread fittings on each side (this means you can thread it onto a garden hose).

Filter: This keeps sediment in the water from clogging the drip emitters. Read the label on your drip lines to find out what the filter should be rated. If you can't determine this from the label, a 200-mesh filter is adequate for all types of drip lines. The filter should also have hose threads on the inlet and outlet side.

Setting Up Your Drip Irrigation System

1. Attach the backflow preventer to your hose bib.
2. Attach the Y-valve to the backflow preventer.
3. Close both sides of the Y-valve and open up the hose bib. If there are any leaks, tighten the Y-valve and backflow preventer. If the faucet itself is leaking, tighten the nut with a

pair of pliers. If it still leaks, you may need to replace its washer or call a plumber.

4. Attach the timer to the Y-valve. Remember: The faucet and hose bib will be open throughout the growing season, so there should be no leaks among the bib, backflow preventer, Y-valve, and timer.

5. Attach the pressure regulator to the timer.

LEFT: A Y-valve, irrigation timer, pressure regulator, filter, female hose beginning, and ½-inch header tubing attached to a hose bib. BELOW: From top: A back-flow preventer, silicon tape, Y-valve, irrigation timer, pressure regulator, filter, female hose beginning, and a series of ½-inch tubing fittings.

6. Attach the filter to the pressure regulator.
7. Attach the adapter for your main line (sometimes called a *female hose beginning*) to the filter.
8. Attach the main line to the adapter, and run the main line to your garden, using elbow and tee fittings as detailed above. You may want to bury it a few inches underground, so you don't trip over it or run over it with the lawn mower. Use a pair of sharp garden pruners, scissors, or a knife to cut the tubing. Seal the end with a figure-eight fitting.
9. Attach the drip lines to the main line. For both drip tapes and ¼ in. tubing, this means punching a hole in the feeder tube with the punching tool, inserting the proper fitting into the hole, and then attaching your drip lines to the fitting. To attach ½ in. emitter tubing, you'll cut the main line and use a ½ in. tee or coupler fitting.

Laying Out the Drip Lines

In a home garden, you'll be changing what you plant in a given area each year and sometimes throughout the year (for example, you may have a tomato plant in a certain corner one year and then lettuce mix the next year). Thus, you'll want to run your drip lines so that the entire square footage of your garden receives water. This usually means running them about a foot apart. Always check the instructions that come with your chosen drip line to make sure you're on the right track.

Stakes are crucial for holding the lines in place. You can often buy stakes designed specifically for the type of drip line you're using, but any two-pronged stake will work. The drip lines can sit on the surface of the soil, or you can bury them just below the surface if you don't like the way they look, in which case you won't need stakes to hold them in place.

Pretty easy, right?

How Long Should I Run My Drip Irrigation System?

This will vary depending on the flow rate of your drip lines and, of course, the weather. Here are some starting points for different types of drip lines:

Drip tapes, low flow (about 20 GPH per 100 ft. of tape with emitters at 8 in.): Start by running your system for 2 hours, 4 times per week.

Drip tapes, high flow (about 40 GPH per 100 ft. of tape with emitters at 8 in.): Start by running your system for 1 hour, 4 times per week.

¼ in. emitter tubing (about ½ GPH per emitter): Start by running your system for 30 minutes, 4 times per week.

½ in. emitter tubing (with ½ GPH emitters): Start by running your system for 30 minutes, 4 times per week.

After your first watering session, poke your finger an inch into the soil. If the soil still seems dry, add 10 minutes to the duration listed. You may even want to add a fifth day of watering if the soil becomes too dry between waterings. Note that a good rainstorm will substitute for one to three of your watering sessions.

As we mentioned above, the caveat when it comes to drip irrigation involves newly transplanted crops and direct-seeded crops. These can dry out even if the subsoil is well watered, because new transplants have few roots to reach the water, and seeds are probably resting in the top quarter-inch of soil. If you have time, the best solution is to check new transplants and seeds every day and water them by hand as necessary. That way you

IRRIGATION FOR CONTAINERS

As we said in the last chapter, irrigation for container gardening is crucial, since containers need to be watered so frequently (up to three times per day in hot, dry weather). This is because there is a limited amount of soil and it can hold only so much water at a time. And since the soil is more exposed to the sun, the water evaporates quickly.

If you have a number of pots clustered close together, then the best option is to set up a drip irrigation system. The framework of the system is the same as for any garden; the only difference is the drip lines themselves. Here's a simple way to set up a drip system for containers, using ¼ in. emitter tubing:

1. Run a ½ in. main line as close as possible to your containers.
2. At each container, punch a hole in the feeder tube and attach solid ¼ in. line (often called *microtubing*). Run this up to the lip of the pot.
3. Attach an elbow fitting at the lip of the pot.
4. Attach ¼ in. tubing with emitters spaced at 6 in. to the elbow, and circle it around the container. For ¼ in. tubing with 8 in. or 12 in. spacing, add a few extra coils.
5. Seal the end of the hose with a plug, and hold the line in place with a stake. You're done!

To water your containers, start by running the system until water just starts to seep from the bottom of the containers. Note how long this takes (probably between 5 and 15 minutes). That will be your watering duration.

Now set the timer to run twice a day. If you have the option of scheduling when it will run, try setting it at around 6:00 AM and 2:00 PM. With larger containers (10 or more gallons), watering twice a day may be sufficient, but if you have smaller containers and are experiencing very hot, dry weather, consider watering as often as three times per day. When you are getting started, make sure to check the moisture in the soil with your finger each day and adjust the system as necessary.

won't overwater other crops. If you're going on vacation or are really busy, consider setting your drip irrigation system to run every day for a week or two if you've just planted new crops and aren't anticipating rain.

Winterizing Your Irrigation System

A drip irrigation system is easy to winterize, because the lines don't hold water when the system isn't running. Thus, you can leave your main lines and drip lines in place over the winter without risk of damage. The same does not apply to some of the other components, however. Before the temperature drops below freezing, turn the water off at the hose bib, open both sides of the Y-valve, and disconnect the timer. This will release any standing water in the system. Then bring the timer indoors. You may also want to turn off the water supply to your outdoor hose bibs and/or attach frost-preventing covers. Seal the open end of the feeder line with a plastic bag and twine to prevent soil from entering the system.

ABOVE: This spinach was direct-seeded along drip tape to ensure proper germination and growth.

part III

GARDEN KNOWLEDGE

"For vegetable plants, every day is a day at the spa."

~ One of our clients, summarizing what he has learned about garden care ~

After the garden is set up, it is time to start thinking about the gardening process itself. The following chapters address the basic skills and information you'll need throughout the growing season. You may not need all of this information at once, but it will be here for you to refer to as you buy supplies, plan where your crops will go, tend to your crops, and harvest your produce.

8

PLANT LIFE 101

ONE OF THE MOST rewarding things about our job is helping people build a connection with the food they eat. That connection begins with an improved understanding of plant life.

We all learn a little about botany in junior high or high school, usually from a few pages of a general science textbook. Unfortunately, much like algebra, history, and state capitals, if you don't use this information in your everyday life, you tend to forget it.

So, even though this isn't a textbook, let's take a quick quiz, to jog your memory a little bit. The quiz has five questions, and they are all multiple choice. Don't spend too much time on this—just take your best guess. Then put down your #2 pencil and turn the page to see how you did.

Question 1:
Which part of a plant do you eat?

A. The flower.
B. The leaf.
C. The stem.
D. The root.

OPPOSITE: Vegetable flowers come in a variety of shapes and sizes.

Question 2:
What is a vegetable?

A. Anything that isn't an animal or a mineral.
B. Anything that grows on a plant and isn't a fruit.
C. Any edible plant product that doesn't grow on a tree.
D. Whatever you want it to be.

Question 3:
Why do plants produce flowers?

A. To get energy from the sun.
B. To reproduce.
C. To scare away animals that want to eat the plant.
D. Who cares? I want a vegetable garden, not a flower garden.

Question 4:
What is an annual plant?

A. A plant that grows from seed to harvest in one season and dies at the end of the season.
B. A plant that is planted once but grows back to be harvested every year thereafter.
C. A plant that lives in England.
D. A plant that is extinct.

Question 5:
Where do edible crop plants come from?

A. They are derived from wild plants all over the world.
B. Greenhouses.
C. Nobody knows.
D. China.

ANSWERS TO THE QUIZ

1. Which part of a plant do you eat?

The answer is:

All of the above.

Depending on the plant, you may eat the root, the stem, the leaves, the leaf stems, the flowers, the seeds, or the fruit. You may even eat something exotic like a tuber or a rhizome.

Here are some common food crops and their most commonly eaten parts:

Asparagus: Shoot
Broccoli: Flower bud
Carrot: Root
Celery: Leaf stem
Corn: Seed
Lettuce: Leaf
Kohlrabi: Stem
Onion: Bulb
Potato: Tuber (OK, maybe tubers aren't so exotic after all)
Tomato: Fruit

We tend to eat the parts of plants that are most flavorful or that contain the highest concentration of nutrients. Different plants put their flavor compounds and nutrients in different places, depending on their survival and reproductive strategies. This is important to understand, because it means the crops in your garden will require different types of care, depending largely on which part of the plant you plan to eat.

If you're going to grow vegetables, though, remember that just because one part of a plant is edible, that doesn't mean the whole plant is! Certain plants are entirely edible, but others have parts (like tomato leaves and rhubarb leaves) that can make you sick. Before haphazardly trying to eat everything in your garden, make sure you know what you are putting in your mouth!

2. What is a vegetable?

The answer is:

D. Whatever you want it to be.

There's no scientific definition of a vegetable and no consistency to how people use the word. When people say "vegetable," they usually mean edible plant products other than sweet-tasting fruits. A vegetable can be a stem, a root, a leaf, a flower, or any other part of a plant (see the answer to the next question for more).

And yes, some fruits are commonly considered to be vegetables. Tomatoes are the classic example, probably because they were officially designated as vegetables by the United States Supreme Court in the 1893 *Nix v. Hedden* decision (botanically speaking, tomatoes are fruits). Other fruits, like zucchini, squash, cucumbers, and eggplants, are also considered vegetables for the same basic reason—they're not sweet.

We only mention this here because we want you to think of your crops in terms of their unique attributes and needs, rather than as members of a generic category. Green beans, potatoes, and asparagus may all be "vegetables," but their life cycles and nutrient requirements are as different as their appearance and flavor. If you decide to try your hand at growing raspberries, strawberries, figs, or apples, you'll find that the same concept applies to "fruit" as well. Every crop is different, and getting to know your plants is one of the best things about gardening.

By the way, if you're curious about that Supreme Court case, Nix and Hedden were at odds because there was an import tax on vegetables at the time, but not on fruit. Nix wanted tomatoes to be fruit, so he wouldn't have to pay tax when he imported them. But Hedden was in charge of collecting import taxes for New York, and he wanted tomatoes to be vegetables so he could tax them. Hedden won.

3. Why do plants produce flowers?

The answer is:

B. They allow plants to reproduce.

We'd love it if our vegetable plants had flowers that could keep away raccoons, deer, and crows, but unfortunately, a plant's flowers typically have only one function: to help it reproduce. Getting energy from the sun is a leaf's job, and scaring off hungry animals is a gardener's job.

It's true that you'll harvest many of the crops in your garden before they ever produce flowers, but producing a flower is the goal that every plant has in mind. The more you understand about a plant's life cycle, the better prepared you'll be to help it along and recognize signs of stress.

So let's take a quick look at a plant's life cycle. You may spend one or two hours a week working in your garden, but your plants are there 24/7, and here's what they're up to when you're not around:

Germinating/Sprouting

A plant's life begins when a seed is placed in a moist environment and it sprouts (germinates). If

you buy transplants, this will already have happened, and if you grow starts indoors, it will happen in your house or greenhouse. When you direct-seed, your plants will begin to sprout a few days or a few weeks after you plant your seeds in the garden.

Growing Roots

After a seed sprouts, it starts sending roots into the soil below it. Roots help anchor the plant in the

ABOVE: Young pumpkins forming from the base of female flowers.

soil, absorb water and nutrients from the soil, and store water and nutrients for the plant to use later (or, in many cases, for you to eat later). A plant's roots will continue to grow throughout its life.

Growing Stems and Leaves

As a plant sends roots downward, it also sends a shoot upward through the soil. This shoot becomes the stem of the plant. Once that stem breaks the surface of the soil and is exposed to sunlight, leaves begin to grow on it. The leaves provide the plant with the energy it needs to grow, and the stem provides support and a pathway for water and nutrients to travel between the roots and the leaves.

Flowering

When a plant thinks it has grown large enough, stored up enough energy, and gotten all of the nutrients it needs from the soil, it starts its reproductive cycle, which means it starts producing flowers. Some plants produce only one flower and some produce hundreds, but the purpose is always the same: seeds.

Since flowering is its only real goal, a plant can start producing flowers too early if it gets stressed. Any number of things, including high heat, poor soil, and lack of water, can cause a plant to "bolt," or produce flowers early. Basically the plant is saying, "I'm stressed out and unhealthy, and I believe I might be dying! I need to reproduce as soon as possible so the world will be blessed with my offspring!"

As we'll discuss later, if you see this happen to one of your plants, usually the best thing to do is cut your losses and harvest what you can. Once the process starts, it can be very difficult to keep under control.

Fruiting

When a plant flowers at the right time, it distributes pollen to other flowers (using birds, bees, bats, the wind, or even you!) and collects pollen on its own flowers. Through a series of events we'd describe in detail if this were a botany book, the pollen fertilizes an ovary at the base of the flower and forms a seed. The ovary begins to ripen, drawing in as much food and water as it can to support the seed. This ripened ovary is what we call a fruit, and if you haven't harvested the plant's leaves, stems, roots, or other structures of the plant, the fruit is what you will eat. If the plant were growing in the wild, the fruit would drop to the ground or be eaten by wildlife, and its seeds would start the whole process over again.

4. What is an annual plant?

The answer is:

A. A plant that grows from seed to harvest in one season and dies at the end of the season.

There are a few main categories that plants fall into based on their life cycle, and we discuss those categories below. It is important to understand the distinctions between these types, so you know whether you will need to replant a crop every spring or it will come back on its own. The majority of plants discussed in this book are grown as annuals and will be reseeded or replanted each growing season.

Annual Plants

Annuals are plants that complete their entire life cycle in a single growing season (usually from spring or summer to fall). The plant will germinate from a seed, set roots, grow its stem and leaves, flower, and set fruit in the course of a few

Bolting refers to the appearance of an undesired flower stalk on your vegetable plant. It commonly occurs in leaf crops (such as lettuce, kale, cilantro, and cabbage) and root crops (such as beets, carrots, or radishes). Bolting can result from a lack of water, excessive heat, lack of fertilizer, or any other stress on the plant. Once the flowering process is triggered, energy is diverted to the flower stalks and away from leaf or root production, decreasing your crop yield.

Overly mature crops will inevitably flower and set seeds, but minimizing stress will help delay the flowering process and ensure healthy leaf and root growth.

Fruiting crops (such as tomatoes, beans and peppers) must flower in order to produce fruits, but excessive stress induces early flowering, which results in minimal plant growth, low yields, and poor tasting fruits.

months. Most vegetable crops are grown as annuals. This means that much of your garden space will be cleared out each winter and replanted the following year.

Perennial Plants

Perennials have a more permanent foundation and grow back for at least several years after they are planted. Some vegetable crops are perennials (asparagus, rhubarb), as are most berries (strawberries, raspberries, blueberries). In the landscape, lawns, woody shrubs, and trees are all perennials. Since they need to be planted in areas where they can live for multiple seasons, we recommend setting aside separate spaces for your perennial crops.

Biennial Plants

Some crops that are grown as annuals are, botanically speaking, actually biennials. This means that, if allowed to live a full life cycle, the plant would germinate, set roots, and grow its stem and leaves the first season, live quietly through the winter, and then flower and set fruit the following season. Examples of biennial plants in your garden are beets, carrots, turnips, and parsley. However, even though these crops are technically biennials, we will treat them as annuals. Most gardeners speak of them as annuals, and the only time their biennial nature is relevant is if they are being grown for seed.

Self-Seeding or Volunteer Plants

Some annual plants (including many garden flowers) will reappear in your garden every year even if you haven't reseeded or replanted them. These are commonly called "volunteers" because they seem to sign up for garden duty on their own initiative. Some volunteer plants are a great joy to see each spring (sunflowers, borage), but others can end up becoming rampant weeds. Over time, you will learn to identify your most common garden volunteers, and you can weed them out at your discretion.

5. Where do edible crop plants come from?

The answer is:

All of the above.

They are derived from wild plants all over the world (including China and sometimes nobody-knows-exactly-where), and today many are grown in greenhouses.

The plants we eat have come from all corners of the globe. Over countless generations, humans have grown and cultivated plants to produce food. Nearly all of the plants you will put in your food garden are "cultivated varieties," meaning that people have long grown them on farms and in gardens. They are different from wild varieties, which tend to grow on their own in the prairies and woodlands surrounding our farms and cities.

The plants that are our food sources are variations on their wild counterparts. The differences between the two are similar to those between domesticated dogs and wolves. If you released your poodle into the backcountry of Yellowstone, it would have a hard time surviving. It has been bred to be dependent on and compatible with people, and its good looks and great personality may have cost it the ability to hunt a buffalo in the wild. The same is true of your garden plants. They have been bred for generations for compatibility with people (to taste great and grow quickly), and they have long been encouraged to do just one thing, produce food. The plants put all their energy into food production, and this comes at a cost: They are less resilient to the ravages of foul weather, parasites, and predators than their wild cousins are.

We also grow plants in our gardens that evolved in climates much different from ours. After all, many popular garden crops (tomatoes, peppers, eggplant, for example) are derived from tropical plants. Because they evolved in very hot areas, they have virtually zero tolerance for cold weather. Which means added challenges when we try to grow them in places like northern Minnesota and Michigan.

Since we have induced these plants to make certain sacrifices (larger fruit on smaller plants, more food in a shorter amount of time, etc.), they need our support in their quest to supply us with an abundant harvest. Much like the support team for a cyclist in the Tour de France, you will be there to fill the plant's water bottle, provide it with snacks, and give it pep talks as it works its way through the growing season.

As you will learn in the course of your first few growing seasons, each crop has its own personality. It grows best when planted at a certain time of year; it may need to be trained on a trellis; it may need some of its branches pruned late in the year. Getting to know the character traits and history of your favorite crops and providing them with the support they need will enable you to garden successfully right from the start!

ABOVE: Many types of vegetables are actually fruits—at least botanically speaking.

9

GARDEN TOOLS: THE ONLY 11 TOOLS YOU'LL EVER NEED

YOU CAN DO NEARLY everything in this book with just a few tools. Some site-clearing or garden-building scenarios may require a few additional tools, but after that, your garden can be easily managed using the tools listed below. You may have some of them already, but if not, they're easy to find at a garden store or hardware store or online. Here are the tools we recommend:

1. **Hand trowel:** Probably the most indispensable tool for the home gardener. You will use your trowel to make planting holes, dig up weeds, and groom the surface of your soil. Look for a trowel that is one solid piece of metal, rather than a metal blade attached to a wood or plastic handle, or a plastic blade. A solid trowel will last forever, while cheaper models inevitably break after five minutes' use. Most trowels are about 12 in. long, which allows them to double as a spacing tool when you're planting.

2. **Hand pruners:** You will use pruners to cut excess or broken branches off your plants, snip off ripe fruit, and cut flowers. You don't need to pay $70, but a decent pair of hand pruners is a good investment. Like hand trowels, the cheapest pairs will break quickly. Also keep in mind that cheap pruners will not cut your plants cleanly, and ragged cuts can leave them more susceptible to diseases. A $10–$20 pair should do the trick.

3. **Scissors:** You will need scissors for cutting twine and snipping off seedlings. Any reasonably sharp pair of general use scissors should work just fine. Pruners do this work as well, but cutting twine can dull them, and pruners can be cumbersome when dealing with very small plants. You're better off with a pair of each.

4. **Knife:** A sharp knife is very useful for harvesting many of your crops. Any standard pocketknife or small kitchen knife will work well.

OPPOSITE: A rake, sod fork, and spade shovel sit ready for action.

5. Spade shovel: You'll need a spade-type shovel for digging beds, turning in compost, edging around the garden, and digging out large weeds. A spade shovel is the standard digging shovel you have probably used before, with a heart-shaped head. It is the best tool for breaking through the surface of the ground. Wood-handled shovels break on occasion, but sometimes a wood handled tool feels nice in the hands. Or you can invest a little more in a solid-shafted metal shovel. We use both types, but whichever type you choose should last for years (and may even come with a warranty).

6. Soft rake: A soft rake is useful for cleaning up debris around the garden and smoothing out the tops of your beds to prepare for planting. These rakes are lighter and more flexible than solid metal hard rakes. Look for a metal or plastic one at any nursery or hardware store.

7. Hard rake: This is a nice tool for grading your beds, smoothing out heavy soil, leveling pathways, and many other tasks. You can buy a solid hard rake at any nursery or hardware store.

8. Garden gloves: Hopefully, you like to get your hands dirty, but even so, it is nice to have a pair of gardening gloves on hand (pardon the pun). We use gloves with breathable fabric tops and rubber palms and fingers. Gloves are great for bigger tasks, like digging up garden beds or pulling out large weeds, so you don't end up with thorns, blisters, or splinters.

9. Garden hose and nozzle: No matter what kind of watering system you plan for your garden, you'll want a reliable hose and nozzle. A hose is essential for watering-in your transplants and hand-watering your germinating crops. Try to find a hose or combination of hoses that easily reaches the farthest edge of

your garden. Look for a nozzle that is able to release a gentle stream of water. (Note that the majority of garden hoses contain lead, which helps make them flexible. If you are concerned about this, look for a garden hose that specifically states that it is lead free.)

10. Tape measure: You will need this when designing and building your garden, and any other time you need to measure longer distances in the garden. Any tape measure will work; we usually use a 20- or 25-foot model.

11. Ruler: Any foot-long ruler or yardstick comes in handy when you're planting transplants or direct-seeding in the garden. A short ruler is easy to carry around, but a yardstick can be set in place while you plant longer sections of your garden beds. You can also use your hand trowel or tape measure as a measuring device, but flat, straight rulers are the best way to get accurate planting distances.

ABOVE: Clockwise from top: two types of hose nozzles, a tape measure, gardening gloves, hand pruners, knife, scissors, hand trowel, and ruler.

Optional Tools

Aside from the essential tools, there are a few other pieces of equipment that come in handy from time to time. A **pitchfork** can be useful anytime you need to move large quantities of straw or fresh manure. A **sod fork** is like a short, thick pitchfork. It's great for removing dug-up sod and for aerating your garden soil. **Mattocks** or **Pulaskis** have one sharp edge that is great for hacking out pieces of sod. They are also helpful for chopping through thick roots of plants that you want to remove when establishing your garden. **Hoes** are great when trying to manage weeds in a large garden. We like to use scuffle hoes (also called hula hoes or stirrup hoes) to weed pathways and around mature plants.

CLEAN YOUR TOOLS!

Cleaning gardening tools seems like a terrible waste of time, but it is a good habit to get into. That's because tools are the quickest way to spread plant diseases across the garden. After using your tools, 1) rinse them off with water to remove dirt and debris, and 2) hang them where they will air dry.

If you know you've been working with diseased plants, or even if you only suspect it, you need to go even further: 1) Wash off the tool, 2) wipe it down with hydrogen peroxide or a bleach solution (1 part bleach to 10 parts water), and 3) leave it to air dry.

BELOW: From left: soft rake, spade shovel, hard rake, pitchfork, sod fork, scuffle hoe, garden hose, mattock, and Pulaski.

10

FERTILIZING YOUR GARDEN

WHAT, EXACTLY, IS FERTILIZER?

FERTILIZING IS AN OFTEN misunderstood gardening concept, and some people think of the word *fertilizer* itself in negative terms, equating it with chemical or synthetic fertilizer. But there are also organic sources of fertilizer, which can be very beneficial to your garden.

Chemical fertilizers are undesirable for a number of reasons. Among other things, they pollute waterways, harm soil microorganisms and earthworms, and can deplete soil micronutrients. They are also often derived from fossil fuels. Fortunately, not all fertilizers are chemical based.

The term fertilizer simply refers to a material that adds nutrients to your soil, to increase the fertility of your garden. Fertile soil produces healthier crops and higher yields. Organic fertilizers are derived from all sorts of natural materials, including mineral deposits, animal wastes (manure, bones, blood, shells), seaweed, and plant wastes (seeds, seed hulls).

Your garden will be much healthier with the addition of organic fertilizer! As we've mentioned several times already, vegetable crops are heavy feeders; in order to be healthy, they need a lot of nutrients from the soil. Just as people are healthiest when they eat foods that are high in vitamins and minerals, plants are healthiest when they have access to soil nutrients. And just as people need to eat on a regular basis, crops need ongoing nutrition throughout the season. As your plants grow and absorb the nutrients from the soil, fertilizers replenish the supply.

Nutrients are often less available in a new garden, because soil microorganisms need time to digest soil minerals and compost before they can release nutrients in a form your crops can use. Cool weather at the beginning of the season also limits their availability. Therefore, in addition to using compost as a source of nutrients in your garden, we recommend adding organic fertilizers when first building your garden, as well as during the growing season and between seasons. This will help maintain the high nutrient levels your crops love.

If you're an experienced gardener, you live in a warm climate, and you're using compost of an exceptionally high quality, you may be able to cut back or eliminate supplemental fertilizers. But for gardeners who have to deal with cold spring weather and are in the process of building their garden soil, organic fertilizer is a tremendous help. Over time, as your compost breaks down and releases its hidden nutrients, fewer

OPPOSITE: Adding a cupful of granular fertilizer before planting.

Organic Garden
Natural Vegan
All-Purpose Fertilizer

Net weight 25 lb.
Covers up to 1500 s.f.

REGISTERED MATERIAL
For Use In
Organic Agriculture
Washington State Dept. of Agriculture

anic Garden Blend 6-2-5

supplemental fertilizers will be necessary, but during the first several seasons these amendments can be crucial for success.

UNDERSTANDING FERTILIZER LABELS

First-time gardeners often get overwhelmed when they look through the selection of fertilizers at their local garden center. Fortunately, as long as you keep a few things in mind, you can avoid confusion and get the right fertilizer for your garden.

THE N-P-K RATIO

Fertilizers go by numbers that refer to the nutrient composition of the product. The package will usually display three numbers in large type, such as 2-5-5, 10-10-10, 0.1-0.05-0.1, or any other combination you can think of. This series of numbers is called the *N-P-K ratio*, and it always refers to the same nutrients in the same order.

N=Nitrogen

Nitrogen is responsible for the early vegetative growth of your plants. It won't help them set flowers or large fruit, but it helps them grow thick stems and big leaves. Nitrogen is not always in a form that plants are able to absorb, and when it does become available to plants (becomes water soluble), crop roots quickly suck it up. It can even wash away in a rainstorm. Nitrogen is notorious for disappearing from the soil more quickly than other nutrients.

P=Phosphorus

Phosphorus has a vital role in photosynthesis and is important for early root growth and flowering in vegetable crops.

K=Potassium (Sometimes Called Potash)

Potassium is also crucial to photosynthesis, and it is important for fruit formation and disease resistance in vegetable crops.

There are many other nutrients that plants need besides these three, and they are usually listed on the package as *micronutrients*.

APPLICATION RATE

All fertilizer packages should specify a "recommended application rate." It is important to follow the recommended rate, because over-fertilization can stress your plants. We provide some approximate application rates below (see "When and How Do I Fertilize My Garden?"), in case your fertilizer label is confusing or lacks this information.

ORGANIC OR NOT?

Make sure the package clearly indicates that the product is certified organic. Many fertilizer brands sport labels that are intended to appear organic or *natural*, even when they contain chemical fertilizers.

ABOVE: Make sure your fertilizers carry a certified organic label.

TYPES OF FERTILIZER

As you stroll the fertilizer aisle in your local nursery or hardware store, you'll notice there are myriad kinds of fertilizer with different N-P-K ratios. You may wonder, Do I have to buy all these different types to have a successful garden? Fortunately, the answer is no. All you need is a dry balanced fertilizer to apply before planting, and either dry balanced fertilizer or liquid fertilizer for supplemental feeding of your crops.

Dry Fertilizers

Dry fertilizers must be mixed into the soil and watered in, so soil microbes can break them down and make the nutrients available to your crops. The nutrients are not immediately available to plants; instead, they are released over a long period of time and thus won't quickly leach from the soil. The nutrients in a fine, dusty fertilizer are available more quickly, while coarser fertilizers supply nutrients over a longer period of time.

SINGLE-INGREDIENT FERTILIZERS

Nutrient deficiencies are a common garden problem, and there are organic fertilizers you can use to address specific nutrient problems. Single-ingredient fertilizers are usually used to supply a large amount of a specific nutrient.

NITROGEN FERTILIZERS

Nitrogen is vital for vegetative growth in plants. High-nitrogen fertilizers can be used to boost heavy-feeding crops in their early stages, and can also help correct a nitrogen deficiency (see chapter 23: Garden Problems and Solutions on diagnosing nutrient deficiencies). Be careful not to overfertilize with high N fertilizers, or fertilize too late in the season, because that can negatively affect fruit and flower formation. Nitrogen fertilizers can be purchased in small boxes or big bags at most garden nurseries.
- Nitrogen fertilizers: Blood meal, cottonseed meal, bat guano, feather meal.

PHOSPHORUS/POTASSIUM/MICRONUTRIENT FERTILIZERS

These nutrients are responsible for many vital plant functions, including root growth, flowering, and fruit development. An extra dose of phosphorus can help transplants set better roots in the spring. If a fruiting crop requires mid- or late-season fertilization, plan to use a formula that is high in phosphorus and potassium and micronutrients (such as calcium, magnesium, boron, and zinc, which are often grouped together in labeling) and low in nitrogen.
- Phosphorus fertilizers: Bone meal, rock phosphate, fish meal.
- Potassium/micronutrient fertilizers: Greensand (high in potassium and micronutrients), kelp meal (high in potassium and micronutrients).

Balanced Fertilizer

A dry fertilizer made up of many different components is called "balanced" or "all-purpose" fertilizer. Ingredients can vary by brand and your location. They may include crab meal, fish meal, bat guano, feather meal, cottonseed meal, bone meal, etc. (The term "meal" refers to the consistency of the product. Just as cornmeal is made

ABOVE: Add fertilizer to your beds before each vegetable planting.

from ground-up corn, so bone meal is made from ground-up bones!) This fertilizer is referred to as "balanced" because it has approximately equal amounts of nitrogen, phosphorus, and potassium. Fertilizers with nutrient breakdowns of 5-5-5, 3-4-4, or 3-2-2 can all be considered balanced.

We recommend balanced fertilizer for your garden because it should make up any nutritional deficiencies your soil has. As you gain more knowledge and experience, you may add other organic fertilizers to address specific crop needs or problems, but if you want to keep things simple, you'll have a highly productive garden using only balanced fertilizer.

Liquid Fertilizers

Organic liquid fertilizers are usually made from processed fish, seaweed, or animal manure. The nutrients in liquid fertilizers are more soluble than in dry fertilizers and can be taken up by your plants more quickly. Thus, liquid fertilizers are great for giving your plants a quick boost if they're nutrient stressed, and they are great for supplemental feeding through the season (especially in container gardens). Note, though, that high concentrations of liquid fertilizer can be harmful to your plants, so you should fertilize periodically with small doses. And even if you plan to use liquid fertilizer, it is still important to add a balanced dry fertilizer before planting.

A liquid fertilizer can have a balanced nutrient breakdown, or it can be high in a single nutrient. Balanced liquid fertilizer will consist of several ingredients and is your best bet for all-around use in vegetable gardening, including in containers. Other types are targeted for more specific results:

High N liquid fertilizer encourages early vegetative growth.

High P liquid fertilizer encourages root

growth in new transplants.

High P and K liquid fertilizers encourage flowering and fruiting.

Liquid kelp provides essential micronutrients.

WHEN AND HOW DO I FERTILIZE MY GARDEN?

For some reason, fertilizing can feel daunting the first few times you do it. But don't worry too much about precision. Organic fertilization doesn't need to be that exact; just try to stay relatively close to the specified application rate.

BEFORE PLANTING

As we've said, we recommend adding dry, balanced organic fertilizer to the soil before planting any crop. Check the label on the package to find out the application rate. If you don't have a scale or don't understand the rates on the package, use these guidelines:

- Most balanced organic fertilizers labeled 3-3-3 (or a similar rating) can be spread at about ¼ cup per 1 square foot (use about ¼ cup per transplant).
- Most balanced organic fertilizers labeled 5-5-5 (or a similar rating) can be spread at about ¼ cup per 2 sq. ft. (use about ⅛ cup per transplant).

For direct-seeded crops: Spread the desired amount of fertilizer on the soil surface. Mix the fertilizer into the top several inches of soil with a rake, hoe, shovel, or hand trowel. Make sure the fertilizer is mixed well; clumps will rot instead of breaking down into usable nutrients. Rake the surface smooth and proceed with seeding.

For transplants: Put the appropriate amount of fertilizer in the hole where the transplant will go,

and mix it into the soil thoroughly with a trowel. If you plan to set out a lot of transplants at once, you can use the fertilizer to mark your spacing.

For containers: Thoroughly mix about ½ cup of balanced organic fertilizer into a 5 gal. pot of soil before transplanting or seeding.

ABOVE: Nutrient-starved plants will remain small and may have unhealthy blue, purple, or yellow coloration.

SUPPLEMENTAL FEEDING FOR DEMANDING CROPS

Heavy-feeding crops need more nutrients because they consume soil nutrients throughout their lengthy growth cycle. (You wouldn't want to sit through an entire football game without a plate of nachos at halftime, right?) You can give your demanding crops a supplemental feeding with either liquid or dry fertilizer. Liquid fertilizer is more quickly absorbed by the plants, so you'll see quicker results, but it is used up more quickly than dry fertilizer. Dry fertilizer takes more time to release nutrients but provides nutrition over a longer period of time.

Don't fret the choice too much. Both options work, so choose whichever you'll be more likely to actually use. You'll find this information in Part IV: Crop Profiles, and in the Reference Tables section at the end of the book.

Dry Fertilizer

Supplemental feeding with dry fertilizer is often called *side-dressing*. Sprinkle fertilizer around the base of the plant or along the edge of the row at the recommended application rate. Mix it shallowly into the soil (no more than an inch, to prevent damage to plant roots) with a trowel or your hand, and then water it in.

Liquid Fertilizer

Mix a solution of the fertilizer in a watering can at the rate directed on the container (a tablespoon and a short mixing stick are useful for this). Water the plants that you want to feed until the mixture has soaked about an inch into the soil.

SUPPLEMENTAL FEEDING FOR CONTAINER VEGETABLES

Because it's so difficult to maintain proper nutrient levels in a container, we recommend supplemental feeding every 1 to 2 weeks for *all* container crops. This can be done with either liquid or dry balanced fertilizer as directed above. *Caution:* Overfertilizing a container planting can be disastrous, so it's vital to use proper application rates when doing so. For a 5 gal. pot, use liquid fertilizer every 1 to 2 weeks as directed on the package, or 2 tablespoons of dry organic fertilizer every 2 weeks.

OPPOSITE: When fertilizing an entire bed, you can use a shovel to help incorporate the fertilizer into the soil.

11

COMPOST

YOU'VE PROBABLY NOTICED that we've mentioned compost a lot in this book so far. That's because compost is a home gardener's primary tool for maintaining high-quality organic soil. Compost is something you can either buy or make at home. Let's look into it.

get the hang of it, it can smell foul and attract rodents if done improperly, especially in an urban environment. If you don't want to try composting during your first years of gardening, or if you don't have the space for a pile, that's OK—high-quality compost is inexpensive and easy to buy.

WHAT IS COMPOSTING?

Composting is the process of letting beneficial bacteria and fungi break down vegetative materials (like weeds pulled from the garden, grass clippings, or rotten vegetables) into a soil-like material that can be applied to your garden. Composting is a convenient, environmentally responsible way to take wastes from your garden and kitchen and turn them into a source of nutrients for your plants and stable organic matter for your soil. It is an integral part of growing food organically, and composting at home is a major step in "closing the loop" for your garden.

It isn't essential to have a home compost pile to be a successful gardener. Although composting is a beautiful process and is relatively easy once you

WHAT IF I DON'T COMPOST?

Sending garden and yard wastes to a landfill is a bad idea! Doing so takes up valuable space and creates methane gas. It also wastes nutrients and organic matter that could return to the soil. If you're not ready for home composting, try to find out whether your town or county offers some way to dispose of compostable wastes. Some municipalities now have curbside pickup or local dumping stations for yard and/or kitchen wastes. If yours doesn't, check with local nurseries and landscaping companies to see if they accept yard waste.

OPPOSITE: Use red wiggler worms in your compost for one of the best organic soil amendments.

HOME COMPOSTING

Composting wants to happen. It's the process by which every ecosystem recycles its nutrients to build soil, and it occurs (at a very slow pace) in any natural environment. When you compost at home, you're doing the same thing, except that you're adding some labor and the right mix of ingredients to move the process along more quickly.

Home composting is easy, but it is important to have a system that works for you and requires only as much attention as you plan to give. Let's discuss two simple home composting systems that are effective in the real world: the traditional catchall open compost pile, and a system that composts kitchen scraps separately from lawn and garden waste.

ABOVE: For larger yards and gardens, a three-pile open compost system can hold all of your kitchen and farm waste.

THE CATCHALL OPEN COMPOST PILE

In a traditional compost pile system, you simply make a pile of your garden, yard, and kitchen wastes and turn it over frequently to help it decompose. This is the easiest way to compost, and it requires no bins, tumblers, or flimsy plastic stuff to make it work.

If you live in a rural or suburban area and have a large yard, this may be the option for you. The disadvantage is that, to keep odors down and pests away, this type of pile needs to have the proper mix of ingredients and be turned frequently. We don't recommend traditional open piles that contain kitchen scraps for city dwellers or anyone with rat or other rodent problems. Incidentally, your compost pile needn't be a plain old pile: If you prefer a more managed look, you can contain it by building a three-bin composter or other structure.

Starting a Catchall Open Compost Pile

1. Choose a small area of your yard (about 6 × 6 ft.) that is out of the way and shaded.

2. Make a pile of your yard waste in this area. Add brown and green materials in layers, or in batches as they become available. (We go into specifics about "brown" and "green" in the "Materials for Composting" chart.) A 3 × 3 × 3 ft. pile is a good size to allow heat to build up from composting and still allow air to circulate through the pile. Don't worry if you don't have enough material to make a pile this large at the outset, since you'll add material over time. If you're adding kitchen wastes, cover them with leaves, straw, or grass clippings.

3. When it rains, cover the pile with a tarp, a sheet of plastic, etc., to keep it from getting

too wet. Remove the cover when the weather's dry to promote air circulation.

4. Don't let your compost pile dry out. Try to keep the materials as damp as a wrung-out sponge. Water the pile if it seems too dry, especially when adding new materials. Keeping it moist will deter pests from nesting in it. If the pile seems too wet, add dry brown materials to soak up the moisture.

5. If your pile contains kitchen scraps, you should turn it at least every 2 weeks to kill pathogens and discourage pests. If the pile contains only yard and garden wastes (because kitchen scraps are being composted separately in a digester or worm bin), you can turn it less frequently, because it will be much less attractive to pests. A frequently turned pile will be ready for use in 2 to 3 months, while an infrequently turned one can take a year or two to break down completely. Finished compost should be dark and crumbly, and smell like garden soil.

If you have room, you can start a second compost pile while the first one is breaking down. A three-bin composter can help you with managing multiple piles. Each time you turn the pile, you move it into the adjacent bin. New materials go into the open bin at one end, and finished compost rests in the bin at the opposite end.

If you're not in a hurry to use the compost you make, and you have the space, you can simply pile up yard and garden wastes (no kitchen scraps!) and let them break down on their own, without worrying about fine points like the brown-to-green ratio. Note that a pile like this won't get hot enough to kill weed seeds or pathogens, and it will take a year or so to break down.

What Should Go into My Catchall Compost Pile?

Microorganisms digest organic matter most quickly with a balance of "brown" and "green" materials (brown = more carbon, green = more nitrogen). Common materials are listed in the chart below.

MATERIALS FOR COMPOSTING

"BROWNS" (HIGHER CARBON)	"GREENS" (HIGHER NITROGEN)	THINGS TO AVOID IN HOME COMPOST PILES
Dry yellow or brown leaves	Kitchen waste: vegetables, fruit, coffee grounds, eggshells, bread, grains, tea bags	Meat, dairy products, oils
Dry brown grass clippings	Fresh green leaves	Dog or cat manure
Plant stalks (corn, sunflowers, etc.)	Green grass clippings	Sawdust or wood shavings
Shredded office paper or newspaper	Fresh weeds (without seeds on them)	Branches or twigs
Straw	Manure from chickens, cows, horses, rabbits	

Aim for a brown-to-green ratio between 50/50 and 75/25 in your pile, but don't worry about being too precise.

COMPOSTING KITCHEN WASTE SEPARATELY

If an open-pile composting system is not properly managed, kitchen wastes can attract rodents, flies, and other unwelcome creatures. By removing the kitchen waste from the pile and composting it separately, you remove the source of attraction for pests. There are two easy ways to do this: in a food digester or in a worm bin. Both can be used successfully in an urban environment or small yard.

A **food digester** is a sealed container (often cone or cylinder shaped) that is partially buried in the ground. Microorganisms and worms from the surrounding soil can enter the bin to decompose the food wastes, but rodents are unable to get in.

A **worm bin** is a sealed box that houses a colony of "red wiggler" worms. The worms chow down on the kitchen wastes that you add, and excrete it back out as worm *castings* (a wonderful organic soil amendment). It's like an ant farm or an aquarium, but it makes compost!

While a food digester or worm bin is great for your kitchen scraps, you probably won't be able to fit all your yard and your garden waste in there too. Either compost that material in a traditional pile (or three-bin system), or have it composted off site. A traditional pile without kitchen scraps won't attract rodents or flies and can be managed much less intensively.

Using a Food Digester

1. Buy or build a food digester, or two. (See the Resources section for information on sellers and building plans.)
2. Find the right location. Specifically, this means

away from the house but easy to access, in full sun or partial shade (in full shade the compost may decompose too slowly).

3. Dig a hole as directed in the manufacturer's directions, usually 18–28 in. deep and 32–36 in. wide. Install the food digester as directed.
4. Start adding your kitchen scraps to the digester. We recommend keeping a plastic or metal container in your kitchen to collect the scraps. A well-sealing lid will prevent odors from escaping.
5. Each time you add food wastes, top them with a thin layer of soil, wood ash, leaves, grass clippings, or compost. This will help suppress insects.
6. When the material has accumulated to within a few inches of ground level, start using your

ABOVE: **A food digester is a clean, easy way to compost small amounts of kitchen and yard waste.**

other digester, if you have one. In most cases, by the time the second digester is full, the contents of the first will be ready to empty and use in the garden. If you produce large amounts of kitchen waste, you may even consider having three food digesters.

What kitchen wastes are suitable to put in a food digester? Vegetable and fruit trimmings and leftovers, rotten or damaged vegetables and fruit from the garden, coffee grounds, eggshells, bread, grains, tea bags.

What kitchen wastes are *not* suitable for home composting? Meat (red meat, fish, poultry) or meat residues (fat, bones, etc.), dairy products, pet waste.

ABOVE: Drill drainage and air holes in an 18-gallon container, stack on top of a container without holes (to catch runoff), and add paper bedding and appropriate kitchen wastes.

Using a Worm Bin

Vermicomposting is a method of using worms to process your food wastes. It requires a sealed container, some "red wiggler" worms *(Eisenia foetida)*, and your kitchen scraps. A worm bin requires more work than the digester, and if you produce a lot of food scraps, one bin may not be sufficient, so consider using two or three. We think you'll find that worms are loving and affectionate pets (OK, maybe not, but worm compost is very space efficient and will provide you with one of the best organic soil amendments).

You can buy ready-made wooden or plastic worm bins, or build your own out of wood. To build a worm bin from everyday plastic storage bins:

- Three or four 10 gal. stackable plastic storage bins with tight-fitting lids
- A drill with a ¼ in. or ½ in. drill bit
- Plenty of shredded newspaper or office paper (but not coated magazine paper)
- 1 lb. of red wiggler worms (available online or possibly at local garden stores)

The assembly is simple:

1. Drill ¼ in. or ½ in. holes around the upper walls and in the bottom of one of the plastic bins. The holes in the walls will allow air to enter the container so the worms don't suffocate, and the holes in the bottom will drain excess moisture from the bin so the worms don't drown.

2. Nest the bin with holes into a bin without holes. The bottom bin will catch draining water and any other materials that fall out (liquid that collects in the lower bin can be used as fertilizer).

3. Moisten a few handfuls of shredded newspaper and add it to the top bin.

4. Place the worms on the newspaper.

5. Place your kitchen scraps on the newspaper, and cover the scraps and the worms with another layer of moist, shredded paper.

6. Put a lid on the top bin. Over time, the worms will digest all of the scraps and the newspaper and turn it into compost called worm castings.

7. Keep adding food scraps and shredded newspaper periodically, until the bin is three-quarters full.

8. When the bin is three-quarters full, your food scraps will have to start going into your third container. Drill holes in the new bin just like you did in step 1.

9. To begin composting in the third bin, either stack it on top of the other two bins and allow the worms to migrate to the new location, or

ABOVE LEFT: Remove finished compost from your plastic bin as it becomes available; you can stack another bin on top and let the worms migrate up to a container of fresh food scraps and bedding. ABOVE: A homemade wooden worm bin uses a variety of materials.

scoop out a handful of the worm-laden compost and add it directly to the new bin.

    A. If stacking, remove the lid from the top bin and rest the new container directly on top of the compost. Once the worms have finished eating the material in the first bin, they will migrate up through the bottom holes of the new one, leaving behind finished worm castings.

    B. If this seems too messy and you don't want to stack the bins, simply repeat steps 1 through 7 to prepare a new worm bin setup with third and fourth bins. Start them off with a scoop of worm-filled compost from the established bin.

10. When the food in the first bin is totally composted (dark brown, crumbly, and no sign of newspaper or food scraps), harvest the finished castings and use them in the garden. Some worms will travel with the compost into the garden, but try to separate out as many clumps of them as possible to return to your bins.

11. Wash out the emptied bins and repeat.

You'll need a dark, relatively warm place in which to keep your worm bins. Consider using a garage, an unfinished basement, a laundry room, or a tool shed. Worm bins can be kept outside when temperatures are warm, but if left in the sun, the worms will overheat and cook to death. Likewise, they will freeze to death if left out during the winter.

What kitchen wastes are suitable to put in a worm bin? Vegetable and fruit trimmings and leftovers, rotten or damaged vegetables and fruit from the garden, coffee grounds, eggshells, bread, grains, tea bags.

What kitchen wastes are *not* suitable to put in a worm bin? Meat (fish, poultry, beef, etc.) or meat residues (fat, bones, etc.), dairy, pet waste.

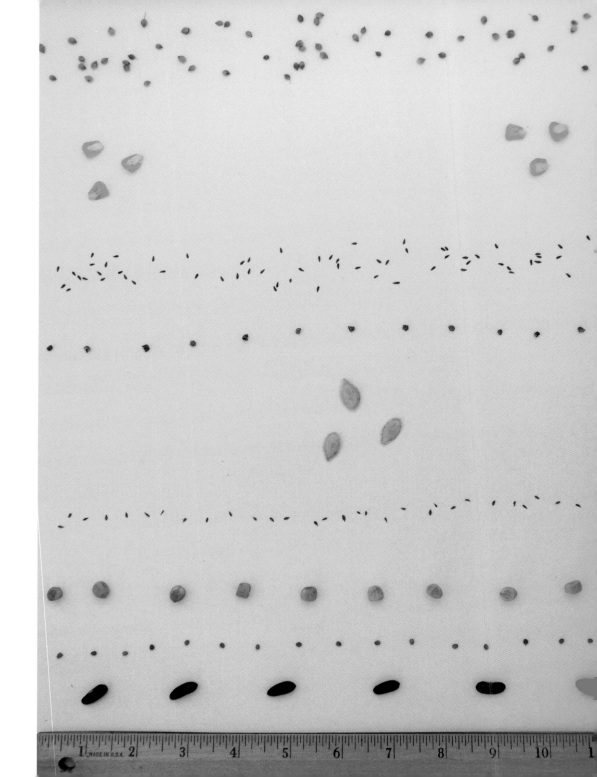

12

ESSENTIAL GARDEN SKILLS

THERE'S NO SUCH THING as a green thumb. Gardening does seem to come naturally to some people, in the sense that they get hooked on it faster than others, but nobody's born knowing instinctively how to garden. People who seem to have a magic touch with plants are just people who have taken the time to learn about what they're growing, and who take a few minutes each day to check on their crops. Soon enough, that will be you!

To be the proud owner of a thriving garden, you'll need certain skills. The good news is, those skills aren't particularly challenging. What's more, you already have several of them. You can learn the others as you go. Let's look at the skills and basic knowledge every gardener should possess.

ACQUIRING SEEDS

You have a few choices when it comes to acquiring seeds for your garden. You can get them directly from a seed company, which means mail-ordering from their catalog or website. You can shop for them at local garden stores, hardware stores, or grocery stores. Sometimes you can get seeds from other local gardeners who collect their own.

If no one you know collects their own seed, we suggest ordering directly from a seed company whenever possible. The advantages are plenty: The seeds will cost less, you will have access to many more varieties, and you will be able to read descriptions of each variety, which will give you a better understanding of each crop's characteristics. The only disadvantage of buying from a seed company is that you need to put in your order at least a few weeks before you expect to start planting.

We recommend keeping copies of a few seed companies' catalogs (most can be ordered from the company websites) around for reference. They contain an incredible amount of useful information. The description in a catalog will give you a good idea as to whether or not a particular crop variety is suited to your growing conditions.

Before placing your order, write out a list of crops you plan to grow this year. Look up each one in the catalog or on the website, and read about the varieties that look most interesting. Once you've settled on the seeds you want, order the smallest quantity possible. A "packet" or "trial size" almost always contains more than enough seed for the home gardener. Remember, tiny seeds

OPPOSITE: Commonly direct-seeded crops shown with relative spacing density per row foot before thinning. From top: cilantro, corn, lettuce mix, beets, squash, carrots, peas, radishes, and beans.

grow into large plants, and you don't need too many to fill up your garden.

DIRECT-SEEDING

Some of the seeds you buy should be planted directly in the garden rather than started in pots and then transplanted—it depends on the crop. Fortunately, direct-seeding is very easy:

1. Based on the information in the catalog or on the seed package, choose the right time of year for sowing the particular crop.
2. Make sure the garden soil is fully prepared for planting. You should have already added the proper amounts of fertilizer and compost. Use a trowel and your hands to break up clumps on the soil's surface that could inhibit the sprouts from emerging.
3. Dig a furrow (shallow trench) or a series of holes to the right depth and with the right spacing (both of which depend on the crop— see Part IV: Crop Profiles for specifics).
4. Drop in the seeds.
5. Cover the seeds with soil, and gently pat the soil down to make sure the seeds make good contact with the soil and are not sitting on the surface.
6. Water the area until it is evenly moist.

Once the seeds are in place, mark the row with some kind of tag specifying the name of the crop, the variety, and the planting date. It's a good idea to put a label at the beginning and end of each row. If you're planting only a single hole (as with squash), place a tag next to it.

When direct-seeding, you need to make sure that the seed and the surrounding soil get evenly wet. The water you add will trigger the germination process—the plant won't start growing until

it gets wet. Sometimes the soil surface can be deceptive: It can appear wet but may still be dry just below the surface. The only way to know for sure is to check. Every time you water in a new row of seeds or seedlings, finger-test to make sure the top inch of soil is moist throughout the area.

ACQUIRING TRANSPLANTS

Early in the spring, vegetable plants in pots (often called "starts") will become available at local nurseries and hardware and grocery stores. There are good reasons to buy some of these for your garden. First, certain crops are difficult to grow from seed and will perform better if transplanted.

ABOVE: A healthy plant will be stout and dark green; an unhealthy, stressed plant may be taller but it will be thin and yellow, purple, or blue, and may flower prematurely. Shown here: tomatoes.

Others simply need to be started indoors many weeks before the weather is warm enough to plant them outside. Letting the experts do that for you—buying healthy, well-cared-for transplants—is a good way to jump-start your garden.

ABOVE: This four-inch pot holds three separate kale plants. ABOVE RIGHT: Carefully separate the plants, trying to leave a root mass and some soil at the base of each plant. Transplant into the garden at the appropriate spacing (12–18 inches for kale). RIGHT: Some plants, like these squash, may be stunted if their roots are disturbed. To keep them healthy, choose the best looking plant, and snip off all others with scissors or hand pruners.

Here are a few tips to help you avoid mistakes when buying transplants:

- Choose healthy, organically grown plants. Read the label that is on or in the pot. It should tell you where the plant was grown, its variety, and whether it was grown organically. Ideally, the source will be a nearby nursery with an organic certification.
- Look for plants that have recently arrived at the nursery. You want dark green, healthy-looking plants, and if the leaves have started to turn slightly blue, purple, or yellow, they are probably not worth buying (even if the price is marked down). Most plants from professional greenhouses arrive healthy and viable, but they often don't receive the care they need from the retailer. Vegetable plants grow quickly, and they quickly use up the soil nutrients in a small pot. If they are kept in a small pot for too long, they can become stressed and may never completely recover.
- Take a close look at the number of plants in the pot. Certain crops usually come one to a pot, such as tomatoes and peppers. Others have a few separate plants bunched in a pot (broccoli, lettuce, and chard may come like this). All too often, an eager gardener will buy a small pot of vegetables, take it home, and plant the whole cluster in a single hole. The plants are then forced to compete with each other for water, nutrients, and sunlight.

So take a good look at the plants in the pot. If you bought broccoli, for instance, you will likely see three or four independent stems coming up from the soil. Congratulations—you just bought four broccoli plants, not one! The problem is, to grow properly, broccoli plants need to be spaced 12 in. apart. So you will need to either remove them from the pot and gently separate them, or cut off all but one plant.

Some plants don't mind having their roots disturbed, but others can become very stressed and end up stunted in their growth if you disturb their roots. If you are unsure what to do or are uncomfortable separating plants, snip off all but one at the base with scissors. Whichever way you go, you will need to separate the transplants to ensure proper health and growth.

Below is a list of plants whose roots should not be disturbed. Be very gentle when transplanting these crops, and always snip off extra plants at the base rather than trying to separate them. Any crop not listed here can handle careful separation.

- Beans
- Cucumbers
- Peas
- Pumpkins
- Summer squash
- Winter squash
- Zucchini

Do not plan to keep a purchased plant in its pot for too long. It's best to shop for transplants only a day or two before you plan to plant them in the garden. It's very easy to set potted plants aside, then forget about them and let them dry out (small pots also dry out more quickly than larger pots).

GROWING YOUR OWN TRANSPLANTS

You may want to try starting seeds indoors and growing your own transplants, rather than buying them at a nursery. This is a fun way to pass the time, especially if you're itching to get started on your garden but it's not warm enough to start planting outside.

Be aware, however, that homegrown transplants

are high-maintenance. You'll need to check on them every day to see if they need water (as we mentioned, small pots dry out quickly), supply them with a lot of light, and administer small doses of liquid fertilizer as they grow. If that sounds like more work than you're interested in doing, consider buying your early and long-season crops as transplants. You will still be able to direct-seed other crops later in the season.

If you decide to grow your own transplants, set up your operation where it will be easy to check on the plants each day. If it is out of the way, you may not notice problems with the young, delicate plants until it is too late—and you don't want to get frustrated before even planting anything in the ground! Also, try for a place that can get a little dirty and where you can safely water your plants (some water may drip from the bottom of the trays).

Leggy **is a term applied to plants that are growing tall, thin stems. This happens when sun-starved plants must search for adequate light. Leggy plants are generally less healthy than those grown in full sunlight and will produce smaller crop yields.**

What You'll Need:

- **A sunny, south-facing window and/ or a fluorescent light fixture (with full-spectrum bulbs) that can be moved up and down on a chain or rope.** If your young plants don't receive adequate light, they will become stressed and get "leggy," which means they grow tall too quickly and produce skinny, unhealthy stems that can easily break.
- **Seed-starting soil mix.** Ideally, this will be a "sterile" soil mix. Ask at your local garden store for soil mixes designed specifically for seed starting. These may be called "germination mix" or "seed-starting mix." They work better than potting soil or garden soil because they are finely sifted to contain only tiny particles. These small particles won't block germinating seeds from emerging, as the larger particles in a potting soil might.

- **Seed trays.** One easy option is to buy a set of plug trays, which should be available at your garden store. Make sure there are drainage holes in the bottom.
- **Plant labels**
- **Seeds**
- **Liquid fertilizer**
- **Watering can/jar**

How to Do It

1. Set up your fluorescent light fixture on a movable chain. You must be able to move the light, since you will want to keep it within a few inches of the plants as they grow. Fluorescent light is good for plants, but due to its low intensity, it needs to be very close to them.

6. Keep the soil continuously moist, until the seed emerges. During germination, the plant is at its most vulnerable and should not dry out at all.
7. Once the plant is visible, start adding small amounts of liquid fertilizer. Mix the fertilizer to the dilution recommended on the bottle, and water with the mixture once a week.
8. Make sure to keep the plants evenly watered. They should never wilt due to lack of water.
9. As the plants grow, adjust the light fixture to keep the bulb 2–3 in. from the top of the plants.
10. Three weeks after germination, if it is still too early to plant outdoors, transfer each plant into a 3–4 in. pot filled with potting soil. If you need to keep it indoors for a long period of time (6 to 8 weeks), you may eventually need to transfer it to an even larger pot.

2. Fill the planting tray with seed-starting mix or potting soil.
3. Make labels for your crops, designating the type of vegetable, the specific variety, and the date you sowed the seed.
4. Sow the seeds to the appropriate depth (see the seed packet or catalog, or this book's crop profiles).
5. Water the tray. Any type of water except distilled water will do. Check the soil to make sure it has soaked up the water evenly throughout.

ABOVE: A fluorescent light hangs a few inches above young plants. As the plants grow, the chains are adjusted to move the light up so that it always remains 2–4 inches above the tops of the plants. If using LED or metal halide bulbs, the light can be fixed farther above the plants.

TRANSPLANTING

Whether you grew or purchased your transplants, they need to be removed from their pots and planted in the garden before their roots run out of space. Before going into the garden, homegrown transplants should spend a few nights outdoors in their pots to "harden off" (get acclimated to cooler temperatures). Purchased transplants will (hopefully) have already been hardened off.

Transplanting is a pretty easy process. Here's how to do it:

1. Choose the appropriate time to move your crops to the garden, based on your growing zone. Make sure the temperature is in the proper range for the crops you're planting.
2. Make sure the garden is ready. If you have recently set up your garden beds, the soil will probably be loose, fertilized, and ready for

planting. If the beds have been in place awhile, loosen up the soil, add the correct amount of fertilizer and compost, and dig a hole big enough for your transplant. If the soil is especially dry, water the hole before planting.

3. Make sure the soil in the pot is moist. This will help the plant's root ball hold together when you remove it from the pot. If the plant is in a plastic pot or tray, squeeze the bottom of the container with your fingers on all sides to loosen up the root ball. Turn the pot sideways or upside down, and gently pull out the plant, holding it by the leaves and not the stem. The plant can recover relatively easily from damage that may occur to its leaves, but moving it by its stem may break it, possibly damaging the plant beyond repair.

4. Place the plant in the prepared hole, cover the roots with soil, and water until the area is saturated. Check the soil with your finger to make sure the area is evenly moist. It can sometimes take much more water to saturate the soil particles than you might think, so it is always wise to perform a finger test.

TOP RIGHT: Eventually, you will be able to accurately space your plants without a measuring tool; but to start out, use a ruler or hand trowel to make measurements. RIGHT: Press the soil down firmly around your transplants to make sure they remain upright and the roots make good contact with the soil. Water your transplants as soon as possible after planting.

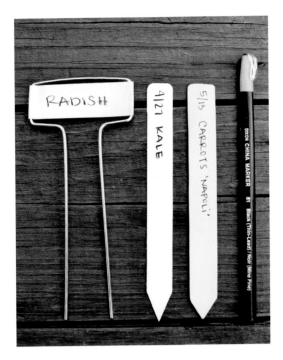

MULCHING

Mulch is an important tool for your garden. It has several uses, including suppressing weeds, conserving moisture in the soil, and limiting fluctuations in soil temperature.

We suggest using mulches made of "organic" materials. By this, we don't mean they are certified organic, but simply that they are derived from natural sources and will decompose over time. Examples include straw and grass clippings. Inorganic mulches are typically made from plastic and do not decompose, although they may degrade in quality due to exposure to sunlight.

We prefer organic mulches because they slowly add nutrients and organic matter to your soil as they break down. Plastic mulches do not add fertility to your soil; in fact, they can become a nuisance, as they often break into smaller, difficult-to-manage pieces.

Mulch applied to pathways will suppress weeds, keep the paths pleasant to walk on, and keep them free of mud in wet times of year. Applied directly to garden beds, mulch will conserve soil moisture (you'll need to water less frequently) and keep weeds down.

Mulch is best applied to your beds after transplants have been placed in the soil and direct-seeded crops have emerged and grown partway to maturity. If it's applied directly over direct-seeded crops, it can prevent them from germinating properly or block sunlight the young plants need to grow. It is important to keep mulch at least 1–2 in. from the stems of each plant. Plants that are in direct contact with mulch may be more susceptible to disease and pest problems.

Mulch can also be applied at the end of the season, to add organic matter and to protect your garden from winter snow and rain, which can leach nutrients from the soil.

LABELING

As we mentioned in "Direct-seeding," it is always a good idea to label your beds with tags specifying the crop, the variety, and the planting date. This is an important step in keeping an organized, manageable garden. It will help you assess whether crops were planted too early, too late, or at just the right time, as well as help you keep track of how long each variety takes to grow to maturity and which varieties perform best. This information will enable you to better care for your plants and more effectively plan next year's garden.

ABOVE: Label your crops with the variety and date of planting, or just the basic crop name.

MULCHES TO USE ON GARDEN BEDS

Compost

Consider using compost as a mulch on your beds. Apply a 2–3 in. layer of compost around the base of maturing crops. In our region (the Pacific Northwest), where weather conditions are cool and wet, compost is the best mulch choice, because other organic mulches tend to create a perfect habitat for slugs (one of our primary garden pests). Note that compost is not a good mulch for pathways, since it will make them muddy and dirty.

Straw

This is probably the most widely used garden mulch and the best choice for many regions. Straw is relatively inexpensive to purchase—though it can be

ABOVE: Straw is one of the very best organic mulches.

difficult to find and transport in urban areas—and since it can be applied in a thick layer, it really helps reduce the amount of water that evaporates from your soil. Apply a 4–6 in. layer underneath your maturing vegetable plants and in your pathways. You can leave straw mulch in place at the end of the growing season to protect the soil through the winter. The following spring, rake it off and reuse or compost it. Make sure not to turn it into the soil in a garden bed, as it can tie up nitrogen as it decomposes.

There is a big difference between straw and hay! Straw is dried grass collected after the seed heads have been removed. High-quality straw should be free of seeds, and it is the best choice for garden mulch. Hay is dried grass that has been harvested specifically for use as animal feed. It may contain seed heads, so it is not a good choice for garden mulch. Remember, hay is for horses! Using hay or poor-quality straw can do more harm than good in your garden.

Grass Clippings

Provided the grass was cut before it set seed, fresh or dried grass clippings make great mulch for beds and/or pathways. Apply a 1–2 in. layer. Any thicker than that, and it may mat down and cause fungus issues, or prevent the soil from absorbing enough air and water.

Shredded Leaves

Deciduous leaves make great mulch for your beds, but you must shred them first. Whole leaves can form a dense mat similar to too-deep grass clippings and lead to fungal problems. Apply a 2–3 in. layer of shredded leaves to your garden beds. *Caution:* Do not use pine needles or leaves from other coniferous plants to mulch your garden beds. These are very acidic and will change the soil's pH.

Burlap

Many people like to use burlap sacks or a roll of burlap as mulch. Burlap is durable (it will last for several seasons), it is easy to pick up and move around if need be, and it is great at suppressing weeds. It can be used to cover garden beds in winter to help protect the soil, and will also keep weeds down in pathways.

Plastic

Some gardeners prefer to use a layer of plastic as mulch on their beds. Black or colored plastic is very effective at weed suppression, and it can help heat up soil during cold weather. You'll need to punch holes through it for your transplants or seeds. If you use plastic mulch, make sure to set up drip irrigation lines underneath it; otherwise, since the plastic prevents rain from reaching the soil, your plants could lose all access to water!

Landscape Fabric

A range of "landscape fabrics" are readily available. These are typically woven plastic materials that allow water penetration but suppress weeds. Landscape fabric can be useful on top of garden beds for weed suppression (you'll need to cut

ABOVE: Shredded hardwood leaves make a great mulch.

small holes to plant through) and is also suitable for pathways. However, if the material is left in place for several seasons, weed seeds will accumulate on top and actually grow roots into the fabric! Trying to clean up landscape fabric that is interlaced with weed roots can be a real nightmare.

MULCHES FOR PATHWAYS ONLY

Bark or Wood Chips

Most plant nurseries, garden stores, and landscaping centers carry bark mulch or wood chips. These are very useful and effective as mulch for garden pathways, but do not mix them into your garden beds. Like straw, they can affect soil nutrient availability. Apply a thick layer (3–8 in.) of bark or wood chips to create a soft pathway that is easy to walk on and work in.

Nut Shells

Gardeners in some areas have access to the empty shells of pecans, hazelnuts, or other nuts, and some like to use these to mulch their pathways. Apply a 4–5 in. layer. Note that nut shells may be difficult to contain in open-sided pathways.

Gravel

Any type of gravel can make a clean, durable pathway. But while it can be a good choice between wood-framed beds or beds with rock perimeters, it can be messy in gardens that lack edging

ABOVE: Choose a mulch for your paths that you like to walk on and feels comfortable for working. Shown here: bark mulch.

materials. Also, as weed seeds settle into your pathways, weeding in gravel can become difficult and tedious. One thing is certain, though: It will last for years!

TRELLISING

Certain crops grow as vines, and they can take up a lot of ground space in the garden. Some can either be trellised or left to sprawl across the ground, while others need trellising to ensure that the stems don't break and that the fruit ripens properly. Let's examine several easy trellises you can buy or build for your garden.

ABOVE: These cucumbers are trained up a piece of twine attached to an overhead beam. ABOVE RIGHT: Cage trellises work well for cucumbers, tomatoes, or any other vine crop.

TWINE TRELLIS

If you are planting any vining crops near an existing structure, you may be able to grow them on pieces of twine attached to that structure. We use this technique when growing tomatoes, pole beans, or snap peas. Simply tie strong twine in a knot to a sturdy, tall structure hanging over or near the plant. Let the twine hang all the way to the ground, and attach it there by tying it to a small stake or wrapping it around a rock. As the pole bean or pea plant or tomato plant grows, gently twist its stalk around the twine so that the plant wraps around and around as it grows. Once it finds the twine, it should have no trouble working its way up.

CAGE TRELLIS

There are many designs and brands of cages available, good for growing tomatoes, cucumbers, or winter squash. The fancier ones can be expensive,

but they are easy to set up and will last for years. Make sure to get a cage that is large enough to handle the full size of your crop. Oftentimes, the smallest tomato cages cannot accommodate a large, healthy tomato plant, so look for a sturdy cage that is at least 4 or 5 ft. tall. These are worth the extra investment. You can make your own cage from a roll of heavy fencing wire.

SINGLE-STAKE TRELLIS

Some crops can be trained up a single stake. We often use single stakes to grow tomato plants. Use any sturdy pole that can be secured in the ground and will be strong enough to hold the weight of the plant. For a sturdy tomato trellis, we buy ½ in. rebar from the local hardware store, have it cut to 6½–7 ft. lengths, and pound them 2 ft. into the ground. However, since a tomato plant does not have vining tendrils, you must tie it to the stake as it grows (which is more work than growing it

in a cage). But this allows for easier pruning and harvesting.

LADDER TRELLIS

You can build a simple "ladder" in your garden with a few easy-to-find materials. We use ladder trellises to grow winter squash, pumpkins, pole beans, and peas. Simply build a rectangular frame and cover it with a piece of wire mesh. Attach two frames at the top to make an A-frame ladder.

TIPI TRELLIS

A "tipi" makes a beautiful trellis for your vining crops. We use these for pole beans and snap peas.

ABOVE LEFT: A ladder trellis works great for vines such as winter squash, cucumbers, and beans. Shown here: birdhouse gourds. ABOVE: A tipi trellis is best suited for pole beans.

poles and let the vines use the poles as a support. When your plants are young, they may need some assistance finding the tipi. Keep an eye on them and help them attach themselves to the trellis. As they grow, use additional twine to tie any escaping plants back onto the trellis.

FENCE TRELLIS

Consider using an existing fence to trellis your crops. If the garden is adjacent to a fence, you can attach twine or net, or use parts of the structure (such as wire panels) to support your crops.

NET TRELLIS

If a fence is not adjacent to the garden but you want to trellis the crop in a straight line across the edge of a bed, you can easily erect a fence-like net trellis. Look for prewoven "pea nets" at garden stores and online. To trellis peas or beans, we use these nets tied to solid posts. We find that using one post at either end and one post in the middle provides enough support for a typical 8 ft. long pea net. If you want to extend the row, simply add another post every 4 ft. As the vines grow up the net, consider tying twine across the front of the plants, to encourage them to stay on the net. This will help keep them from pulling off as they get heavy with fruit.

Tipis can be constructed from long bamboo poles or other tall stakes such as branches or purchased garden stakes. Select three or four poles of similar length and diameter (we often use three bamboo poles that are 7 ft. long). Lash the tops together as seen in the photos, and push the bottom ends of each pole as deeply as you can into the garden bed. A properly constructed tipi should remain stable without any extra staking. Use twine to wrap lines or crosses around the poles so that the vines have guides to help them grow up the trellis. Alternatively, you can plant only at the bases of the

HOOP HOUSES AND FLOATING ROW COVERS

A hoop house is a great way to protect your plants from insect pests or severe weather. It consists of a series of metal or plastic hoops over which you drape protective materials. Such materials can include greenhouse plastic, bird netting, shade cloth, or floating row cover. The most broadly useful of these is floating row cover (common brand

ABOVE: Nylon or twine netting makes a great trellis for peas, beans, or any other vine crop.

names are Reemay and Agribon), a polypropylene blanket that protects crops from cold weather, insects, and birds while still allowing light and moisture to pass through, so you can leave them on throughout the day.

BUILDING YOUR OWN

Hoop houses and row covers are not essential garden supplies, but if you end up with a serious infestation of leaf miners or flea beetles, or if you want to grow crops through the winter, they can work wonders. Here's how to build your own:

ABOVE: A hoop house of floating row cover can help keep plants warm and reduce pest damage.

What You'll Need

Hoops: Use white PVC water pipe, gray PVC electrical conduit (available at any hardware store), or #9 wire (buy this from an agricultural supplier). Plan on one hoop per 3–4 ft. of bed length. A 6–7 ft. length works well for a 4-ft.-wide bed. Shorter lengths will create a lower profile, and longer lengths will let you grow tall crops under cover. If you're using PVC, you'll need to buy two pieces of 2 ft. long (½ in. diameter) rebar for each hoop.

Row cover: You'll probably have to order this online (see the Resources section) or from a particularly well-stocked nursery in your area. The cover should be at least 6 ft. longer than your bed, and about 2 ft. wider than the length of the hoops (see the following instructions).

Weights: You will need several weights to hold the row cover in place. Almost anything will work; we like to use bricks or small rocks. Plan to use eight weights for a 4 × 8-foot bed. For PVC, you can use ready-made *snap clamps* instead (see Resources), to secure the row cover to the hoops.

How to Do It

1. Make your hoops: Cut the PVC pipe or #9 wire to size to fit in an arc over your bed. Use heavy wire cutters to cut the #9 wire; PVC is easily cut with a hacksaw.

2. Cut your row cover about 6 ft. longer than the bed and about 2 ft. wider than the length of the hoops. This will give you enough excess to secure the sides and ends with weights. Row cover 10 ft. wide works well for 7 ft.

hoops. If you order online, you'll probably have to buy a roll that's at least 50 ft. long, but you can easily cut it down to size.

3. Set the hoops: For a #9 wire hoop, simply bend the wire into an arc and drive the ends into the soil. To set up a PVC hoop, hammer a 2-ft. rebar stake 12–18 in. deep on each side

ABOVE LEFT: A short piece of rebar is hammered into the soil on either side of the bed and makes an anchor for the PVC pipe as it arcs over the bed. ABOVE: For wooden framed beds, a ¾-inch piece of PVC is held to the side of the bed with 1-inch pipe clamps. A length of ½-inch conduit fits perfectly inside the clamped piece to create a sturdy hoop.

of the bed where you want to place the hoop. Slide one end of the PVC over the rebar stake and bend it over to slide over the opposite one. Place one hoop at each end of the bed, and one every 3–4 ft. in between.

4. Pull the row cover over the bed. Bunch the fabric at one end of the bed and secure it with a weight or clamp. Then stretch the fabric to the opposite end until it's tight, and weight or clamp that end. Place the rest of the weights or clamps along the sides of the cover to secure it (one every 3 ft. or so).

5. Pull your row cover off periodically to check the crops and the moisture level of the soil. Otherwise you can leave it in place.

A couple of notes on row covers for wood-framed raised beds:

- The row cover must be wide enough to reach the ground so you can secure it with the weights. If the fabric does not reach the ground, cut the hoops shorter or secure the cover with snap clamps instead of weights.
- An alternative to securing the hoops by driving them into the soil is to make custom holders using ¾ in. PVC and ¾ in. pipe clamps.

Some advanced row cover techniques:

- You can use greenhouse plastic (see the Resources section for suppliers) instead of floating row cover for additional warming and frost protection when growing cool-season crops, but you'll have to remove the covers when the sun is out, so you don't overheat your crops. Plastic cover heats the bed up more than row cover but requires much more ongoing management.
- Pulling shade cloth (see Resources) over the hoops in the hot summer months will help

you grow cool-loving crops such as lettuce and spinach.

- You can cover hoops with bird netting (see Resources) to protect fruiting crops such as strawberries, which are particularly appealing to our avian friends.

ABOVE: A hoop house covered in shade cloth protects heat-sensitive plants from the midsummer sun. Shown here: young lettuce transplants.

WEEDING

Weeding is easy; the trick is knowing which plants are weeds. To put it most simply, any plant that you don't want in your garden is a weed.

If you transplant crops into the garden, they should be easy to keep track of, since you know what they look like and where you placed them. Direct-seeded crops should also be easy to recognize, since they will emerge from the soil in a straight row or a block, whereas weeds appear all over the garden beds and pathways in random patterns.

Even a vegetable plant that is growing out of place can be considered a weed. Keep in mind that everything in the garden is arranged to make the most of the space without forcing crops to compete with each other for water, nutrients, and sun. So any additional plants can compromise the system and reduce the vitality of your crops. It is very important to keep your garden as weed-free as possible.

Weeds are easiest to remove when they are still small. Spending 15 to 30 minutes every week

ABOVE: Use your hands or a trowel to cultivate the surface of the soil on a regular basis to easily kill weeds while they are small. ABOVE RIGHT: Large weeds will compete with your vegetables, reducing their size and vigor. Shown here: potatoes becoming overwhelmed by weeds.

clearing newly emerged weeds from your garden will eliminate the need to spend more time later, when it may take all afternoon to pull up large weeds with well-established root systems. Think of it this way: The more often you weed, the less time you will spend weeding!

The other advantage of weeding when plants are small is that you remove the risk of the weeds setting seed in your garden. One weed can produce thousands of viable seeds, and if these are allowed to drop into your garden, you will be weeding out their offspring for years to come.

If you do end up with larger weeds, take the time to remove as much of the root as possible. If you chop off only the top, the plant will quickly regrow from the remaining root system.

A SKILL FOR CONTAINER GARDENERS: REPOTTING PERENNIALS

Although the majority of vegetables you grow in containers will be annuals, the list may also include a few perennial vegetables and perennial herbs. If your gardening efforts succeed, those perennials will live to grow bigger with each season. However, maybe because you have limited space, or you decide you don't really need 10 pounds of mint each summer, you'll want some plants to stay the same size each year. At the same time, there may be others that you want to grow into bigger pots each year, to increase their yield. You may even decide to separate a large plant into several smaller containers.

Whatever size you want the plants to be, it is a good idea to repot perennials every year or two. This allows you to provide them with new soil and prune back their roots to promote new, healthy root growth. Here's how to go about it:

1. If you plan to graduate a plant to a bigger pot, move it up gradually: Buy a pot 1½ or 2 times larger each year, rather than going straight for the tenfold increase you ultimately want to achieve. If you don't want the plant to get any bigger, then simply reuse the same pot. If you are separating the plant into sections, find a few smaller pots.

2. In the spring, after the last frost date, remove the plant from the pot. If you plan to reuse the pot, clean it out before replanting (as directed in chapter 6: Creating a Container Garden).

ABOVE: A vigorous perennial will eventually outgrow its pot and must be root pruned and/ or repotted in a bigger container. To root prune, snip off or cut roots that wind around the plant.

3. Prune the roots. Chances are, your plant will have built a relatively large root system over the course of the past year. If it is in a small container, the roots will likely wrap around the sides and bottom in a circle so that, when you remove the plant from the pot, the soil retains the shape of the pot because the roots are holding it together. If this is the case, take a sharp knife and cut through the circling roots in a few places. If they are densely tangled, it is all right to remove whole sections of the excess roots.

   If the plant was in a larger pot, the roots may not have filled the entire space, but it is still a good idea to trim the root system's outer edges before repotting. Root pruning encourages healthy new root growth.

4. Divide the plant if necessary. To break the plant down into several smaller plants, look for natural divisions in the stems or roots and carefully pull the sections apart. If you are repotting into the same size pot or a larger one, examine the plant for any unhealthy or tangled sections that can be removed and composted.

5. Replace at least half of the existing soil with fresh potting soil. Fertilize it according to the directions given for the crop in this book's crop profiles.

6. Replant your perennial and water-in the plant.

OPPOSITE: Loosen the roots of a perennial when repotting to initiate healthy new root growth.

13

KNOW YOUR CLIMATE

THE GUIDELINES, INSTRUCTIONS, and information we provide in this book apply to every area of the United States. However, because we live in such a vast land, gardeners need to take several climatic factors into consideration. Different parts of the country get different amounts of rainfall, have different high and low temperatures, and get different amounts of sun. Understanding how your region's climate affects your crops will help you plan your garden activities throughout the season

PLANT HARDINESS ZONES

The United States Department of Agriculture (USDA) has created a map of North America that divides it into "Hardiness Zones" based on the average annual minimum temperature. There are 11 such zones, with many of them divided into A and B subcategories. Knowing your zone helps you understand which plants (and specific varieties) grow best in your area and when to plant them. It also gives you a sense of your seasonal irrigation needs.

OPPOSITE: Starting a garden will make you more aware of weather patterns and the changing of the seasons.

Got your zone? The next step is to figure out your first and last frost dates. At first glance the terminology seems a little backward: *First frost* refers to the first frost of the fall, which signals the end of the main growing season. *Last frost* refers to the last frost of the spring, or the start of the main growing season. Thus, because it comes at the beginning of the growing season, throughout this book, we will always present the "last frost" date first!

Frost dates aren't absolutes, and you can grow crops earlier and later in the year, but the majority of your production will happen between your zone's last frost and first frost dates.

The following table lists approximate first and last frost dates for each zone. Keep in mind that these dates are based on yearly averages; in a particular year, a frost may occur several weeks earlier or later than the average date. Still, you can plant your garden based on these average dates. If you want to get more precise about your town or county, check out the United States National Arboretum's website for an online hardiness zone map (see the Resources section), or ask a local plant nursery or your county agricultural extension office. Specific dates for your area should be easy to find. If you know your zip code and have internet access, try: www.garden.org/zipzone.

LAST AND FIRST FROST DATES

USDA HARDINESS ZONE	LAST FROST DATE	FIRST FROST DATE
1	June 15	July 15
2	May 15	August 15
3	May 15	September 15
4	May 15	September 15
5	April 15	October 15
6	April 15	October 15
7	April 15	October 15
8	March 15	November 15
9	February 15	December 15
10	January 31	December 15
11	No frost	No frost

ZONE	AVG. ANNUAL LOW
2	-40°F through -50°F
3	-30°F through -40°F
4	-20°F through -30°F
5	-10°F through -20°F
6	0°F through -10°F
7	10°F through 0°F
8	20°F through 10°F
9	30°F through 20°F
10	40°F through 30°F

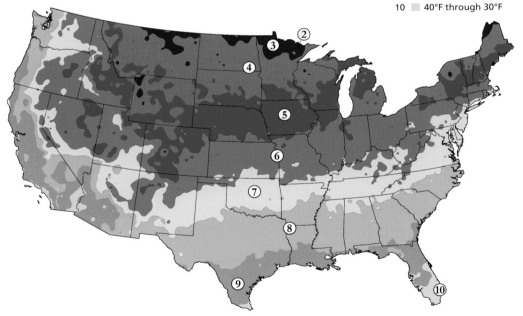

The USDA Hardiness Zone Map; zone 1 is the coldest and located only in Alaska; zone 11 is the warmest and located only in Hawaii. © *The National Arbor Day Foundation.*

REGIONAL DIFFERENCES

Although the crops covered in this book can be grown in any part of the country, your specific location will determine when they can be planted outside, how quickly they will grow to maturity, and how many times you will be able to plant them in the course of a year. From a plant's perspective, the following are the key climatic differences between regions:

- **Season length:** Unless you live on the equator, the hours of daylight your garden receives will change throughout the year (longer days in summer, shorter days in winter). This varies by latitude. The amount of sunlight your garden receives dictates how quickly crops are able to grow.

- **High and low temperatures:** Usually correlated with your latitude, temperatures are also influenced by altitude, proximity to large bodies of water, and surrounding population density (areas with more buildings and pavement absorb more heat and are warmer than rural areas). Freezing temperatures signal the beginning and end of the main gardening season. Similarly, extreme heat can bring about the end of certain crops.

- **Precipitation:** Some areas receive very little rain during the growing season, and others may see rain almost every day (possibly negating the need for supplemental irrigation during parts of the season).

Let's take a quick look at the major regions of the United States, and how their climates affect plant growth.

Northeast

The Northeast is known for severe winter storms and sweltering, humid summers; the contrast between the seasons can be astounding. The relatively short duration of the warm season makes it important that garden transplants be started early in the year and kept inside until the danger of frost is past. The warm summer nights help crops grow quickly, so progress in the garden can be very fast.

Southeast

Most areas of the Southeast have a pretty typical, cyclical growing season … only warmer. Since the winters are milder than in northern regions, spring crops can be planted earlier and will grow later in the season. The longer growing season allows many crops to produce larger yields than they can in cooler areas. If you live in an area that rarely experiences temperatures below freezing (32°F), you may have the opportunity to grow many crops during the entire year.

In the warmest parts of the Southeast (like southern Florida), crops can be grown on an alternate schedule under which "spring" planting happens in the fall and the growing season lasts through the winter. Some vegetable crops may struggle with extreme heat in the summer months in these areas, so the planting schedule is organized around high temperatures rather than around the freezing temperatures of winter.

Midwest

The Midwest has a climatic pattern similar to that of the Northeast: very cold winters and very warm, humid summers. The Midwest is known to have some of the best native soil for growing food, and its climate is ideal for many crops. There are abundant spring and summer rains, which can sometimes reduce the need for watering. As in the Northeast, it is crucial to wait until the danger of frost is past, which usually occurs in early or mid-May.

Great Plains

The Plains can undergo even shorter, more extreme shifts in temperature than the Northeast or Midwest. The last frost of spring may happen as late as June, and the first frost of the fall can come in September. Fortunately, summer weather is hot enough that crops are able to grow very quickly in the short window that they have. Make sure your crops are planted as soon as the weather warms up, so they have time to grow to maturity before fall temperatures start to drop.

Southwest

Areas of the Southwest experience the hottest temperatures in the country. Because of the nature of the landscape, many parts of the Southwest see wide variations in temperature in the course of a single day: It's not uncommon to have a 40°–50° shift in temperature between day and night. Southwest winters can be very cold and dry, but summers are hot enough to keep even the most heat-loving crops happy. Arid parts of the Southwest may require a daily watering schedule.

Northwest

Much of the Northwest is known for its maritime climate. This means that, although the area sits at relatively high latitude, the warming effect of the Pacific Ocean keeps temperatures mild. While winter temperatures stay relatively warm, summers remain relatively cool. Crops can often be planted out earlier than in other regions, but they take longer to mature due to the consistently cool evenings. Growing certain cold-tolerant crops year-round is possible in much of the Northwest.

Central and Southern California

Parts of California are warm enough to grow vegetables year-round. The timing of crop planting in these areas is much more variable than in other regions, and you can often get in multiple plantings in a single year. As in the Southwest, some vegetable crops may struggle with extreme heat in the late summer months, so the planting schedule is organized around high temperatures rather than the freezing temperatures of winter.

Hawaii

The Hawaiian Islands are a truly tropical location, which means that you can typically get in two full growing seasons every year. The growing timetable is based on dry and wet seasons rather than summer and fall. The wet season starts around November and continues through the spring. Generally, "spring" planting happens around January and then again around July or August.

Alaska

The very northern reaches of the United States have some of the most extreme growing conditions imaginable. The winter is very dark and cold, and the last frost of spring may happen very late, but summer days are very, very long. Some crops may be difficult to grow to maturity in Alaska, but many of the short- and half season crops will grow tremendously fast and large during the summer months.

OPPOSITE: Peas are one of the most beautiful and delicious crops for the home garden.

14

CROP PLANNING

BEFORE WE START TALKING about specific crops, let's spend a minute thinking about how crops interact with each other in the garden, so you can better imagine what your garden may look like as you select your crops.

There are plenty of ideas out there about how best to organize your crops. Some people believe that different plants should be mixed together so as to discourage pests or create visually interesting garden scenes. We recommend planting in individual rows and/or groups of the same plant. This has several advantages:

- When a particular crop is ready to be removed from the garden, you will be able to clear a whole row or section of the bed, leaving adequate space to plant another crop.
- Some crops have growth forms that make them incompatible with other plants. By planting your crops in groups, it's easier to keep compatible plants together and incompatible plants apart.
- Concentrations of the same crop are easier to manage—to apply fertilizers at the right time, thin the plants, etc.

Since there are virtually infinite crop combinations, it is impossible to give a set of exact rules for planting. But below are some general guidelines that should make garden planning easier. Over time, you will gain a better understanding of why crop spacing is so important and exactly how much space a plant will take up once it is mature.

GROWTH FORM

Tall crops: Plants that either have tall growth forms or are trellised on tall structures should be sited where they will not shade other, shorter garden crops. Good places to start are the north side of the garden or far to the east or west. *Examples: tomatoes and trellised vining crops (pole beans, cucumbers, peas, winter squash), flowers.*

Medium height crops: These are crops that grow only about 2–3 ft. tall. Some of them benefit from staking, so that they remain upright when loaded with fruit (a good example is a pepper plant), but generally they don't need large or complicated trellising. Because they are relatively short, these plants won't cast too much shade over other parts of the garden. *Examples: broccoli, peppers, kale, chard, bush beans.*

Short crops: Some crops are very short (6–12 in.). These include root crops such as carrots (where most of the growth is below ground)

OPPOSITE: Lettuce mix, spinach, and head lettuce.

and salad greens (like lettuce and spinach). Short crops are great because they can be fitted into areas where taller crops might not go and can be planted next to taller crops (as long as the short crops still receive sun exposure, i.e., anywhere but on the north side of a tall crop). You can plant a row of carrots or lettuce just to the south of a row of tomatoes, and both will perform fabulously. *Examples: beets, carrots, lettuce.*

Sprawling crops: Some crops grow as vines. These can be trellised so that they fit into the "tall crops" category, but most will also grow well if left to sprawl across the ground.

Letting them sprawl has advantages and disadvantages. On the plus side, you won't need to build or buy a trellis, and the plants won't cast

ABOVE: A row of maturing carrots behind a row of tiny carrot seedlings. LEFT: Front to back: kale and spinach, cilantro and carrots, lettuce, onions, potatoes, garlic. OPPOSITE: Winter squash trailing out of a raised bed.

shade across the garden. On the other hand, if you let them sprawl, they may take up quite a bit of square footage; also, their fruits may be more likely to rot. *Examples: pumpkins, cucumbers, winter squash.*

LIFE SPAN

Another way to think about your crops is in terms of their life span. Some will be ready to harvest and remove from the garden after only a month or six weeks, some will live for three to four months, and some will take all season long to reach maturity. It is helpful to know how long a plant will be in the garden, so you can plan to replace it with another crop once it is finished.

Long-season crops: In most climates, these crops are planted once a year, usually in spring or early summer. They are called long-season because it takes a long time for them to grow from seed to harvest. For example, you may start tomatoes from seed indoors in March, transplant them into the garden in May, and harvest them in August and September. Plan to keep long-season crops in place through the whole growing season.

Half season crops: These plants are generally planted twice a year. Half season crops take a few months to grow to maturity, so they are often planted in spring and then again in the middle of summer. The Brassicas (broccoli, cabbage, kale, etc.) are usually grown as half season crops. For example, we usually plant kale in April and then again in mid-July. Once the spring half season crops are harvested, replace them with short-season crops or a fall planting of half season crops.

Short-season crops: Short-season crops may take only a month or six weeks to reach maturity, so they can be planted several times during the season. These are the crops that are often "succession-planted." For example, cilantro (which grows very fast and then flowers very quickly) should be planted every two weeks during the growing season if you want a consistent supply. Many short-season crops are intolerant of high heat and so are best grown in spring and fall. In the summer they may bolt very quickly, which means they send up a flower stalk before they have grown to a suitable size for eating.

Keep in mind that you should only put in small amounts of your short-season crops each time you plant. If you plant too much at once, you may be overloaded with the crop one week and then have none at all the next week! Growing them in small amounts leaves space open in the garden to plant your next succession.

Perennials: These are crops that are planted once and come back year after year. Most vegetable crops, by contrast, are annuals, which means they must be planted from seed every year. When planting perennials, remember that you will be setting aside the space for the indefinite future. Some perennial crops last only a few years, but many can last a decade or longer.

CROP ROTATION

In a small garden, true crop rotation is very difficult. But there are several plant families that should be rotated to new spots each year, so that diseases and pests don't build up in the soil. Plant these in a new location each year (after a few years they will end up back where they started, but that is OK):

Alliums: garlic, leeks, onions, scallions

OPPOSITE: A row of bush beans (foreground) is planted on the south side of a pole bean trellis (background).

Brassicas: broccoli, cabbage, cauliflower, collards, kale

Cucurbits: cucumbers, pumpkins, summer squash, winter squash

Nightshades: eggplant, peppers, potatoes, tomatoes

Your other crops can be worked around these rotating crops to fill in the available spaces.

LAYING OUT YOUR GARDEN

Now it's time to apply all these concepts to your own vegetable garden. Here's how we suggest you divide your space and choose where to place each crop:

1. Make a list of the crops you would like to grow. You can come up with these off the top of your head or use this book's crop profiles section as a reference.
2. Use the Crop Size, Spacing, and Scheduling chart in the Appendices to categorize your chosen crops as long-, half-, and short-season crops, and as tall, medium-sized, or short crops.
3. Draw a simple map of your garden space.
4. Label your map with your chosen crops. When possible, keep tall and trellised crops on the far north, east, or west sides of the garden. Also when possible, group plants with other crops in the same plant family. Note which crops will come out during the course of the season, and decide which short- or half season crops to replace them with.
5. When you're actually planting the garden, be sure to follow the plant spacing recommendations very closely. Overcrowding your vegetables will result in more problems and less harvest!

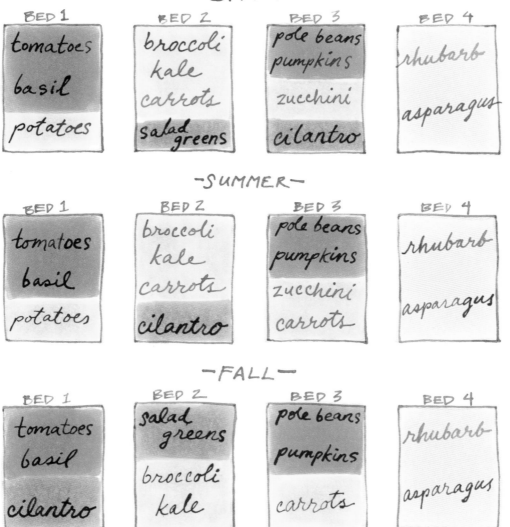

-SPRING-

BED 1
tomatoes
basil
potatoes

BED 2
broccoli
kale
carrots
salad greens

BED 3
pole beans
pumpkins
zucchini
cilantro

BED 4
rhubarb
asparagus

-SUMMER-

BED 1
tomatoes
basil
potatoes

BED 2
broccoli
kale
carrots
cilantro

BED 3
pole beans
pumpkins
zucchini
carrots

BED 4
rhubarb
asparagus

-FALL-

BED 1
tomatoes
basil
cilantro

BED 2
salad greens
broccoli
kale

BED 3
pole beans
pumpkins
carrots

BED 4
rhubarb
asparagus

COUNTERCLOCKWISE FROM OPPOSITE TOP: Step 1: Write out a list of the crops you want to grow. Step 2: Separate the plants into groups based on their life spans. Step 3: Draw a simple map of your garden, writing in the names of your crops in their beds for each season. Using this plan, you can replace short- and half-season crops as the seasons progress. Step 4: Also consider which tall plants should go at back (north side) of bed to prevent shadow.

15
STORING YOUR HARVEST

NO MATTER HOW WELL your crop plantings are timed and how many succession plantings you do, a large portion of your seasonal harvest will become available simultaneously. You'll be eating some of your crops immediately, but you will also very likely want to keep some of the food for a few weeks or even a few months. This book's crop profiles use the following designations to help you make the most of your harvest:

Counter: Some crops keep best at room temperature; the cooling effect of the refrigerator can adversely affect their texture or speed up the decomposition process. *Examples: tomatoes, winter squash, pumpkins*

Fridge: Many crops will keep anywhere between one week and six months in the refrigerator. Unless otherwise specified, plan to keep the produce in a closed container such as a plastic bag or a lidded glass or plastic storage container. For longest storage, remove excess water before refrigerating. A little moisture keeps the produce fresh and crisp, but standing water in the bottom of the container encourages rot. *Examples: salad greens, turnips, beets, carrots.*

Freezer: If you have access to freezer space, and a little time to process your harvest, you can keep many crops throughout the winter. Some can be chopped and placed in sealed containers and frozen directly, while other crops should be either fully cooked before freezing or "blanched." Blanching kills many of the enzymes that cause produce to decompose, leading to longer storage life.

To blanch vegetables, bring a pot of water to a rapid boil (1 gal. or larger is ideal) and prepare a large pot or bowl of ice water on the side. Chop your vegetables, and drop them into the boiling water. They can go straight in, to be scooped out with a sieve or large slotted spoon, or lowered into the water in some kind of metal basket or slotted container. Start timing once the water returns to a boil. The boil time for each vegetable—it will be short, so don't walk away!—is listed in its profile. Remove the vegetables from the boiling water and drop them immediately into the cold water. When they have cooled (about the same amount of time as they boil), place them on kitchen towels and gently pat them dry. Place them in plastic bags or other containers and freeze them immediately. *Examples: zucchini, carrots, beans, Brassicas.*

Some fruits and vegetables store best if they are spread out on a tray and frozen before going into storage containers. Tray freezing allows the pieces to freeze individually and not stick together in a solid mass. *Examples: blueberries, strawberries, raspberries.*

OPPOSITE: Harvest your thyme and hang it to dry for year-round use.

Dried: Some vegetables and many herbs keep best when dried or dehydrated. The simplest way is to hang them individually or in bundles in a warm, dry, location for several weeks. Check on them regularly to ensure no mold develops. You can also use a dehydrator if you have one. Once dried, most herbs can be stored in glass spice jars; vegetables such as onions and garlic can be stored in a pantry or on the kitchen counter. *Examples: rosemary, thyme, oregano, garlic, bulb onions*

Canning: Most any vegetable or herb can be incorporated into a canning recipe. High-acid foods can be canned in a boiling water bath, while low-acid recipes should be canned in a pressure canner. We recommend consulting one of the many excellent books on canning to see how it's done (some are listed in the Resources section).

Outside: Some crops can be stored right in the garden—you can harvest them as you need them over an extended period. Others may do best if stored, after harvest, in a protected outdoor location such as a shed or garage.

If you end up with more of a certain crop than you know what to do with, consider contacting a local food bank or soup kitchen. Many of them now accept fresh produce from home gardeners. As you gain experience in the garden, you can even intentionally grow extra to donate to those in need. (Check out the Plant a Row for the Hungry program for more information, in the Resources section.)

ABOVE: Garlic bulbs hanging in a warm, dry location.

part IV

CROP PROFILES

"Better than any argument is to rise at dawn and pick
dew-wet red berries in a cup."
~ *Wendell Berry* ~

We want your first garden to be a success, so you'll stay with it and continue to develop your gardening skills for years to come. With that in mind, we've developed a list of crops you should consider growing your first few seasons. We've selected them based on ease of care, popularity, and suitability for the home garden.

These crops grow well almost everywhere, and they tend to be somewhat forgiving of rookie mistakes. As a group, they offer you the opportunity to learn the whole range of basic gardening skills. Obviously, you'll want to raise crops that are familiar to you and that you know you want to eat, but consider also throwing in an unknown or two, just for fun.

A few quick notes on using the profiles:

1. For more information on techniques mentioned in each profile's "How to plant" section, see chapter 12: Essential Garden Skills.

2. The "When to plant" section refers to first and last frost dates. Use the related chart in chapter 13: Know Your Climate to find your own first and last frost dates.

3. More information on pests and diseases can be found in chapter 23: Garden Problems and Solutions.

16
ANNUAL VEGETABLES

ANNUAL CROPS ARE TYPICALLY planted in the spring or summer and harvested sometime later that year. These plants will die at the end of the season and will need to be replanted the following year. It's a great joy to see how fast an annual plant can grow, going from seed to maturity in just a few months.

Most (but not all) annual vegetables fall into one of four major plant families: Alliums (onions, leeks, garlic), Brassicas (broccoli, cabbage, kale), Cucurbits (squash, pumpkins, cucumbers), and Nightshades (tomatoes, peppers, potatoes). These plants have a wide range of growth forms, including climbing vines, wide bushes, and short round roots. They take anywhere from three weeks to six months to complete their life cycle.

OPPOSITE: A basket of radishes.

BEANS: "GREEN" AND OTHER BEANS
POLE BEANS: Tall Crop (vine), Long Season Crop
BUSH BEANS: Short Crop, Short Season Crop
FAVA/BROAD BEANS: Medium Height Crop, Half Season Crop

Phaseolus vulgaris, Vicia faba

One of the oldest domesticated crops, beans originated in South America and were brought to Europe in the late 1400s. Some beans are eaten fresh in their shell (your everyday green bean), and some are removed from their shells and dried for long-term storage (such as pinto beans and black beans). Despite the differences in what we do with them, most types of beans are closely related and have similar growth habits. They are easy to grow and produce a ton of food for the amount of space they use. Most home gardeners grow beans for fresh eating rather than for drying and storage. Beans are rich in protein, iron, potassium, folate, and vitamins C and A.

Farmers use many different terms when talking about beans. Here are a few definitions:

BUSH BEANS: These are bean plants that don't need a trellis. They are short (typically about 18

157

in. tall) and generally set all of their fruit during a short period of time (over the course of 1 or 2 weeks).

POLE BEANS: These are plants that like to climb and so require a trellis. Pole beans can grow 6 ft. or more in a season, and they generally set fruit over a long period of time (several months).

GREEN BEANS/SNAP BEANS: A green bean/snap bean is any bean we harvest before the seeds inside the pod grow to maturity. We eat them shell and all. Not all "green beans" are green; there are also yellow, red, purple, and striped varieties. Snap beans can be either bush beans or pole beans, and some varieties are available as both types.

DRY BEANS/SHELLING BEANS: These are beans that are allowed to grow to maturity and dry out. The shells are removed before eating. Some types of snap beans are used in this way, but typically different varieties (such as kidney beans and black beans) are grown specifically for drying. These can be either bush beans or pole beans, and some varieties are available as both types.

BROAD BEANS: An entirely separate species, but grown in much the same way. The term *broad bean* is used interchangeably with *fava bean*. They are both eaten fresh and dried for long-term storage.

ABOVE LEFT: Pole bean seedlings wrap themselves around a trellis as they grow. ABOVE: Bush beans are shorter plants that grow only 1-2 feet tall and don't require a trellis.

What you eat: The fruit.

Recommended varieties: BUSH TYPES: Provider, Jade, Royal Burgundy (purple!), Indy Gold (yellow!). POLE TYPES: Fortex, Kentucky Wonder, Blue Lake Pole.

Hardiness: Broad beans are frost tolerant, but the others are not.

Seed information: BEANS: Germination temp. 60°–90°F, optimal 80°; germination time 16 days at 60°, 6 days at 86°. Seed viability 3 years. FAVA BEANS: Germination temp. 40°–75°; germination time 7–14 days. Seed viability 2–6 years.

Mature plant size: BUSH BEANS: 18 in. tall and wide. POLE BEANS: Up to 6–8 ft. tall when grown on a trellis. FAVA BEANS: 4–5 ft. tall.

How to plant: Direct-seeding is the most common way to plant beans.

BUSH BEANS: Plant seeds about 1 in. deep and 2 in. apart, and space the rows 6 in. apart. Thin to 1 plant every 4 in.

POLE BEANS: Plant seeds 2 in. deep and 2 in. apart, and space rows 1 ft. apart. Thin to 1 plant every 6 in. On a tipi trellis, plant 6 seeds per pole and thin to 3 plants per pole.

FAVA BEANS: Plant seeds 2 in. deep and 2 in. apart, and thin to 1 plant every 6 in. They are not climbing plants, but fava beans are tall and unwieldy, so you can seed them next to or inside a trellis and tie them up as they grow.

When to plant: Beans need warm soil to germinate, so wait until after your last frost date (usually the middle of May or early June) to direct-seed them. In cool soil, darker seeded beans germinate better than lighter ones.

Fava beans germinate best in cool soil and should be planted in early fall or very early spring.

How much to plant: 12 bush bean plants will yield about 1 lb. of beans; 16 pole bean plants will yield 10–15 lb. over the course of the season, or 1–2 lb. each week. 1 fava bean plant will yield 1–2 pounds.

For a consistent supply of bush beans, put in a new planting every 2–3 weeks. Your last planting should go in early to mid-August—any later, and they won't have time to set fruit before they are killed by frost.

Pole types will produce for the entire growing season, so you only need to plant those once per year.

Some people like to start the season with a sowing of both bush and pole beans. The bush beans will give you an early supply while you wait for the pole beans to start producing.

Most home gardeners feel adequately supplied by a single trellis of pole beans (16 plants) and 2 or 3 plantings of bush beans (12 plants per planting).

When to fertilize: Before planting.

General care: Watch for slug or snail damage in young plants. Pole beans need to be trellised; you can use a tipi or net type. Pinch the growing tips when the plant reaches the top of the trellis (see the Peas profile).

Pests: Potential pests include slugs, Mexican bean beetles, aphids, leafhoppers, leaf miners, and flea beetles.

Diseases: Beans are fairly disease resistant, but potential problems include powdery mildew, downy mildew, rust, and anthracnose.

Container suitability: BUSH TYPES: Good. Try growing them in a 3 gal. pot or larger (any container at least 8 in. deep). Space plants 4 in. apart. POLE TYPES: OK. 5 gal. pot or larger (any container at least 12 in. deep). Remember, you must provide a trellis for pole types. FAVAS: not recommended.

When and how to harvest: Both pole and bush

varieties should be picked when the width is about that of a pencil, but pick them thinner for French dishes calling for *haricot verts*. Fava bean pods will be much thicker (the width of a carrot).

Storage and preservation:

FRIDGE: Fresh beans keep longer if you leave the tops on. Store them in a sealed container or plastic bag (40°–45°F is ideal).

FREEZER: Blanch for 3–4 min., dry and freeze immediately.

DRIED: Shelling beans will store for several years in a glass jar or other container.

CANNED: Use a pressure canner.

What Beans Can Teach You: How to Inoculate Seeds

Why you do it: Whereas most plants remove nitrogen from the soil, beans actually add it. This remarkable feat is the result of a relationship beans have with a certain soil bacterium. The bacterium takes nitrogen from the air and converts it into a form that will stay in the soil. This nitrogen boost helps the beans grow and will also aid the growth of future crops planted in the same soil. To ensure a healthy population of bacteria near your plant roots, purchase bacterial inoculants for your seeds. These are available from plant nurseries, but they're much less expensive when ordered directly from a seed company.

How you do it: In a small bowl, moisten the seeds lightly with a spray bottle. Sprinkle them with

ABOVE LEFT: Harvest your beans before they become too large and tough for fresh eating. LEFT: Inoculating your seeds will help produce more vigorous plants.

inoculant, and mix until they're evenly coated. You're ready to plant!

Also useful for: Peas, fava beans, clovers, soybeans.

BEETS
Short Crop, Half Season Crop

Beta vulgaris

Beets are thought to have originated somewhere around the Mediterranean. They fall into four general categories:

GARDEN BEETS: The type we discuss below. These have been bred for their delicious leaves and roots.

SUGAR BEETS: A type bred for high sugar content. These are rarely eaten, but are processed into refined sugar.

MANGEL-WURZELS: These are bred to be used as livestock feed. They are OK for eating when the roots or leaves are picked small, but chances are, you won't find many people growing them at home.

CHARD: Swiss chard is a type of beet bred to produce large leaves instead of a large root, but these plants are almost genetically identical to garden beets. (Chard is discussed in the Cooking Greens profile.)

Garden beets are a great crop because you can eat both the leaves and the roots, kind of like two vegetables in one. Most beets you have seen were probably dark red (the juice will stain everything, so be cautious in the kitchen), but there is a rainbow of other colors available, including yellow, white, pink, and striped varieties.

Beets are also incredibly nutritious. The leaves have a good supply of vitamins A and C, calcium, phosphorus, potassium, and iron. The roots are

rich in phytochemicals such as folate, betacyanin, and betaine.

What you eat: The root and the leaves.

Recommended varieties: Early Wonder (early red beet), Chioggia (red and white stripes), Golden Detroit (yellow-orange), and Detroit Dark Red and Bull's Blood (very dark red).

Hardiness: Young plants can tolerate frost. Large beets will rot when exposed to hard frosts, so it is best to harvest them in the fall before very cold weather sets in.

Seed information: Germination temp. 50°–80°F, optimal 77°; germination time 16 days at 59°, 5 days at 77°. Seed viability 5 years.

Mature plant size: Up to 18 in. tall, including greens, and 4 in. wide.

How to plant: Beets are best direct-seeded. Sow seeds ½ in. deep, 1 in. apart. Thin to 1 plant every 4 in.

When to plant: Start seeding beets a few weeks before your last frost date (around late March or early April). Put in your last planting in late July.

ABOVE: Space your beets at least 4 inches apart.

How much to plant: 2–4 plants will yield about 1 lb. of roots. To have a consistent supply, succession-plant them as often as once a month. Try starting with 2–3 row ft.

When to fertilize: Before planting and 3 weeks after they emerge. Use ¼ cup balanced fertilizer per 3 plants, or liquid fertilizer.

General care: Thinning is crucial for beets to size up properly. Keep an eye out for downy mildew on your beet leaves. Remove any leaves showing signs of mildew.

Pests: Minimal. Flea beetles, aphids, and leaf miners.

Diseases: Downy mildew and scab.

Container suitability: Not recommended.

ABOVE: An Early Wonder red beet and Golden Detroit beet ready to eat.

When and how to harvest: Harvest beets at any size, very small if you like to roast or bake them whole. It's best to pull them before they grow larger than a baseball (they can become very tough if allowed to grow too large). Simply pull the whole plant out of the ground by the leaves, using a trowel to help lift the roots if necessary. Cut the leaves off and rinse them, and wash the roots.

Storage and preservation:

FRIDGE: Beet roots and leaves are best stored in the refrigerator in a plastic bag or a glass or plastic container. Dry the leaves and roots before putting them away. Leaves will keep about a week, and roots can store up to 6 months.

FREEZER: Fully cook beets, tray-freeze, then place in freezer bags.

CANNED: Try canning pickled beets.

What Beets Can Teach You: How to Side-Dress Fertilizer

Why you do it: Beets can be a little finicky—they like very fertile soil. Give them an extra dose of fertilizer after they've started growing, to get the roots to size up.

How you do it: Three weeks after planting, take ¼ cup of balanced fertilizer and sprinkle it alongside 3 beet plants (or about 1 ft. of the row); you will be using 1 cup for every 4 ft. With a trowel or your hand, mix the fertilizer into the top 2 in. of soil around the beets. The fertilizer should then be watered into the soil.

Also useful for: While the amount and type of fertilizer used to side-dress other crops may vary, the application method is the same and can be used on Brassicas, summer and winter squash, Brussels sprouts, tomatoes, peppers, eggplant, corn, and cucumbers.

BOK CHOY

(ALSO CALLED BOK CHOI,
PAC CHOI, PAK CHOY)
Short Crop, Short Season Crop

Brassica rapa chinensis

Bok choy has been used in Chinese cuisine for hundreds, if not thousands, of years. In recent years it has gained in popularity around the world because it is delicious, it grows quickly, and it is relatively easy to grow. Like other vegetables in the "cabbage family," it is rich in vitamins A and C and a wide variety of minerals.

What you eat: The leaves.

Recommended varieties: Joy Choy, Black Summer; Shuko is a great baby variety. Look for varieties described as "slow bolting."

Hardiness: Handles light frost well.

Seed information: Germination temp. 45°–90°F, optimal 85°; germination time 20 days at 50°, 4 days at 85°. Seed viability 3–4 years.

Mature plant size: 8 in. (baby size) to 18 in. tall.

How to plant: Bok choy grows best in cooler temperatures. Hot weather or intermittent cool

ABOVE: Harvest bok choy by cutting the roots from the base of the bulb right at soil level.

and hot may cause the plants to bolt. Bok choy is an especially good choice in cooler regions, even during the summer. Direct-seed or transplant. Space plants 6 in. apart for baby size, 1 ft. apart for full size.

When to plant: Direct-seed or transplant in early spring or late summer.

How much to plant: Can be harvested baby sized or full sized. Consider planting 5–10 plants in the spring and again in the early summer. Since the crop grows quickly, if you want a regular supply, plant 2 or 3 plants every 2 or 3 weeks while weather remains relatively cool.

When to fertilize: Before planting.

General care: Watch carefully for signs of insect damage (see the list of potential pests below).

Pests: Your biggest problems will likely be flea beetles, aphids, slugs, and snails. Other potential pests include cabbage loopers, cutworms, imported cabbageworms, root knot nematodes, and root maggots (the larvae of cabbage root flies).

Diseases: Clubroot, downy mildew.

Container suitability: Good. 1 gal. size per plant or larger, or anything at least 6 in. deep.

When and how to harvest: Cut the plant at the base, where the stalk meets the soil, with a sharp knife or pair of hand pruners.

Storage and preservation:

FRIDGE: Stores well for a week or two in a sealed container or plastic bag.

FREEZER: Blanch 2 min., dry and freeze immediately.

What Bok Choy Can Teach You:
How to Harvest "Baby" Vegetables

Why you do it: Many vegetables are most tender when they are still immature. The plants may grow to a much larger size if left in the garden for a longer period of time, but when they're picked early, the taste is milder and the texture more tender. Harvesting baby vegetables means you get to eat the crop earlier.

How you do it: Harvest bok choy when the plant reaches 6–10 in. tall. Certain varieties are cultured specifically as baby types, but any variety can be harvested when young to attain the same results.

Also useful for: Beans, beets, carrots, salad greens, summer squash.

BROCCOLI, CABBAGE, CAULIFLOWER
Medium Height Crop, Half Season Crop

Brassica oleracea

Broccoli, cauliflower, and cabbage are all variations on a single species of plant, originating from wild cabbage in Europe. At first this seems hard to believe, but once you start growing them in the garden you can see how similar the young plants look and how similar their needs are. A wide variety of Brassicas are grown in the home garden; other members of this family include Brussels sprouts, bok choy, turnips, rutabagas, kohlrabi, and mustard greens. These plants are sometimes called *cruciferous* crops because their four-petaled flowers resemble tiny crosses.

Though they are somewhat needy and can be a little tricky to grow the first time, Brassicas are well worth the effort, since the quality of homegrown types will far surpass what you can find in the grocery store. In addition to vitamins A and C and a variety of minerals, these plants contain high levels of healthful phytochemicals.

What you eat: BROCCOLI, CAULIFLOWER: The

immature flower. CABBAGE: The leaves.

Recommended varieties: Matching your varieties to the seasons is important with broccoli and cabbage. For early-spring planting, use varieties that need fewer days to maturity, and for summer planting use varieties that take longer. The latter are usually labeled as best for "fall production."

BROCCOLI (SPRING PLANTING): Blue Wind, Gypsy, Packman, Bay Meadows, Fiesta.

BROCCOLI (SUMMER PLANTING FOR A FALL CROP): Arcadia, Marathon, Diplomat.

CABBAGE (SPRING PLANTING): Tendersweet, Golden Acre, Red Express.

CABBAGE (SUMMER PLANTING FOR A FALL CROP):

ABOVE LEFT: Use a knife to cut the broccoli head from the stem of the plant. ABOVE CENTER: Some plants may produce miniature heads due to stress or just bad genetics; harvest and replant the area with a new crop. ABOVE RIGHT: An overly mature broccoli, cabbage, or cauliflower will open up into small yellow flowers.

Melissa, Ruby Perfection, Danish Ballhead.

CAULIFLOWER: Snow Crown, Fremont.

Hardiness: Brassicas handle frost well.

Seed information: Germination temp. 45°–90°F, optimal 85°; germination time 20 days at 50°, 4 days at 85°. Seed viability 3–4 years.

Mature plant size: Up to 24 in. tall and 12 in. wide.

How to plant: These crops are easiest to grow when transplanted into the garden, and plant starts are usually available at nurseries during the growing season. If growing your own transplants, start them indoors up to 4 weeks before last frost. Brassicas like to be planted deep, so you can bury them up to their first set of true leaves when transplanting. Space plants 1 ft. apart.

You can also direct-seed these crops. Wait until late spring (2 weeks before your last frost date), and then bury groups of 3 seeds in the ground at 1 ft. spacing. When the plants emerge, thin to 1 plant per foot. Planting Brassicas in different areas of your garden each year will greatly reduce pest and disease problems.

When to plant: Although Brassicas are tolerant of the cold, you'll have fewer problems if you wait until late spring to transplant them. For a consistent supply, put in a new planting of each every month. Set out your last plants or seeds in mid-July or early August.

How much to plant: Cabbage and cauliflower each yield a single head; once you cut them, they're done producing. Consider how many heads of cabbage or cauliflower you'd eat in a week (or month or year), and plant accordingly. Broccoli yields a single large head and then sends out smaller side shoots after you cut the main head. The overall harvest from each plant is about a pound. Consider planting 4 or 5 plants of each type in the spring and another 4–5 plants in midsummer for fall harvest.

When to fertilize: Before planting, and at 3 and 6 weeks after transplanting. Use ¼ cup balanced fertilizer per plant, or liquid fertilizer.

General care: Watch plants carefully for signs of insect damage. As with bok choy, many pests will be interested in these crops (see list below). As the plants grow, the lower leaves may start to turn yellow or brown and die. Pull these off to improve air circulation.

Pests: Your biggest problems will likely be aphids, root maggots (the larvae of cabbage root flies), cutworms, slugs, snails, imported cabbageworms, and cabbage loopers. Other potential pests are flea beetles, and root knot nematodes.

Diseases: Alternaria blight, clubroot, downy mildew.

Container suitability: BROCCOLI, CABBAGE: OK, but expect smaller heads than in the garden. 5 gal. size per plant or larger, or anything at least 12 in. deep. CAULIFLOWER: OK, but they can

ABOVE LEFT: After the main head is harvested, broccoli will produce a series of great tasting, miniature florets. ABOVE CENTER: Remove any tough, damaged outer leaves from cabbage and cauliflower. ABOVE RIGHT: Cut the cauliflower from the stem with a knife, just under the base of the head. This technique also works with broccoli and cabbage.

be easily stressed in a container and form *very* small heads.

When and how to harvest: BROCCOLI: Cut the head off a few inches down the stem with a sharp knife. Cut when individual beads are swollen up, but before the beads start to separate. A head of broccoli is a compact bunch of flowers that should be cut before they open up and bloom—if left too long, it will turn into a large yellow bouquet! If your broccoli plants have smaller heads than you are used to seeing in the store, that is OK. Just make sure to harvest them before they start to flower, and they'll still taste great. Harvest the smaller side shoots in the same fashion.

CABBAGE: Cut the head off when it looks full size and feels tightly packed inside when squeezed.

CAULIFLOWER: Cut the "curd" (what the flower is called) when it has fully sized up, but before it

starts to separate (don't worry if it has opened a little).

Storage and preservation:

FRIDGE: Broccoli and cauliflower both store well for a week or two in a sealed container or plastic bag. Cabbage is a great keeper; it may last up to 6 months in a bag in the refrigerator. If the outer layer of leaves starts to get funky, just peel them off and use the good part that remains underneath.

FREEZER: Blanch 3 min., dry and freeze immediately.

What Broccoli Can Teach You: How to Set Up Brassica Collars and Mulch Rings

Why you do it: Brassicas are a tasty treat for a number of bugs. One is the cabbage root fly, which lays its eggs near the base of your plants. When the eggs hatch, the larvae (called root maggots) love to eat the roots of broccoli, cauliflower, and cabbage. Additionally, wandering cutworms may chomp down the stem of newly planted Brassicas (and leave the rest of the plant to die).

How you do it: To protect against root maggots, place a small ring of mulch around the base of each plant. Try using bark mulch or sawdust. The flies don't like to lay their eggs in this type of material, and if they do, the maggots may have a harder time making it into your soil. For cutworms, protect the stem with a 3 in. high ring made of the cardboard tube from a toilet paper roll, or a ring cut from an old plastic plant pot. Push the ring 1 in. into the soil. This prevents cutworms from reaching the stem of the plant.

Also useful for: Root maggot mulch ring: Brussels sprouts, onions, leeks, tomatoes. Cutworm collar: any new transplant or young seedling.

ABOVE: Planting brassicas in cardboard collars can help prevent cutworm damage.

BRUSSELS SPROUTS

Medium Height Crop, Long Season Crop

Brassica oleracea

Brussels sprouts are actually the same species as broccoli, cabbage, and cauliflower, but the process of growing them is a little different. Brussels sprouts may be the coolest-looking plant in the garden. They grow about 3 ft. tall and look like a miniature cabbage tree. Anyone who says they don't like Brussels sprouts should be required to harvest them from a home garden, cut them in half and roast them with olive oil, salt, and pepper (or spend a year in Alcatraz).

The "B" in Brussels sprouts is often capitalized because it refers to the capital of Belgium, the country where the modern-day Brussels sprout was cultivated.

In addition to vitamins A and C, Brussels sprouts are loaded with potassium, iron, folate, riboflavin, and antioxidants.

What you eat: The lateral sprouts.

Recommended varieties: Bubbles, Churchill, Roodnerf, Jade Cross, Oliver.

Hardiness: Brussels sprouts tolerate frost well.

Seed information: Germination temp. 50°–95°F, optimal 85°; germination time 20 days at 50°, 4 days at 85°. Seed viability 3–10 years.

Mature plant size: Up to 36 in. tall and 24 in. wide.

How to plant: Brussels sprouts are best transplanted. Space plants 18 in. apart. You can direct-seed them by planting 3 seeds in one spot every 18 in., and thinning to 1 plant after they've emerged.

ABOVE LEFT: In late summer, remove the top 6-8 inches of the Brussels sprouts plant so the plant will develop larger sprouts. ABOVE CENTER: Pull individual sprouts from the stem, or harvest the entire stalk at once by cutting the plant down at soil level. ABOVE RIGHT: Remove yellowing leaves to increase air circulation and light penetration.

When to plant: Brussels sprouts are a long-season crop, which means you plant them in the spring, they grow throughout the season, and they are ready to harvest in the fall. Mid- or late May is a good time to transplant Brussels sprouts. You can also try planting them in the early fall so they will produce sprouts in the spring, but in many locations overwintering crops may die in hard winter frosts.

How much to plant: 1 plant will yield a little less than 1 lb. of sprouts. Try planting 4 or 5 plants.

When to fertilize: Before planting, and at 3 and 6 weeks after transplanting. Use ¼ cup balanced fertilizer per plant, or liquid fertilizer.

General care: Use Brassica collars (see broccoli profile) at planting. Watch for slug or snail damage on younger plants and for aphids and cabbage loopers on larger plants. Clean up dying leaves as the plant matures. When the plant starts to form a cabbage-like top (late summer, early fall), cut it off. This will allow the plant to send more energy into the sprouts and increase sprout size. Eat the top after you cut it off!

Pests: Primarily aphids, cabbage loopers, and imported cabbageworms. Other potential problems are flea beetles, root knot nematodes, slugs, and root maggots (the larvae of cabbage root flies).

Diseases: Alternaria blight, blackleg, clubroot, downy mildew.

Container suitability: Not recommended.

When and how to harvest: When sprouts feel tight and dense when squeezed, you can pull or cut them off the main stem. They are easy to break off if you simply use your thumb to push them downward. Exposing the sprouts to a few frosts while still on the plant will improve their flavor, but make sure to harvest all of your sprouts if temperatures drop into the lower 20s, because they will start to rot after a few hard freezes.

Storage and preservation:

FRIDGE: Store in sealed containers or plastic bags for several weeks.

FREEZER: Blanch 3–4 min., dry and freeze immediately.

OUTSIDE: Will store on the stalk for several weeks after reaching maturity.

What Brussels Sprouts Can Teach You: How to Clear Dying Leaves

Why you do it: Brussels sprouts live in the garden for a long time, and during the season, their lower leaves will start to yellow and brown. If these leaves are removed, it will improve air circulation and help sunlight reach the sprouts on the stalk. This minimizes fungal problems, increases sprout size, and improves the general health of the plant.

How you do it: When a leaf starts to look yellow or otherwise funky, break it off! It should come off rather easily without damaging the plant. As much as possible, avoid leaving the stubs of the leaves: These are potential places where diseases can establish themselves.

Also useful for: You should prune dying leaves off of any plant. The most important are other Brassicas (broccoli, cauliflower, cabbage, kale), tomatoes, and summer and winter squash.

CARROTS

Short Crop, Half Season Crop

Daucus carota

Carrots are yet another amazing garden crop: They don't need much space, they taste delicious, they are versatile in the kitchen, and they keep forever. If you are trying to get children interested in gardening, let them plant and harvest carrots.

Carrots are thought to have originated thousands of years ago in present-day Afghanistan. Carrot scientists (let's pretend there is such a thing) believe that the earliest carrots were purple in color and developed into yellow and orange roots much later. These days, most carrots eaten in the United States are orange, but if you want to mix things up, you can grow purple, yellow, white, red, and striped varieties in your garden.

Carrots are loaded with beta-carotene and potassium and are said to lower blood cholesterol when eaten raw. Clearly, if you eat enough carrots, you may end up with superpowers (X-ray vision, strong teeth, etc.).

What you eat: The root.

Recommended varieties: Scarlet Nantes, Purple Haze, Bolero, Napoli.

Hardiness: Carrots tolerate frost well.

Seed information: Germination temp. 41°–95°F, optimal 75°; germination time 50 days at 41°, 6–8 days at 77°. Seed viability 2–5 years.

Mature plant size: Greens up to 24 in. tall.

How to plant: Carrots are best direct-seeded (transplanting them diminishes root size). Sow ¼ in. deep, and sow them thickly (2 or 3 seeds per inch) in rows 6 in. apart. Thin to 1 plant per inch. Carrots are slow to germinate (they can take 2 or 3 weeks to emerge from the soil),

so make sure to keep them well watered until they emerge.

When to plant: Start direct-seeding carrots in early April. For a consistent supply, put in a new planting every month. Put your last planting in by mid-July so they can size up before winter.

How much to plant: A 1 ft. row of carrots (about 6 plants) will yield about 1 lb. Carrots store well, so if you want to have a big stash for winter eating, put in a big planting in early or mid-July. Consider planting 10–20 row ft. in the spring and again in the summer.

When to fertilize: Before planting.

General care: Watch for slug damage to young seedlings! Carrots should be weeded regularly, as they grow slowly and don't compete well against other plants. If the soil dries out too much between waterings, the roots may split. Planting into loose, deeply worked soil will reduce "forked" roots (which happens when a carrot grows into an obstruction, such as a rock). Forked roots are still tasty to eat, but won't yield as well.

Pests: Carrots are often a pest-free crop. Potential problems are slugs, carrot rust flies, aphids, and nematodes.

Diseases: Generally, diseases aren't a problem with carrots. Most likely are Alternaria leaf blight and rust.

Container suitability: Good. Use 3 gal. pots or larger, or anything at least 9 in. deep. Space 2 in. apart.

When and how to harvest: It is hard to tell when a carrot is ready from above ground, so don't hesitate to pull one up to check after the recommended days-to-maturity for your variety (this will be listed on the seed packet). Carrots can be harvested when the roots are

any size, but they are generally best when the roots are ¾ to 1 inch in diameter. To pull by hand, simply dig your fingers slightly into the soil until you can grab the body of the carrot, and wiggle it until it comes free. If you have a lot of carrots to harvest at once, use a spading fork or shovel to dig them up. To prevent stabbing the carrots themselves, drive the shovel into the soil a few inches away from the plant and keep the tool completely vertical until the shovel is as deep as it can go. Now, pull the top of the handle toward the ground to lift up the carrots. Trim the tops and wash the soil off using a spray nozzle on your garden hose. In the winter, you can leave carrots in the ground and dig them up as you need them. They actually become sweeter when stored in the ground and exposed to cold temperatures. If you expect temperatures lower than the upper 20s, cover them with a 12 in. layer of straw or shredded newspaper mulch to protect them from frost damage.

Storage and preservation:

FRIDGE: Carrots can store for months in a plastic bag. The roots will keep longest if you cut off the tops immediately after harvest.

FREEZER: Chop into ½ in. pieces, blanch 3 min., dry and freeze immediately.

OUTSIDE: Can store in the ground for several months, even during the winter.

ABOVE LEFT: It is essential to properly thin your carrots so that plants are 1–2 inches apart.
ABOVE: Pull carrots right out of the ground with your hands. Use a trowel to loosen the soil if necessary.

What Carrots Can Teach You:
How to Thin Your Direct-Seeded Crops

Why you do it: Carrots need enough space to produce a big root. If individual plants are too close, you may get a mess of stringy, narrow carrots.

How you do it: Once your seedlings have emerged from the ground, check to see how close they are. If they're growing close together, start at one end of the row and cull until they are spaced at least 1 in. apart. (Wash the seedlings you've pulled, and toss them in a salad—microgreens!)

Also useful for: Any direct-seeded crop may need thinning. Especially important are beets, turnips, and beans.

CELERY, CELERIAC (CELERY ROOT)

CELERY: Medium Height Crop,
Long Season Crop
CELERIAC: Short Crop, Long Season Crop

Apium graveolens

Derived from wild Mediterranean plants, celery is a beautiful, delicious vegetable, ideal for flavoring soup stocks and as an after-school snack. Because it requires a long period of consistently mild temperatures (not too hot and not too cold!), celery can be a tricky crop to grow. Celeriac is a lesser-known variety that is grown for its large root rather than its fleshy stalks. Both have similar flavor and can be used in a wide variety of dishes.

It should be noted that there is a compound in celery and celeriac that can cause severe allergic reactions similar to those caused by peanuts and peanut butter.

What you eat: CELERY: The stem. CELERIAC: The root.

Recommended varieties: CELERY: Utah. CELERIAC: Diamante.

Hardiness: Celery does not tolerate frost well.

Seed information: Germination temp. 45°–80°F, optimal 60°; germination time 20 days at 50°, 4 days at 85°. Seed viability 3–10 years.

Mature plant size: Plant foliage can be up to 24 in. tall and 12 in. wide.

How to plant: Soaking the seeds before planting will speed up the slow germination process (see the Parsley profile). Because the plants require a long, cool season, grow them as transplants if possible, or buy transplants if they are available. Space plants 12 in. apart.

When to plant: Celery should be direct-seeded or transplanted in the early spring 2 or 3 weeks before the last frost.

How much to plant: 1 plant will yield a little less than 1 lb. of celery. Try planting 5–10 plants.

When to fertilize: Before planting, and at 3 weeks after transplanting. Use ¼ cup balanced fertilizer per plant, or liquid fertilizer.

General care: Watch for slug or snail damage on younger plants and for aphids on larger plants. Make sure to provide continuous, ample water: Celery is virtually all water and can become quickly stressed if the soil dries out at all.

Pests: Aphids, flea beetles, root knot nematodes, slugs, and root maggots.

Diseases: Alternaria blight, blackleg, clubroot, downy mildew.

Container suitability: Not recommended.

When and how to harvest: For celery, cut the plant at the soil line when the stalks have reached about 8–10 in. tall, late in the season. Harvest celeriac root when the bulb is 2–4 in. in diameter. Trim the excess fibrous roots off the

bottom of the main root, and cut off the leafy top-growth.

Storage and preservation:

FRIDGE: Store in sealed containers or plastic bags for several weeks. Celery will keep a few weeks, celeriac up to 8 months.

FREEZER: CELERY: Blanch 2 min., dry and freeze immediately. CELERIAC: Chop, fully cook, then freeze.

ABOVE: Harvest individual celery stems or harvest the entire plant by cutting at the base just above soil level.

What Celery Can Teach You: How to Field-Blanch

Why you do it: Celery is known for its sweet, fleshy stalks. Their taste and texture can be accentuated if sunlight is blocked from the plant in the weeks leading to harvest.

How you do it: When the celery stalk has reached its mature size, cover each plant with a paper bag. Leave the bag over the stalk for a week and then harvest.

Also useful for: Leeks, lettuce, rhubarb.

COOKING GREENS:
CHARD, COLLARDS, KALE

Medium Height Crop, Half Season Crop

Brassica oleracea, Beta vulgaris

Kale and collards are in the same family as cabbage, while chard is related to beets. But although they have distinct genetic pathways, the management of these crops is very similar. All three are typically grown as cooking greens, which means that the leaves are typically too tough and bitter to be eaten raw. Cooking softens and mellows the leaves.

More people say, "I just don't know how to use it!" about these crops than about any other. But it is worth learning how to cook these greens, since they produce an incredible amount of food for the space they take up, and they are among the most nutritious vegetables you can grow, with high levels of potassium, vitamin A, and vitamin C.

What you eat: The leaves.

Recommended varieties: CHARD: Rainbow. COLLARDS: Champion. KALE: Red Russian, White Russian, Nero Di Toscana.

Hardiness: All of these greens handle frost well.

Seed information: Germination temp. 45°–90°F, optimal 85°; germination time 20 days at 50°, 4 days at 85°. Seed viability 3–4 years,

Mature plant size: Up to 36 in. tall and 12 in. wide.

How to plant: If possible, plant cooking greens from transplants. Starts should be available at nurseries during the growing season. Space them 12 in. apart. Like the other Brassicas, kale and collards like to be planted deep, so bury them up to their first true leaves when transplanting. You can also direct-seed these crops.

Wait until about late spring, and then sow 3 seeds for every 1 ft. of row space. When they emerge, thin to 1 plant per ft. Planting these crops in different area of your garden each year will greatly reduce pest and disease problems.

When to plant: Although these greens are tolerant of the cold, you'll have fewer problems if you wait until mid- or late spring to start transplanting them. Since they can be harvested over an extended period, it is usually possible to plant one crop in the spring and one in the late summer (for fall harvest). Set out your last plants for fall eating mid-July to early August.

How much to plant: Since each plant will produce for weeks or even months, you may not need as many plants as with other crops. A mixed planting of 6–10 plants (some kale, some chard, and some collards) in the spring and again in midsummer will provide a diverse array of cooking greens throughout the season.

When to fertilize: Before planting.

General care: Watch plants carefully for signs of insect damage, as various pests will be interested in eating these crops (adding Brassica collars as described in the Broccoli profile will help). To keep your plant producing, pull off unharvested lower leaves just as they're starting to brown and die.

Pests: Primarily slugs, aphids, snails, cabbage loopers, and imported cabbageworms. Other potential problems are flea beetles, root knot nematodes, and root maggots (the larvae of cabbage root flies).

Diseases: Downy and powdery mildew are the biggest challenges with these crops. Some plants will outgrow an onset of mildew, but often you may be better off removing them and starting over. Fortunately, these crops will grow well during most of the year, so you can

often remove diseased plants and still have time for another planting. You may also have trouble with Alternaria blight, blackleg, and clubroot.

Container suitability: Good, but expect smaller plants and leaves than in the garden. Use a 3 gal. pot per plant or larger, or anything at least 12 in. deep.

When and how to harvest: Pull off individual leaves, only a few from each plant at a time.

Storage and preservation:

FRIDGE: Cooking greens store well for a week or two in a sealed container or plastic bag.

FREEZER: These freeze well if they are chopped up and placed in sealed freezer bags immediately upon harvest; make sure they are dry first. Or blanch 3–4 min., then dry and freeze immediately.

What Cooking Greens Can Teach You: Single-Leaf Harvesting

Why you do it: Each of these crops will produce quite a bit of food. The trick is to harvest the leaves properly and at the right time. If stripped of their leaves too early, the plants will not have enough energy to regenerate and keep growing. Likewise, if you strip too many leaves at once (even from a mature plant), you reduce its potential for future production.

How you do it: Don't harvest any leaves until the plant is at least 1 ft. tall. When it is producing large, healthy leaves, strip leaves individually, starting with the largest ones (typically the

ABOVE LEFT: Pull off the largest kale leaves and allow the plant to continue growing. ABOVE: A chard plant from which leaves have been recently harvested.

lowest leaves on the plant). If you have a number of plants, take one or two leaves from each plant rather than stripping one plant entirely. If you systematically take only the largest leaves and allow the plants to grow between harvests, your cooking green harvest can last for several months. To properly harvest single leaves, grab the leaf by the stalk and gently pull downward. It should easily tear off the stem.

Also useful for: This same technique can be applied to some salad greens (such as spinach and leaf lettuces).

CORN

Tall Crop, Long Season Crop

Zea mays

Corn, which is thought to have evolved in central Mexico, is now the most widely planted crop in the United States. As with any other crop, there are many varieties to choose from. Much of the corn you see along the roadsides of the Midwest is "field corn," grown primarily as livestock feed and for use in processed foods. In the home garden we want to grow varieties known as "sweet corn." These produce big ears of succulent corn just right for fresh eating, boiled or grilled. To grow corn properly, chew on a stalk of grass and wear overalls.

Corn is rich in vitamin B1, folate, fiber, and vitamin C.

What you eat: The seeds.

Recommended varieties: Corn likes high temperatures, so it is important to select varieties that are known to grow well in your climate. We like Luscious and Delicious. It is also fun to grow popcorn varieties at home!

Hardiness: Not cold tolerant—plan to keep an eye on your corn, and harvest it as soon as it ripens.

Seed information: Germination temp. 60°–95°F, optimal 77°; germination time 12 days at 60°, 4 days at 77°. Seed viability 1–3 years.

Mature plant size: Up to 6 ft. tall and 2 ft. wide.

How to plant: Corn is easy to grow when either transplanted or direct-seeded. It may be possible to find corn transplants in the spring, but most gardeners will want to direct-seed. The soil temperature should be pretty warm (50°F). Plant 2 kernels in each hole, 1 in. deep and 12 in. apart, in well-prepared, loose soil, and cull the less vigorous of the 2 once they have emerged (in some holes only one plant will emerge).

When to plant: Wait until 2 weeks after the last frost, which means in many locations that you can plant out sometime around mid-May but still have time to plant through early June.

How much to plant: Plan to leave a garden bed entirely to corn. If you have space, try to plant at least 20 plants to ensure pollination. If you know you will be eating quite a bit of corn during the summer or if you want to freeze some of the crop, consider expanding into more beds.

When to fertilize: Before planting, and at 3 and 6 weeks after transplanting. Use ¼ cup balanced fertilizer per plant, or liquid fertilizer.

General care: Watch plants carefully for signs of insect and animal damage. Ripening ears of corn are particularly attractive to larger animals such as raccoons and birds. Consider covering the crop with bird netting when the ears begin to ripen.

Pests: Corn has plenty of potential pests, including cutworms, aphids, corn earworm, and the aforementioned animals.

Diseases: Anthracnose, rust.

Container suitability: Not recommended. Suitable for container growing if you plan to grow for decoration only (expect very small ears of corn).

When and how to harvest: It will not be immediately obvious when your corn is ready to harvest. Once the ears have sized up, select an ear, peel back the top of the husk, and pinch one of the kernels. The kernel should be fat and should squirt out a milky white juice when popped. If the kernels still appear flat and emit a watery-looking juice, they are not yet ripe; if they are tough and seem difficult to pop, they may be overripe. More than in almost any other crop, the sugars in corn very quickly convert to starches after harvest, which means it will be sweetest if eaten soon after harvest. If you know you will be eating your corn for dinner, wait until that day to pick it.

ABOVE: Plant several rows of corn to ensure proper pollination. ABOVE RIGHT: A ripe kernel will emit a milky white juice when pinched.

If you try growing a popcorn variety, simply let the ears dry out on the stalk, collect them when dry, and store them on the kitchen counter or in a cabinet.

Storage and preservation:

FRIDGE: Store in a plastic or glass container for up to 2 weeks.

FREEZER: Blanch ears 7–10 min. depending on size, dry and freeze immediately.

DRIED: Popcorn.

CANNED: Must use a pressure canner. Add to a recipe like salsa.

What Corn Can Teach You:
How to Plant for Wind Pollination

Why you do it: Many crops are pollinated by insects and other creatures, but some (like corn, wheat, and other grains) are pollinated by the wind. The flowers are designed so that their pollen will be picked up by the wind and carried to nearby plants. If a corn plant is not surrounded by other corn, the pollen won't reach the other flowers and the plants won't set seeds (your ears of corn).

How you do it: Plant your corn in a separate section or bed of your garden. It is generally suggested that you plant at least four rows in order to get proper pollination. The more rows you plant, the better your chances of success.

Also useful for: Wheat, rye, barley, any other grain (most of which are not common home crops but are fun to grow nonetheless).

CUCUMBERS
Sprawling Crop or Tall Crop (if trellised), Long Season Crop

Cucumis sativus

Cucumbers are a delicious and refreshing summer crop, great for adding crunch to sandwiches and salads, or eating all by their lonesome. They are closely related to summer squash, zucchini, and pumpkins and are thought to have originated in the area that is now India.

Cucumbers are mostly water (90–95 percent but still give you a healthy dose of potassium and antioxidants. They are almost always picked "green," which refers to their color but also the fact that they are immature fruit. If left on the vine,

a cucumber will eventually ripen to yellow. At that point it is mature but also very bitter and not so good for eating (although there are types that are intended to be eaten yellow, such as the "lemon cucumber").

The tradition of canning is often thought of primarily in terms of cucumber pickles. Certain varieties are grown for fresh eating and others for pickling, but most varieties are good for both.

What you eat: The fruit.

Recommended varieties: Marketmore 76, Genuine.

Hardiness: Cucumbers can't tolerate frost, and grow best at 60°F and up.

Seed information: Germination temp. 65°– 100°F, optimal 86°; germination time 6 days at 68°, 3 days at 86°. Seed viability 2–5 years.

Mature plant size: Up to 5–6 ft. tall in a trellis, or 5–6 ft. long if spread on the ground.

How to plant: In cooler climates, cucumbers are best grown from transplants. If you're using a cage with a 2–3 ft. diameter, place 2 plants in each cage. If you're using a cage trellis (see chapter 12: Essential Garden Skills for more information), place 1 plant in each cage. If you're not using a trellis, space plants 2 ft. apart. Cucumbers can be direct-seeded once the soil has warmed above 60° (in many areas this is sometime around late May or early June).

When to plant: Cucumbers like it warm, so it's best to wait until the weather has really warmed up to set out transplants. If the weather is still cool and rainy, don't be afraid to wait.

How much to plant: Expect to harvest 2–5 lb. of cucumbers per plant. 1 or 2 plants are plenty for most gardeners, but if you plan to make a lot of pickles, add another 3 or 4 plants.

When to fertilize: Before planting, and at 3 and

6 weeks after transplanting. Use ¼ cup balanced fertilizer per plant, or liquid fertilizer.

General care: Watch for slug, snail, and cutworm damage on young seedlings. Cucumbers like plenty of water when setting fruit, so make sure they have an ample supply. Underwatering may lead to very thick skin on your fruit.

Pests: Cucumber beetles, leaf miners, and squash bugs may try to eat the foliage.

Diseases: Powdery mildew, downy mildew, Verticillium wilt, and black rot.

Container suitability: Good. Use 3 gal. pots or larger, or anything at least 9 in. deep.

When and how to harvest: Harvest cucumbers when they're about the size—depending on the type—that you'd expect to see in the grocery store. After the first harvest, check the plants every 2–3 days to make sure the cukes don't get too large. Frequent harvesting encourages the plant to produce more fruit and keeps the skins from getting tough.

Storage and preservation:

FRIDGE: Cucumbers keep best at 40°–50°F, but will do better in the refrigerator than if left out at room temperature. Expect them to keep a few weeks.

CANNED: Pickles.

What Cucumbers Can Teach You: How to Trellis Vining Crops

Why you do it: Cucumbers grow as a vine and can take up a lot of space in your garden if left to sprawl out. If you put them on a vertical trellis, they will grow up instead of out. This maximizes the use of your valuable garden space, and also keeps the fruit off the ground, reduces the risk of disease by improving air circulation around the plant, and enhances ripening by increasing sun exposure.

How you do it: Circular tomato cages sold in nurseries work great for cucumbers, or you can fashion your own from welded wire fencing or steel reinforcement mesh for concrete. The bigger your cage, the less your plant will sprawl (a 6 ft. tall by 3 ft. diameter cage is ideal, but even a 4 ft. tall basket type of cage will help. Immediately after transplanting, place the cage over the cucumber. If the plant is having a hard time finding its way up the trellis, help it out by tying it in place with a piece of twine (make sure not to pinch the stem).

Also useful for: Pole beans, peas, tomatoes, winter squash.

ABOVE: Cut the cucumber from the plant with scissors or a knife.

EGGPLANT

Medium Height Crop, Long Season Crop

Solanum melongena

Eggplants are beautiful, colorful, unique, and among the most fun crops to grow. Rich in fiber, potassium, and manganese, the eggplant is a night-shade and is related to tomato, potato, and pepper (and tobacco!) and is considered a native of India. Eggplants come in a variety of colors, including purple, white, pink, and green, and can range from 12 in. long to only 1 or 2 in.

The French word *aubergine* is used in many places outside the United States to refer to eggplant (and the dark purple color typically associated with it).

Like tomatoes and peppers, eggplants love hot weather. In cooler regions, they may have trouble reaching their full potential: The plants may grow tall and look healthy, but they often will not set as much fruit as they would in a very hot climate. If you're lucky enough to have a large eggplant harvest, we recommend filling an empty guitar case to the brim and taking them to a friend's house for dinner:

"Are you going to play us a song?"

"No—I just wanted to make some baba gha-noush…."

What you eat: The fruit.

Recommended varieties: There are many shapes and sizes of eggplant from all over the world. European and American eggplants are the large purple or purple-white types often seen in grocery stores; try Nadia or Rosa Bianca. Asian types can be long and slender, with few seeds, tending to ripen earlier than other types; try Ping Tung. There are also white, green, and striped varieties (hopefully, some resourceful plant breeder will develop a hot-pink variety soon).

Hardiness: No frost tolerance whatsoever. Egg-plants should be harvested before the first frost or they will rot.

Seed information: Germination temp. 60°–95°F, optimal 85°; germination time 21 days at 60°, 5 days at 85°. Seed viability 5–8 years.

Mature plant size: Up to 36 in. tall and 12 in. wide.

How to plant: Plant your eggplants from trans-plants, 12 in. apart. These should be available at local nurseries. If starting transplants at home, start seeds 8 weeks before the last frost.

When to plant: After the last frost. If the weather remains cool in spring, wait an extra week or so to make sure the plants are not exposed to too much cold.

How much to plant: In ideal conditions, 1 plant should produce 6–10 or even up to 15 fruits. Consider planting 3–5 plants.

When to fertilize: Before planting, and at 3 and 6 weeks after transplanting. Use ¼ cup bal-anced fertilizer per plant, or liquid fertilizer.

General care: If placed out at the proper time in a warm location, eggplant does not require a tremendous amount of cultural care, but check regularly for pest or disease problems. The fruits can become heavy, and the plants may benefit from staking once the fruit sets, so they don't tip over.

Pests: Eggplant is susceptible to a fair number of pests. Most common are aphids, hornworms, and leaf miners. Also leafhoppers, flea beetles, potato beetles, mites, and nematodes.

Diseases: Verticillium wilt, blossom-end rot. Eggplant can be susceptible to any tomato or potato diseases.

Container suitability: OK, but expect slightly smaller plants and fruit than in the garden. A plant can grow in a container as small as 1 gal., but larger is always better: A 3 gal. pot is the optimal size.

When and how to harvest: Harvest eggplants as soon as they are a size that you like. They can be harvested early, when still small, and they may have a softer texture at this stage. Removing fruit quickly will allow the plant to ripen more fruit during the course of the season. To harvest, simply cut the stem an inch above the top of the fruit with scissors or a sharp knife. Upon close examination, you will see tiny spikes on the undersides of the leaves and on the plant stem. These are sharp, so pay attention when you are pinching flowers or harvesting the fruit.

Storage and preservation:

COUNTER: Refrigerators can be a little too cold for eggplants, so keep them out on a counter. They will keep a week or two in the kitchen.

FREEZER: Eggplant can be blanched and frozen, or cooked in preparations like baba ghanoush and then frozen.

What Eggplant Can Teach You:
How to Remove Late-Season Blossoms

Why you do it: Once a fruiting plant (tomato, pepper, eggplant, etc.) gets established and starts producing fruit, it often will continue to set flowers until the end of the season. But since summer will inevitably come to an end, flowers set in the fall will never have the chance to develop into fruit. Removing the flowers during the last few weeks of the season tells the plant to put its energy into developing the fruit that is already set rather than making new fruit. This will help the last few eggplants size up fully before cold weather hits.

How you do it: When the end of the season is in sight (usually around mid- or late September), start pinching off all new blossoms. Continue to do so for the remainder of the season.

Also useful for: Peppers, tomatoes, winter squash.

ABOVE: To harvest eggplant, cut the stem above each fruit with scissors or hand pruners.

FENNEL (ANNUAL)

Short Crop, Half Season Crop

Foeniculum vulgare var. azoricum

Annual fennel, also known as Florence fennel or *finocchio*, is a relatively fast growing, tender vegetable. Closely related to the hardy perennial fennel herb, Florence fennel is known to be a finicky plant and may occasionally bolt before maturing into a nice-sized bulb, but the mild taste of a fresh, well-grown fennel can't be beat.

What you eat: The stem and leaves.

Recommended varieties: Orion.

Hardiness: Mature plants are tolerant to light frosts.

Mature plant size: 12–18 in.

How to plant: Direct-seed or transplant. Space plants 6–8 in. apart.

When to plant: Seeding or transplanting should be done in spring after the last frost and again in midsummer.

How much to plant: 2–6 plants in spring and again in summer.

When to fertilize: Before planting.

How it grows: Seedlings may take 60–80 days to reach maturity. The stem will swell at the base, creating a stout bulb that sits on the surface of the soil. Short feathery leaf fronds grow from the top of the bulb and can be used like a fresh herb.

General care: Disturbed roots, excessive heat, or lack of water may induce bolting. Keep plants mulched and well watered through the season. Clip off emerging flower stalks with hand pruners to allow the plant a chance to fully develop.

Pests: Slugs, aphids.

Diseases: Powdery mildew.

Container suitability: Good. 1 plant per gal. of pot size.

When and how to harvest: Ideal bulbs are about the size of a tennis ball, but small plants can be used as well. Cut bulb from the roots with hand pruners at soil level, just as you would harvest a head lettuce, cabbage or kohlrabi.

Storage and preservation: Fennel is generally best used fresh.

FRIDGE: Store in a sealed container or plastic bag for several weeks.

What Annual Fennel Can Teach You: Use What You've Got

Why you do it: Florence fennel can be a difficult plant even for experienced growers. Sometimes, despite your best efforts, a plant will become stressed and will not produce the volume of

ABOVE: To harvest fennel, cut the bulb from the roots at soil level.

food that you were hoping for. Instead of discarding a bolted, small plant, find a way to incorporate it into a recipe.

How you do it: If your fennel is bolting, rather than forming a large bulb, harvest the plant as is, and taste it to make sure it is not overly bitter or tough.

Also useful for: Many stressed plants can still be salvaged and used in the kitchen. Harvest stressed plants; if they taste good, eat them. Either way, clearing them from the garden will make room for another crop.

GARLIC
Short Crop, Very Long Season Crop
(9 months)

Allium sativum

Garlic is a member of the Allium family, which also includes onions, scallions, shallots, and leeks. It is thought to have originated in central Asia and has been a highly valued crop for ages (it was used as currency by the ancient Egyptians).

Garlic is rich in manganese, vitamin B6, and vitamin C. Today it is said to fight off both vampires and the common cold. Garlic grows best when planted in the fall so that it can "vernalize" during the winter. When a crop requires vernalization, it means that the plant will grow best after being exposed to cold temperatures. One interesting thing about garlic is that, contrary to common grocery-store labeling, it comes in many varieties and several distinct types:

SOFTNECK: Softneck garlic has a flexible central stem, and the bulbs tend to have many small cloves and thick wrapper skins. This is the type you usually see in the grocery-store. Softneck is widely

grown because it keeps very well all winter long.

HARDNECK: Hardneck (sometimes called *stiffneck*) garlic has a stiff central stem and fewer and larger cloves than softneck. It is grown for specialty markets like restaurants and farmers markets. It generally does not store as long as softneck garlic but is easier to peel and, many people feel, has a better taste. Hardneck garlic is the source of the "garlic scapes" you may see at farmers markets in the spring.

ABOVE: Pull mature garlic plants from the ground when one-half of the leaves have turned brown. Use a shovel or trowel to loosen the soil if necessary.

What you eat: The bulb, the scapes.

Recommended varieties: SOFTNECK: New York White. HARDNECK: Russian Red. ELEPHANT: Most seed companies list elephant garlic as a variety unto itself.

Hardiness: Plant in fall for harvest the following spring. Garlic can be planted in the early spring, but generally the heads will not be as large as those of fall-planted garlic.

Seed information: Seed garlic bulbs are best stored at 60°F.

Mature plant size: Up to 18 in. tall and 4 in. wide.

How to plant: Plant 1 garlic clove for each plant that you want. Choose large, healthy-looking cloves. Plant 2 in. deep and space 6 in. apart.

When to plant: Garlic is planted in the fall. It can generally be planted any time starting around mid-October, but wait a little later if fall temperatures remain warm. If garlic is planted too early, it will sprout before the worst winter weather hits and may be damaged by the cold. Generally, planting around November 1 is a good rule. Fall-planted garlic will emerge early in the year (weather dependent), sometime in January or February.

How much to plant: 1 clove will produce 1 head of garlic. Consider planting 10 plants. If you have space, try 50–60 plants, so you have a head of garlic for each week of the year!

When to fertilize: Before planting. Top-dress the area with compost in the spring once the garlic has emerged, and feed with ¼ cup balanced fertilizer per 2 plants.

General care: It is important to keep garlic well weeded, as competition from weeds will stress the plants and reduce the size of the heads.

Pests: Garlic is generally pest free but may be affected by nematodes.

ELEPHANT: This variation of garlic has just a few very large cloves in each head and is milder in flavor than hard and softneck varieties. It is actually a different species from the other types of garlic, and is closely related to leeks.

ABOVE: Cut the scape from the top of your garlic plant while it is still curled up.

Diseases: Generally disease free. Rust can be a problem in some areas.

Container suitability: OK. Use a container at least 12 in. deep. Allow for 1 gal. of soil for each plant. Expect smaller heads than if grown in the ground.

When and how to harvest: In midsummer the garlic tops will begin to turn brown. Once half of the stem has turned brown and started to dry out, the garlic can be harvested. Hang it in a warm, dark place for several weeks to cure, to increase storage life.

Storage and preservation:

DRIED: Store dried bulbs in a well-ventilated, cool, dry area like a kitchen counter or a closet.

CANNED: In pickled vegetable recipes and salsas.

OUTSIDE: Can be hung in a protected, cool, dry location in a shed or other outbuilding.

FRIDGE: Garlic scapes are best kept in a plastic bag in the fridge. Bulbs don't do well in the fridge.

What Garlic Can Teach You:
How to Cut Scapes from Hardneck Garlic

Why you do it: A garlic scape is the elongated, curly stem that emerges from the central stem of hardneck garlic plants in early summer. It's actually the precursor of the garlic's seed head. The scapes are delicious, and removing them will ultimately result in a larger bulb of garlic. This is best done when the scape has about one full loop in it. If you wait too long, they will straighten out and become tough and stringy. Even if they straighten out, cut them off to encourage larger heads of garlic.

How you do it: In early summer, once the scapes emerge and curl, break them off immediately above the top leaf of the plant. Cook and enjoy.

MELONS: CANTALOUPE, HONEYDEW, MUSKMELON, WATERMELON
Sprawling Crop or Tall Crop (if trellised),
Long Season Crop

Cucumis melo, Citrullus lanatus

The term *melon* is somewhat broad and can be applied to fruits of a few distantly related groups, including muskmelons (cantaloupe, honeydew, casaba) and watermelons. Rich in vitamins A and C and lycopene, melons originated in various parts of Africa and India and are related to cucumbers, summer squash, and winter squash. Like winter squash, many types are vine growers and need ample space (or a trellis) in the garden, so look for bush varieties if you plan to grow them in a small space. More so than other squash, melons *love* hot weather. Thus the plants are best suited to Southern climates, but they can grow well just about anywhere, provided you choose the best varieties for your area.

Some farmers in China are known to raise watermelons in square glass boxes. The fruit grows to fill the box and ends up a perfect square shape, making it easier to stack and ship! Feel free to grow your own watermelons in squares, pyramids, or even dodecahedrons.

What you eat: The fruit.

Recommended varieties: MUSKMELON, CANTALOUPE: Athena, Haogen, Jenny Lind. HONEYDEW: Earlidew, Honey Pearl. WATERMELON: Moon and Stars, Sugar Baby.

Hardiness: Not frost tolerant. Melons like really hot weather, so they may not grow well in only moderate summer temperatures.

Seed information: Germination temp. 65°– 100°F, optimal 86°; germination time 8 days at

thin down to 1 plant when seedlings emerge. Space plants 3 ft. or more apart.

When to plant: Direct-seed or transplant melons 4 weeks after the last frost.

How much to plant: Depending on variety, a melon vine will yield 1–6 fruits.

When to fertilize: Before planting, and at 3 and 6 weeks after planting. Use ¼ cup balanced fertilizer per plant, or liquid fertilizer.

General care: Sow or plant in well-prepared, fertile soil. Weeding around young plants will help them get off to a healthy start. Once the plant is established, additional weeding should be unnecessary.

Pests: Squash bugs, whitefly.

Diseases: Like other squash, melons are affected by downy or powdery mildew.

Container suitability: Not recommended.

When and how to harvest: Harvest once fruit are fully sized. MUSKMELONS: Mature fruit should smell sweet and easily slip off the stem of the plant. WATERMELONS: Harvest when the leaf closest to the fruit has died back, or the stem near the fruit begins to turn brown.

Storage and preservation:

FRIDGE: Melons will keep for 2 weeks in the refrigerator.

FREEZER: Cut into 1–2 in. pieces or balls, tray-freeze, and pack into freezer containers. Will keep 1–2 months.

What Melons Can Teach You: Assessing Ripeness

Why you do it: It can be tricky to pick a melon at just the right time, and unripe melons will not be as sweet and tender as mature fruit.

How you do it: A ripe cantaloupe or other muskmelon should give off a sweet smell when ripe. Put your nose right up to the fruit and check for

65°, 3 days at 86°. Seed viability 2–4 years.

Mature plant size: Up to 6–10 ft. long.

How to plant: Melons can be set out from transplants or direct-seeded into the garden. Transplanting is helpful in cooler climates to get a jump on the season. As with other Cucurbits, they are sensitive to disturbances to their roots and should be transplanted very carefully. If direct-seeding, sow 3 seeds in each hole and

ABOVE: Cut the stem above each melon when the fruit starts emit a sweet aroma.

sweetness. The fruit should also easily slip off the stem of the plant when ready (what farmers term "full slip"). For a watermelon, check the stem and leaves close to where the fruit attaches to the vine. When it is ripe, the stem and closest leaf should be turning brown and dying back. A ripe watermelon should feel heavy and make a dull, hollow sound when tapped. Ultimately, you'll need to harvest a few melons and taste them to get some experience—you'll know when you get it right!

Also useful for: Assessing the ripeness of melons is a skill unto itself, but harvesting and tasting to learn when a crop is at its peak is a great skill for most vegetables.

ONIONS, LEEKS, SCALLIONS

ONIONS: Short Crop, Long Season Crop
LEEKS: Short Crop, Long Season Crop
SCALLIONS: Short Crop, Short Season Crop

Allium cepa, Allium porrum

Like garlic, these are all members of the Allium family and share that unique "oniony" flavor. They are rich in chromium, vitamin C, and fiber. Varieties such as "bulbing" onions can take 7 or 8 months from seed to harvest, while others, such as scallions, are ready to harvest in as little as 50 days. There are multiple varieties of all three plants, particularly onions. To extend your harvest and menu options, consider growing some of each.

What you eat: The bulb and the leaves.

Recommended varieties: ONIONS: Ailsa Craig, Copra, Ruby Ring. LEEKS: King Richard. SCALLIONS: Evergreen Hardy White.

Hardiness: Onions should be harvested before the first frost or they will begin to rot. Leeks are more frost tolerant and can often keep in the garden through the late fall. Scallions are also frost tolerant and may keep throughout the winter.

Seed information: Germination temp. 50°–90°F, optimal 70°; germination time 14 days at 50°, 7 days at 70°. Seed viability 1 year.

ABOVE: Harvest onions and leeks at any size. The top of a mature onion will flop toward the ground.

Mature plant size: Highly variable. ONIONS: 18 in. tall and 2–6 in. wide. LEEKS: 18 in. tall and 1–3 in. wide. SCALLIONS: 12 in. tall and very thin.

How to plant: If possible, plant your alliums from transplants or "sets." Sets are small, dried miniature onion bulbs that can be planted directly in the ground. The bulbs should be set in holes 6–9 in. deep, in well-prepared soil. Space bulbing onions and leeks 6 in. apart and scallions 3 in. apart. Growing onions or leeks from seed is also possible, but in order to mature in time, they must be started very early in the year.

When to plant: Onions and leeks started from seed should be sown indoors in early to mid-January. This is much earlier than other transplants, so to preserve your sanity, we recommend buying these plants from a nursery for at least your first few years of gardening. Scallions, however, grow very quickly and can be grown as transplants or direct-seeded throughout the season.

How much to plant: Since onions and leeks are good storage crops, planting size should be based on your plans for winter storage. If you don't have the space or interest to keep crops through the winter (at least for now), try planting 1 row each of onions and leeks and planting a couple of successions of scallions.

When to fertilize: ONIONS AND LEEKS: Before planting, and at 3 weeks after transplanting. Use ¼ cup balanced fertilizer per plant, or liquid fertilizer. SCALLIONS: Before planting

General care: Of all your crops, alliums are generally the most pest and disease free. Once planted, keep the area as free as possible from weeds.

ABOVE LEFT: Cut back onion roots before planting to initiate healthy, new growth. ABOVE: Plant seedlings deep in the soil to create long, blanched stems.

Pests: May be affected by aphids or thrips.

Diseases: Downy mildew.

Container suitability: Good, but expect smaller plants and bulbs than in the garden. Scallions are particularly adept at container growing and grow well in 1 gal. pots or larger.

When and how to harvest: Bulbing onions are ready to harvest once the stems start to turn brown and die back. Leeks will stop growing and the outermost leaves will start to turn yellow and brown when they are mature. Both onions and leeks can be harvested earlier than this, but they will be smaller. To harvest, carefully loosen the soil around the plants, so as not to damage the plant, and then gently lift the entire plant from the ground. You can cut off long roots with scissors or a sharp knife and pull off any outer leaves that look yellow or otherwise undesirable.

Storage and preservation:

FRIDGE: Store scallions, green onions, and freshly harvested onions in a glass or plastic container for several weeks. Leeks store well in a plastic bag in the fridge for up to a month.

DRIED: When dried, some varieties of onions store well for several months. After harvest, allow them to dry in a sunny spot for a few days, then place them in a well-ventilated mesh bag in a dark, cool location such as a closet, pantry, or garage.

COUNTER: Dried onions will keep well on the counter for a few weeks.

OUTSIDE: For longer storage, keep leeks in the garden as long as possible and harvest as needed. They may be damaged by very cold weather but in temperate regions will often keep through much of the winter.

What Onions Can Teach You: Proper Planting Depth

Why you do it: Members of this family are interesting because, while they produce relatively tall aboveground stems, the best-tasting part of the plant is usually underground. Some varieties produce large underground bulbs (onions), while others produce thick, tasty stems (leeks, scallions). The aboveground portions are edible and delicious, but the belowground sections are usually considered the best parts for eating.

How you do it: These plants can be planted anywhere from 6 in. to 9 in. deep. The deeper you plant the base, the more of the growth will be underground and therefore more tender and better for eating.

Also useful for: Though this technique is not directly applicable to many other crops, it is similar to the strategies you use when planting potatoes.

PEAS (SNAP PEAS)

SNAP PEAS: Tall Crop (needs trellising, although dwarf varieties need much shorter trellis), Half Season Crop
SHELL PEAS: Medium Height Crop (can grow with or without a trellis), Half Season Crop

Pisum sativum

Fresh snap peas are a reason unto themselves for having your own garden. They are delicious raw or cooked, they're one of the earliest crops you can plant and harvest, and they are highly nutritious (containing vitamins C and B6, folate, iron, healthful phytochemicals, and a fair amount of vegetable protein).

Peas are thought to have originated in central Asia, and they were then cultivated by humans for centuries before a scientist named Gregor Mendel used them to develop the principles of genetics. Mendel chose peas because they are fast and easy to grow and easy to cross-pollinate. His observations helped him figure out how hereditary traits are passed from generation to generation, principles that apply to everything from peas to humans, tomatoes to aardvarks (among other things).

Peas fall into two general categories. SHELL PEAS are typically grown to maturity on the vine and then removed from the shell before eating. SNAP PEAS are harvested before they are fully mature on the vine and usually eaten whole with the shell on. They are the best choice for a first-time gardener since they are more productive and easier to grow than shell peas. If left on the vine too long, the pods become tough, at which point they can be shelled.

What you eat: The fruit.

Recommended varieties: Sugar Snap or Super Sugar Snap are the classic choices for snap peas. Try Dwarf Gray Sugar for a shorter type.

Hardiness: Peas can tolerate temperatures down to 22°F when they are young (before they flower), but frost tolerance is low for mature plants.

Seed information: Germination temp. 40°–75°F, optimal 77°; germination time 36 days at 41°, 6 days at 77°. Seed viability 3 years.

Mature plant size: Up to 6 ft. tall, or 3 ft. for dwarf varieties, and 3 in. wide.

How to plant: Set up either a tipi or net trellis. Dig a 1 in. deep trench along the trellis. Inoculate the seeds (see the Beans profile for specifics) and sow in the trench at 2 seeds per in. Thin to 1 plant every 2 in. If you can find them at a nursery or grow them yourself, peas grow well from transplants. Plant these at 1 plant every 2 in.

When to plant: You can set out transplants as early as late February and as late as mid-May. Direct-seed peas mid-March through late April. They don't germinate or grow well when temperatures get above 75°F, so it's best to sow them early. You can also try planting peas for fall harvest by direct-seeding them in early to mid-July.

How much to plant: Expect to harvest 7–8 lb. from an 8 ft. row of peas. A single tipi trellis or 8 ft. row should be adequate for most home gardens.

When to fertilize: Before planting.

General care: Watch for slug or bird damage to young plants. If young plants have a hard time finding the trellis, help them by wrapping the tendrils around it and securing them with twine if necessary.

Pests: Slugs, snails.

Diseases: Powdery mildew is inevitable with many pea varieties, but you can usually get a good harvest before this fungus destroys the crop.

Container suitability: Good. Use 1 gal. pots or larger, or anything at least 8 in. deep. Space plants 2 in. apart. Trellis peas in a pot by using thin bamboo poles or twine, or you can build a tipi trellis if the pot is large enough.

When and how to harvest: Harvest snap peas when they're plump, but before the shells get tough. The first peas will appear at the bottom of the plants. Harvest every 2 days to make sure you get to them before they are tough.

Storage and preservation:

FRIDGE: Peas keep well in plastic bags for several weeks, but are best eaten right away.

FREEZER: Blanch 1–2 min., dry and freeze immediately.

What Peas Can Teach You: How to Pinch Growing Tips

Why you do it: Snap peas need to be grown on a trellis to be productive in a garden. Amazingly, though, some varieties can grow past and overwhelm even the tallest trellis. By limiting their height, you encourage them to direct their energy to their flowers and fruit.

How you do it: When the pea vines reach the top of your trellis, use your fingers to pinch off (or scissors to cut) the main stem at the desired height. The vines will continue to flower and fruit on the remaining vine. You can also eat the shoots that you pinched off—they're great in salads!

Also useful for: Pole beans, cucumbers, tomatoes, and any other trellised crop.

ABOVE LEFT: Harvest peas before they become too swollen, at which point they will lose their good texture and taste. ABOVE: Cut the tops from the pea plants when they have reached the top of your trellis.

PEPPERS

Medium Height Crop, Long Season Crop

Capsicum annuum

Some people like sweet peppers and some people like hot peppers, but almost everyone likes some kind of pepper. Peppers originated in Central and South America and were first taken to Europe by Christopher Columbus. They contain ridiculously high amounts of vitamins A and C.

The wild pepper has been domesticated into hundreds of sweet and hot varieties. Generally speaking, bell and hot pepper plants like the same conditions—namely, hot, sunny, dry weather. Most new gardeners are surprised to find out that green bell peppers are not a crop in themselves but merely unripe bell peppers that eventually will turn yellow, orange, or red. Similarly, all hot peppers will eventually turn from green into a rainbow of bright, ripe colors.

What you eat: The fruit.

Recommended varieties: BELL PEPPERS: Lipstick, California Wonder, King Arthur. HOT PEPPERS: Early Jalapeño, Hungarian Hot Wax, Habanero.

Hardiness: Peppers should be harvested before the first frost or they will rot. When nearing the end of the season, harvest full-sized but unripe fruit a little early so that the last fruits can size up. Unripe peppers will ripen off the plant after harvest.

Seed information: Germination temp. 60°–95°F, optimal 85°; germination time 21 days at 60°, 7 days at 85°. Seed viability 2–3 years.

Mature plant size: Up to 36 in. tall and 12 in. wide.

How to plant: Pepper transplants should be available at local nurseries; plant them 12 in.

ABOVE TOP: Peppers love growing in containers.
ABOVE: Harvest peppers by cutting the stem above each fruit with a knife or scissors.

apart. If starting transplants at home, start seeds 8 weeks before the last frost.

When to plant: Peppers should be planted out any time after the last frost. If the weather remains cool in late spring, wait an extra week or so to make sure the plants are not exposed to too much cold weather.

How much to plant: Your plants should produce several peppers. In ideal conditions, a plant may produce 10–15 peppers; in cooler climates, half that much. Try planting 2 or 3 plants of each variety that you like.

When to fertilize: Before planting, and at 3 and 6 weeks after transplanting. Use ¼ cup balanced fertilizer per plant, or liquid fertilizer.

General care: If a pepper plant is placed in a warm location at the proper time, not a tremendous amount of care is necessary before harvest. Peppers can become heavy, and the plants may benefit from staking once the fruit starts to set, so the plant doesn't tip over.

Pests: Peppers have a fair number of pests. Most common are aphids, hornworms, and leaf miners, but also leafhoppers, flea beetles, potato beetles, mites, and nematodes.

Diseases: Blossom-end rot, stem rot.

Container suitability: Good, but expect slightly smaller plants and peppers than in the garden. A pepper plant can grow well in a container as small as 1 gal., but a 3 gal. pot for each plant is ideal.

When and how to harvest: Harvest peppers as soon as they are sized up and ripe. Removing ripe peppers quickly will allow the plant to ripen more fruit during the course of the season. Bell peppers will turn yellow, orange, or red when allowed to fully ripen. Once a pepper turns color, the taste and nutritional benefits improve greatly. To harvest, cut the stem 1 in. above the top of the pepper with scissors or a sharp knife.

Storage and preservation:

FRIDGE: Keep in a plastic or glass container for up to 2 weeks.

FREEZER: Bell peppers freeze well. Immediately after harvest, cut out the stem and seeds of the bell pepper, cut into slices (if desired) and freeze in a sealed freezer bag. You can tray-freeze them if you want to make sure they don't stick together.

DRIED: Hot peppers will store all winter if properly dried out and are great for winter cooking. To dry, simply hang by a string in the open air.

CANNED: In recipes like salsa.

What Peppers Can Teach You: How to Create a Microclimate

Why you do it: Of all the crops you will grow in your garden this year, peppers are one of the most heat loving. These are plants that do particularly well in places such as Mexico and New Mexico. They thrive on dry, hot weather. In order to have any chance at growing peppers in cooler climates, look for creative ways to simulate these conditions as much as possible.

How you do it: There are several common techniques for creating a hot microclimate in your garden. First, look for spots that are naturally the warmest. If any part of the garden sits up against the wall of your house, this would be a good location for peppers. The wall will act as a heat sink that both reflects extra daytime heat toward the garden bed and keeps the area warmer at night as the daytime heat is slowly diffused. Building a small cloche or cold frame for your pepper plants creates a greenhouse effect and keeps the area warmer both in the daytime and at night. Another idea is to place rocks around the pepper plants. The rocks will accumulate heat during the sunny parts of the day and then dissipate it during the night.

Also useful for: Creating warm microclimates can also help your tomato, basil, and eggplant crops. At the same time, creating a cooler microclimate can be useful for heat-intolerant crops in warm regions during the height of summer. You can do this by planting them in a partially shaded area of the garden, or setting up a shade cloth to protect them (see chapter 12: Essential Garden Skills for more information). Heat-sensitive crops include salad greens such as lettuce, arugula, and spinach.

POTATOES

Short Crop, Long Season Crop

Solanum tuberosum

Potatoes are a very satisfying crop to grow at home. There's nothing quite like digging into a garden bed and uncovering the hidden crop. Even more than carrots, kids *love* digging up potatoes. Potatoes often get a bad rap for being devoid of nutrition, but in actuality they are good sources of vegetable protein, vitamin C, B vitamins, copper, iron, and potassium.

Potatoes originated in the Andes mountains in South America. Farmers there developed countless potato varieties in myriad colors and sizes, but unfortunately, when potatoes were introduced into Europe, the genetic diversity of Andean potatoes was left behind.

In fact, many people posit that Ireland's Great Famine of the mid-1800s occurred because all of the potatoes then grown in Ireland were the same variety and therefore had no genetic variability.

When a fungus started destroying the potatoes, few of the plants were resistant to the disease, and many potatoes in the country were lost! This serves as a cautionary tale to promote crop diversity in modern-day farms and gardens: Don't put all your eggs (or potatoes) in one basket!

What you eat: The tuber.

Recommended varieties: Most potato varieties grow well, but our favorites are Yukon Gold, Superior, Red Gold, Purple Viking, Yellow Finn, Ozette, and Red Norland.

Hardiness: Although potatoes are set out early in the season, the plants themselves are not tolerant of frost.

Seed information: Seed potatoes are best stored at 40°–50°F until planting time.

Mature plant size: Up to 36 in. tall and 12 in. wide.

How to plant: Potatoes are almost always planted using pieces of the tubers themselves. You can order seed potatoes or buy them from a nursery, or buy organic potatoes from the grocery store. Leave small potatoes whole, or cut midsize potatoes in half and large ones into quarters. Aim to plant pieces about the size of golf balls, but make sure each chunk has at least 1 or 2 eyes on it. Dig 8 in. deep holes spaced 1 ft. apart for each piece, and add ¼ cup of balanced fertilizer to the hole and mix with a trowel. Place 1 piece of potato in each hole with the eye facing up, and fill the hole with half of the soil you removed (to a depth of 4 in.). Cover with the remaining 4 in. once the vines have grown 6–8 in. out of the soil.

When to plant: Planting potatoes is a St. Patrick's Day tradition (March 17), but they can be sown any time from mid-March through mid-June.

How much to plant: Each potato plant will yield

1–3 lb. of potatoes. Try planting 4–8 plants.

When to fertilize: Fertilize at planting time as directed above, and at 3 and 6 weeks after planting. Use ¼ cup balanced fertilizer per plant, or liquid fertilizer.

General care: Other than hilling and fertilizing, potatoes are a relatively maintenance-free crop.

Pests: Flea beetles and Colorado potato beetles are potential insect pests.

Diseases: Scab can cause cosmetic blemishing to the tubers. If scab shows up in your patch, choose resistant varieties in the future.

Container suitability: Good if a large enough container is used. Try a 20 gal. trash can or a large plastic storage container. Make sure to drill drainage holes in the bottom.

When and how to harvest: You can harvest baby new potatoes about 60 days after you see the plant emerge. For maximum yield, wait

ABOVE: To plant, cut each potato into golf ball-sized pieces; make sure each has at least one eye. ABOVE RIGHT: Harvest potatoes once the tops of the plants turn yellow and brown and begin to die back.

until the foliage begins to brown and die back. Drive a spade or garden fork into the ground about 1 ft. to the side of the plant. Be careful not to cut or stab your potatoes, because it will shorten their storage life (you may inevitably cut a few, but just make sure to eat those first). Gently lever the tubers up, and pull out any you've exposed. Now, using your hands or a trowel, dig thoroughly through the soil for the remaining potatoes.

Storage and preservation:

FRIDGE: For small quantities, wash and dry potatoes and store them in a plastic bag in the fridge for a week or so.

DRIED: For long-term storage, wash the tubers, let them air dry, and store them in a paper or netting bag at 40°–50°F (garages and clean basements are great places to keep them).

What Potatoes Can Teach You: Hilling Soil around Your Crops

Why you do it: Hilling potatoes makes them more productive by increasing the volume of soil around the plant, which helps tuber formation. Also, it prevents the potatoes from turning green by preventing light from reaching the potatoes closest to the soil's surface.

How you do it: When the plants reach 6–8 in. tall, mound garden soil around them until only the top 3 or 4 branches are exposed.

Also useful for: Leeks.

ABOVE: Plant potatoes in trenches and cover with soil as vines grow.

RADISHES
Short Crop, Short Season Crop

Raphanus sativus

Radishes are the great, underappreciated prince of the garden. Rich in vitamin C and calcium, they are wonderful because they grow so quickly and take up very little space.

Radishes can be ready to harvest in as little as three weeks after sowing, which means they are often the first crop ready to eat in the spring. After months of impatient waiting, the first harvest (however small) from your spring garden is always cause for celebration. Like many garden crops, radishes are available in a variety of colors and sizes, including white, purple, red, and pink.

What you eat: The root.

Recommended varieties: Cherriette, Easter Egg (several different-colored varieties in a package together), Cherry Belle.

Hardiness: Radishes can handle cold temperatures but will not store for long periods in the ground.

Seed information: Germination temp. 45°F, optimal 65°; germination time 7 days at 45°, 3 days at 65°. Seed viability 2–3 years,

Mature plant size: 6–12 in. tall.

How to plant: Direct-seed, then thin to 1 plant per inch.

When to plant: Direct-seed your radishes any time of year once the soil temperature is 45°F or higher.

How much to plant: For a continual harvest, plan to seed short rows every 2 weeks during the growing season.

When to fertilize: Before planting.

General care: Due to their short growing cycle,

there is not too much to worry about after seeding your radishes. Sow them into fertile, well-prepared soil and thin the row to 1 plant per inch once seedlings emerge. Make sure the surface of the soil remains moist while plants are germinating. If underwatered, the roots can become prematurely woody and pithy, so make sure beds don't dry out too much.

Pests: Radishes are susceptible to slug and snail damage and may also have problems with leaf miners and root maggots.

Diseases: Not very common, but could be affected by downy or powdery mildew.

Container suitability: Good. A patch of radishes can grow well in a container as small as 1 gal., but larger is always better (and it allows for more radishes).

When and how to harvest: Harvest radishes as soon as they are sized up and ripe. Removing ripe radishes will allow the remaining, smaller plants to develop.

Storage and preservation:

FRIDGE: Radishes will store well in a plastic bag for several weeks.

FREEZER: Blanch 1–2 min., dry and freeze immediately.

OUTSIDE: They won't last as long in the garden as they do in the fridge. Since they can be grown for much of the year, radishes are commonly grown in many successions and eaten fresh rather than grown for storage.

CANNED: Radishes are a great addition to any pickling recipe.

ABOVE: Harvest the largest radishes first to allow smaller roots to size up.

What Radishes Can Teach You: Harvesting at the Right Time for Best Taste

Why you do it: Radishes grow very quickly, and they keep in the garden for a relatively short period of time. Young, ripe radishes are tender and delicious, but those left too long in the garden can split open and become woody and unpalatable.

How you do it: Early in the spring, start direct-seeding radishes into the garden. Depending on temperatures, they will be ready to harvest somewhere between 3 and 6 weeks after sowing. If you enjoy this vegetable, it is important to follow the principles of succession planting (planting small amounts, more often). What is most important is to harvest your radishes right when they become ripe. Fortunately, harvesting is very easy: They will often push themselves mostly out of the soil, enabling you to simply pluck them up one at a time. The key is to keep an eye on them and pull them from the garden as soon as they reach a usable size (½–2 in.). The plants may even start to send up flower stalks soon after they reach edible size. Some will continue to grow much past the desirable size, and unharvested specimens can approach the size of a baseball, but at that point they will almost certainly be too tough for eating.

Also useful for: Learning the proper time to harvest is crucial for virtually every crop in your garden. Some crops (such as carrots) can store well in the ground for several months without losing flavor and texture, but others (radishes, head lettuce, broccoli) are not nearly as good if the proper window is missed. Finding the exact timing for each crop takes a little experience, and radishes provide a good way to acquire it.

SALAD GREENS: HEAD LETTUCE, LEAF LETTUCE, ARUGULA, SPINACH
Short Crop, Short Season Crop

Lactuca sativa, Eruca vesicaria sativa, Spinacea oleracea

This is possibly the most common story related by a first-time vegetable gardener:

"I done went out and planted all my lettuces in the spring, hopin' for a good harvest, and dadgummit if every one of them heads weren't ready at the exact same time! I was givin' out heads of lettuce to my brother Donald, my aunt Bessie, the neighbors up the way, you name it! Then I realized I didn't have nothin' for salad eatin' for the rest of the time!"

Salad greens grow quickly and generally do not keep for a long time in the garden once they are mature. To maintain a consistent supply, it is essential to plant them multiple times during the season (and not all at once in the early spring).

Derived from wild greens in the Mediterranean, lettuces and many other salad greens are well known for their reluctance to grow in hot conditions. If these plants overheat, they bolt. When plants bolt, the leaves become bitter and generally useless for consumption. Bolting is an indication that the plant is stressed; it starts to flower early in an effort to produce seeds, so that it can reproduce before its demise.

There are many different types of salad greens, all of which are rich in vitamins (A, C, K), folate, potassium, and countless other nutrients:

HEAD LETTUCE: Lettuce can be grown as a "head," allowing each plant to size up fully for harvesting all at once. Lettuce heads can be open and leafy (green and red leaf types, oak leaf types,

CLOCKWISE FROM TOP LEFT: Cut head lettuce from the roots at the base of the head, at soil level. Harvest individual spinach leaves or cut the whole plant back to the base. Cut arugula leaves when they are 6–8 inches tall. Cut lettuce mix when leaves are 6–8 inches tall.

and French crisp or Batavian types), tall and elongated (romaine), or actual "heads" (butterhead, Bibb, Boston, iceberg types). When we refer to head lettuce, we mean any of these types, not just iceberg. For an earlier harvest of tender leaves, you can pluck individual leaves from head lettuces when they're partially mature (you won't get a full head this way, but you'll be able to harvest leaves on multiple occasions).

BABY LETTUCE, LETTUCE MIXES: Lettuce grown as baby lettuce is direct-seeded thickly in a row and cut about 1 in. above the ground when the leaves are still relatively young (4–5 in. tall). This results in a salad of particularly tender baby greens. You can often get 2 to 3 additional cuttings from 1 seeding. Many seed companies sell packages of premixed lettuce seed varieties for a multicolored and multitextured salad.

SPINACH: Spinach can be grown like baby lettuce for raw use in salad, or you can harvest individual larger leaves for cooking. It is particularly sensitive to heat and is therefore usually grown only in the spring and fall.

ARUGULA: Another popular salad green, known for its spicy flavor. It is typically planted and harvested like baby lettuce.

What you eat: The leaves.

Recommended varieties: HEAD LETTUCE FOR SPRING AND FALL GROWING: Deer Tongue, Winter Density (romaine), Flashy Trout Back, Nancy (butterhead). HEAD LETTUCE FOR SUMMER GROWING: Parris Island Cos, Black Seeded Simpson. BABY LETTUCE/LETTUCE MIX: We recommend getting a premixed package of

ABOVE: Plant small sections of salad greens each week for a continual supply.

lettuces that contains a variety of green and red types. SPINACH: Regiment. ARUGULA: Roquette (Rocket), Surrey.

Hardiness: Most salad greens can handle cold temperatures. Established spinach and arugula and lettuces may live through the winter if covered.

Seed information: Germination temp. 40°F, optimal 65° (above 75° and germination is very poor); germination time 7 days at 40°, 3 days at 65°. Seed viability 2–3 years.

Mature plant size: HEAD LETTUCE: Up to 12 in. tall and 6–8 in. wide. BABY LETTUCE/LETTUCE MIX AND OTHER LEAFY GREENS: 6–8 in. tall.

How to plant: Direct-seed or from transplants. In the spring, head lettuces and spinach starts will likely be available at local nurseries. Transplants work well, but due to their fast-growing nature, most of these crops can be direct-seeded into the garden. For head lettuce, space plants 8 in. apart. For baby lettuce and arugula, direct-seed thickly in rows (for the amount of seed, imagine you're sprinkling Parmesan cheese on a pizza). For spinach, space plants every inch for baby leaves, or every 3–4 in. for large cooking leaves.

When to plant: Direct-seed any time of year once the soil temperature is 45°F or higher. For a continual harvest, plan to seed short rows every week during the growing season. Once temperatures reach consistently above 75°, lettuce seed may have a difficult time germinating. During the hottest part of the summer, plant salad greens in cooler, shadier spots. Placing them in the shade of taller vegetable plants (such as tomatoes) may help you continue your harvest through the hottest part of the summer.

How much to plant: For a continual harvest, seed short rows (1–2 ft. long) every week throughout the growing season.

When to fertilize: Before planting.

General care: Sow salad greens into fertile, well-prepared soil. They like a lot of water, so make sure the soil remains moist, especially in warmer weather. Proper irrigation may slow the bolting process. Once bolting has started, it is irreversible. Pull bolting plants to make room for successions of other crops.

Pests: Salad greens are susceptible to slug and snail damage and may also have problems with aphids, leaf miners, and root maggots.

Diseases: Not very common, but could be affected by downy or powdery mildew, white mold, or gray mold.

Container suitability: Good. Salad greens will grow well in a container as small as 1 gal., but larger is always better. If planting multiple successions in pots, remember to fertilize between each planting.

When and how to harvest: The harvest method for each type of green is slightly different:

LETTUCE, FULL HEADS: Cut the plant off at the base once the head has reached mature size (usually 8–10 in.). Remove damaged outer leaves, and pull the remaining root mass from the soil for composting.

LETTUCE, INDIVIDUAL LEAVES: Pull 3 or 4 leaves from each plant (as you do with kale). Repeat once a week until the plant stops producing. This is commonly done when heads are about half size (4–6 in.) but can be done at any size.

BABY LETTUCE/LETTUCE MIX: Cut a section of the row down to 1 in. above soil level. A healthy stand of lettuce will regrow within a week or two and allow for a second and sometimes a third harvest.

SPINACH: Spinach can be harvested like baby lettuce (cut at about 1 in. above the soil) for salad use, or you can pick individual leaves. Pull 3 or 4 leaves per plant once a week.

ARUGULA: Arugula is harvested like lettuce mix.

Storage and preservation:

FRIDGE: Salad greens will store well in a plastic bag for several weeks.

OUTSIDE: Since they can be grown for much of the year, salad greens are commonly planted in many successions and eaten fresh rather than grown for storage.

What Salad Greens Can Teach You: Succession Planting

Why you do it: Salad greens grow relatively quickly. While certain crops (such as tomatoes or peppers) are considered "long season" and are planted once in the spring, and it takes them all season to ripen their crop, plants such as lettuce and spinach mature much more quickly and are called "short season" crops. To have fresh salad greens available throughout the season, it is important to learn how to plant multiple successions of these short-season crops.

How you do it: Succession planting is very easy. The general idea is to plant small amounts of a crop on multiple occasions. Planting your short-season crops in this way will prevent you from being overloaded with a vegetable one week and completely lacking it the next.

Also useful for: Succession planting is applicable to many crops in this book. Some of the most common succession-planted crops are bush beans, beets, broccoli, cabbage, carrots, cauliflower, chard, kale, collards, scallions, and radishes. Less common but still possible are corn, peas, and potatoes.

SUMMER SQUASH: ZUCCHINI, YELLOW CROOKNECK, YELLOW STRAIGHTNECK, PATTYPAN
Sprawling Crop, Half Season Crop

Cucurbita pepo

Summer squash is another fun and exciting crop to grow: It's delicious, it grows quickly, and it produces like crazy. This New World crop includes a range of types that grow exactly the same way but whose fruit can be very different. You can find an incredible amount of variety in summer squash types.

Try to avoid summer squash burnout by not growing too many plants (one to three is usually plenty for a home garden). Home gardeners are known to deliver excess zucchini harvests anywhere they can think of, including neighbors' doorsteps and inside parked cars at the library. So if you have neighbors who garden, be sure to keep your windows rolled up and doors locked at zucchini harvest time.

Plan to pick the squash when they're young and tender instead of baseball bat size. If you forget to harvest some and they end up bigger than your head, start looking for recipes for zucchini bread, zucchini fritters, and zucchini relish. Summer squash contains folate, potassium, vitamin A, and a hint of manganese.

What you eat: The fruit.

Recommended varieties: Most varieties seem to perform well. We like Yellow Crookneck, Zephyr, Sebring, and Sunray (all yellow types); Jackpot and Raven (zucchinis); and Sunburst (pattypan).

Hardiness: Frost kills summer squash plants.

Seed information: Germination temp. 65°–100°F, optimal 86°; germination time 6 days at

68°, 3 days at 86°. Seed viability 3–6 years.

Mature plant size: Up to 24 in. tall and 36 in. wide.

How to plant: Summer squash can be easily grown by direct-seeding or from transplants. Space plants about 2 ft. apart. For transplants, add and mix ¼ cup of balanced fertilizer into each planting hole. To direct-seed, fertilize as above, and then plant 3 seeds about 1 in. deep in each planting hole. Thin to 1 plant for every 3 seeds.

When to plant: Set out transplants in late April through early July. Direct-seed any time between late May and early July.

How much to plant: Each plant will yield 3–6 lb. of squash. For your first year, don't plant more than 2 unless you are really, really psyched about summer squash.

When to fertilize: Before planting and at 3 and 6 weeks after planting. Use ¼ cup balanced fertilizer per plant, or liquid fertilizer.

General care: Watch for insect damage when the plants are young. Prune dying lower leaves off to slow the spread of mildew.

Pests: Squash vine borers, squash bugs, and cucumber beetles.

Diseases: Powdery mildew, downy mildew.

Container suitability: OK. 5 gal. pot per plant or larger, or anything at least 13 in. deep.

When and how to harvest: Use pruning shears to clip fruit from the plant. Harvest at any size you like. Clip them small (6–8 in. long) for salads, sandwiches, and light cooking. As they get bigger, seeds start to form inside, and the flesh becomes a little pithy. Larger squash are best used for zucchini bread and squash fritters. Check the plants at least every other day so you can harvest at the desired size.

Storage and preservation:

COUNTER: Summer squash stores best at 40°–50°F but quickly loses its texture if stored in the refrigerator. Keep it on the counter!

FREEZER: Blanch 3–4 min., dry and freeze immediately.

What Summer Squash Can Teach You: How to Encourage Insect Pollination

Why you do it: Summer squash is an insect-pollinated crop, which means it needs the help of winged friends to transfer pollen from the male to the female flowers. Encouraging these insects to find a home in your garden is a great idea.

How you do it: Flowering plants attract and provide a food source for pollinating insects. Try planting annual flowers such as alyssum,

ABOVE: Harvest zucchini by cutting the stem above each fruit with scissors or a knife. Smaller fruits have the best taste and texture.

bachelor's button, black-eyed susan, calendula, cosmos, marigold, nasturtium, sunflower, and zinnia in your garden, or include perennials such as bee balm iris, delphinium, lavender, lobelia, rhododendron, and rosemary in the landscaping near your garden.

Also useful for: Any fruiting plant appreciates having insect pollinators around (beans, berries, cucumbers, fruit trees, peas, tomatoes, winter squash).

TOMATOES

Tall Crop (needs trellising),
Long Season Crop

Lycopersicon esculentum

Tomatoes are an incredible crop and probably the most popular garden vegetable. The tomato originated in South America and eventually made its way into the cuisine of just about every culture on the planet. There are many stories about the slow adoption of tomatoes in parts of Europe due to its similarity to poisonous nightshade plants. But eventually the temptation of the sweet, prolific fruits won out over the fear of a horrible death, and pizza was born. Tomatoes contain vitamins A and C and a host of healthful phytochemicals such as lutein and lycopene.

There are two main types of tomato plants you can grow. This is an important distinction, so remember to look for the type on each seed packet or plant tag:

Determinate tomatoes grow to a certain height, then flower and set fruit over a short period of time. Determinate tomatoes can be left to sprawl or given a shorter trellis. They are generally grown for preservation and canning; many determinate types are Roma or plum tomatoes.

Indeterminate tomatoes will continue to grow larger and larger through the season and continue to set fruit for many weeks (until the end of the season, when they are killed by frost). Indeterminate tomatoes require a tall trellis (either a single pole or a circular cage or fence). Most cherry tomatoes and many slicing tomatoes are indeterminate varieties.

Tomatoes come in a variety of shapes and sizes. Some principal categories are:

CHERRY, GRAPE: Small, very sweet tomatoes usually eaten whole.

ABOVE: Trim off lower leaves and plant the stem of the tomato plant underground. The buried stem will grow roots, leading to a more vigorous plant.

PLUM, ROMA: Medium-sized fruit, usually with an oblong, narrow shape (similar to a plum), used for sauces and for canning.

SLICING, BEEFSTEAK: Large tomatoes used for slicing for sandwiches, for caprese salad, you name it.

What you eat: The fruit.

Recommended varieties: CHERRY: Sungold, Sweet 100, White Currant. SLICING: Stupice (heirloom), Moskvich (heirloom), Big Beef, Black Prince (heirloom). ROMA: Window Box Roma, San Marzano.

Hardiness: Frost will kill tomatoes.

Seed information: Germination temp. 60°–90°F, optimal 77°; germination time 14 days at 59°, 6 days at 77°. Seed viability 3–7 years.

ABOVE: Snip off extra shoots from the bases of the leaves as your tomato plant grows. ABOVE RIGHT: Ripe tomatoes feel soft to the touch.

Mature plant size: Up to 6 ft. tall and 36 in. wide.

How to plant: It's crucial to start with large, healthy transplants. Look for plants with dark green vegetation in 4 in. or larger pots. Space plants 18 in. apart. If planting with a single pole trellis, drive the post in place first. Next, snip the lowest side branches and the bottom set of leaves off of your transplants, and dig a hole deep enough for each plant to be buried up to the next lowest set of leaves. (Tomatoes set new roots out of the buried stem, so planting them this way gives them the opportunity to develop a large root structure very quickly.) Add ¼ cup of balanced fertilizer to the hole and mix with a trowel. Set the plant in the hole and fill it back in with soil. If you're using a circular cage, place it over the plant (take care not to puncture your drip irrigation system).

When to plant: Tomatoes are best planted in late spring, mid- to late May in most areas.

How much to plant: Tomato yield is variable, but you'll likely harvest 3–6 lb. per plant (up to 10 lb. in ideal conditions). We recommend starting with 1–6 plants for your first year.

When to fertilize: Before planting, and at 3 and 6 weeks after planting. Use ¼ cup balanced fertilizer per plant, or liquid fertilizer.

General care: Prune and train your tomatoes to their trellis. After the plants have started ripening their first fruits, you can stop watering them. This will reduce the size of the tomatoes and the overall yield of the plants, but will encourage ripening and improve flavor.

Pests: Tomato hornworms, aphids, slugs, nematodes.

Diseases: Early and late blight, anthracnose, Verticillium and Fusarium wilt.

Container suitability: Good. Use 5 gal. pots or larger, or anything at least 12 in. in. deep.

When and how to harvest: Tomatoes taste best when ripened on the plant. They're ready when fully red (or yellow, orange, or purple) and slightly soft to the touch. Harvest by cutting the stem just above the tomato, or by breaking it off with your hand. Tomatoes also ripen well off the vine if held at room temperature. This is useful for large tomatoes that don't fully ripen on the vine, and in the fall when temperatures aren't high enough to ripen the fruit outdoors.

Storage and preservation:

COUNTER: Tomatoes should be stored at 60°–70°F. A basket on the counter is perfect. Avoid the fridge unless you like mealy, tasteless tomatoes.

FREEZER: You can puree fresh tomatoes, drain the excess liquid, and freeze them immediately, or you can cook the puree to the desired thickness and then freeze.

DRIED: Sun-dried tomatoes.

CANNED: Tomato sauce, salsa, whole or sliced tomatoes, paste.

What Tomatoes Can Teach You: How to Prune

Why you do it: Pruning helps ensure high yields of fruit and greater ripening success, especially with indeterminate types. It will limit the overall number of tomatoes, so the plant can produce and ripen higher-quality fruits. It increases air circulation through the plant (which helps keep disease down) and improves sunlight penetration (which helps with ripening). Late-season pruning reduces the production of late-season tomatoes, so that the plant has a better chance of ripening existing fruit. Generally speaking, determinate tomatoes need considerably less pruning than indeterminate types.

How you do it: The ideal tomato plant has two to three main stems, with single lateral branches radiating from each stem. We recommend pruning tomatoes once a week to keep them under control. Prune by breaking excess branches off with your fingers, or use pruning shears if branches are too large to break.

A. At transplanting time, check the crotch of each branch. Break off any new branch growing from the crotch. Also, break off any forming flower buds.

B. Continue to check branch crotches each week and break off new branches. Also, break off any flower buds that appear for 2–3 weeks after transplanting.

C. If using a single pole-type trellis, tie the main stem of the plant to it. If the plant develops other large stems that compete with the main stem, keep only one or two of them and make slings with twine to support them. If you're using circular cages, the cage will support these additional stems. Cut off any additional main stems that develop.

D. Keep this basic structure going as the plant grows. Prune off any yellowing, dying, or diseased leaves. The plant will continue to grow, set new flowers, and fruit.

E. Starting in mid-August, prune off any new flower buds. This will keep the plant from setting fruit too late into the fall.

F. This process sounds kind of complicated, but don't hesitate! You'll get more and more comfortable each time you prune.

Also useful for: Pruning tomatoes is a skill unto itself, but the basic technique of selectively removing foliage can help you with managing diseases and improving air circulation for any fruiting crop.

TURNIPS, RUTABAGAS, KOHLRABI

TURNIPS, KOHLRABI: Short Crop,
Short Season Crop
RUTABAGA: Short Crop, Half Season Crop

Brassica rapa and Brassica napobrassica

Members of the Brassica (or cabbage) family, turnips, rutabagas (also called Swedes), and kohlrabi are often-ignored crops in home vegetable gardens, and we think that's a shame. These crops are easy to grow and surprisingly tasty. Their roots are high in vitamin C, and the leafy greens are a great source of vitamin A, folate, and calcium.

Turnip and rutabaga are closely related (the rutabaga is a cross between a turnip and a cabbage), and varieties can sometimes be difficult to distinguish from each other. Rutabaga tends to be larger and more elongated, and has an orange

ABOVE TOP: Pull mature turnips right out of the soil. ABOVE: Harvest mature kohlrabi by cutting the plant from the roots right at soil level.

hue to the flesh. Both are grown primarily for their roots. Kohlrabi is very similar in growth habit to these crops, but it is grown for its swollen stem instead of its root structure. In reality, all three crops appear as roundish bulbs sitting on the surface of the soil.

In Ireland and Scotland, Halloween enthusiasts make their jack-o'-lanterns from large rutabagas and turnips rather than pumpkins!

What you eat: TURNIP/RUTABAGA: The root. KOHLRABI: The stem.

Recommended varieties: TURNIP: Purple Top White Globe, Hakurei. RUTABAGA: Laurentian. KOHLRABI: Kohlribi (purple), Gigante.

Hardiness: Brassicas handle frost well.

Seed information: Germination temp. 45°–90°F, optimal 85°; germination time 20 days at 50°, 4 days at 85°. Seed viability 3–4 years.

Mature plant size: Up to 18 in. tall.

How to plant: Direct-seed. Thin plants to 4 in. apart.

When to plant: Direct-seed these crops any time of year once the soil temperature is 50°F or higher. They are generally grown as a spring crop and can be sown again in midsummer for a fall harvest.

How much to plant: Start with a short row, 1–2 ft. long.

When to fertilize: Before planting. Use ¼ cup balanced fertilizer per 3 plants.

General care: These crops are less prone to insect and disease problems than most other Brassicas. Watch plants carefully for signs of insect damage. As the plants grow, the lower leaves may start to turn yellow or brown and die. Pull these off to improve air circulation. Make sure to harvest the crops before they exceed their mature size, as they can become woody and unpalatable if left in the garden too long.

Pests: Likely pests include aphids, cabbage loopers, cutworms, slugs, snails, and imported cabbageworms. Other potential problems are flea beetles, root knot nematodes, and root maggots (the larvae of cabbage root flies).

Diseases: Alternaria blight, clubroot, downy mildew.

Container suitability: OK, but expect smaller roots and stems than in the garden. 1 gal. size per plant or larger, or anything at least 6 in. deep.

When and how to harvest: TURNIP AND RUTABAGA: Pull the roots from the ground when they have reached the desired size. They can be harvested small for tender, sweet "baby" versions. KOHLRABI: Cut with a sharp knife or hand pruners just below the base of the stem.

Storage:

FRIDGE: These crops store well for several weeks in a sealed container or plastic bag.

FREEZER: Blanch 2–3 min., dry and freeze immediately.

What Turnips Can Teach You: Obscure Vegetables Can Be Delicious

Why you do it: To expand the diversity of your garden and your diet. To show off your culinary sophistication.

How you do it: Try planting a short row of turnips or rutabagas in the spring or late summer, and see if you enjoy preparing and eating these crops.

Also useful for: Bok choy, pac choi, pak choi, and bok choi.

WINTER SQUASH, PUMPKINS, GOURDS

Sprawling Crop or Tall Crop (if trellised),
Long Season Crop

Cucurbita maxima, Cucurbita moschata, Cucurbita pepo

Q: What makes a squash a winter squash?
A: You eat it during the winter.

The term "winter squash" has become somewhat confusing, because we are no longer required to put up a supply of storage crops in order to make it through the winter (although some of us choose to do so anyway). Winter squash should be thought of as both storage squashes (butternut, acorn, spaghetti, etc.) and pumpkins. Like summer squash, these plants originated in South America and are full of vitamin A, calcium, and potassium.

Overall, winter squash are very similar to summer squash, but with a few major differences. One is that, while many summer squashes are bush-type plants, meaning they have a somewhat short growth habit, winter squashes are typically vining types, which means they can trail for 10–20 ft. and, if you're not careful, spread to consume your entire garden.

The other principal difference is that while summer squashes produce fruit relatively quickly (within a couple of months), the winter squashes need much more time to properly ripen their fruit and are not usually ready to harvest until early fall. The goal of growing winter squash is to have some residual garden harvest to eat long after the hot, sunny days of summer.

Gourds grow just like winter squash, except that the fruit is inedible. We wanted to mention them because they're fun to grow and the fruit is great for crafts and decorating. There are even varieties that you can make into birdhouses!

What you eat: The fruit.

Recommended varieties: WINTER SQUASH: Butternut, Delicata, Acorn. PUMPKIN: New England Sugar Pie (for eating), Howden and Charisma (for jack-o'-lanterns), Dill's Atlantic Giant (for record-breaking giant pumpkins).

Hardiness: All winter squash should be harvested and brought inside before the first frost. Freezing conditions will lead to rapidly rotting fruit.

Seed information: Germination temp. 60°F, optimal 85°; germination time 14 days at 60°, 3 days at 85°. Seed viability 4–5 years.

Mature plant size: There are both vining types and bush types of winter squash. As you might have guessed, the vining types are long (up to 6–10 ft.) and sprawling, and the bush types are taller and more compact (3–4 ft. wide, 2–3 ft. tall).

How to plant: Winter squash and pumpkins can be set out from transplants or direct-seeded into the garden. As with summer squash, they are sensitive to disturbances to their roots and so should be transplanted very carefully. If direct-seeding, sow 3 or 4 seeds in each hole and thin down to 1 plant when seedlings emerge. Space plants at least 3 ft. apart. Many seed packs will direct you to plant squash in "hills" or "mounds." These terms are simply old-fashioned ways to refer to a place to plant squash; there is no need to build an actual hill for the seeds—just space them as far apart as directed. You can also plant winter squash on sturdy trellises (ladder types are best). Make sure to use vining types for this application.

When to plant: Direct-seed your winter squash 2 weeks after the last frost. This means that in many locations you can seed them in mid- to

late May to ensure they have enough time to ripen before the first frost.

How much to plant: A healthy winter squash or pumpkin can produce between 2 and 6 fruits per plant. Consider planting 2 or 3 plants.

When to fertilize: Before planting, and at 3 and 6 weeks after planting. Use ¼ cup balanced fertilizer per plant, or liquid fertilizer.

General care: Sow or plant in well-prepared, fertile soil. Weeding around young plants will help them get off to a healthy start. Once the plant is established, additional weeding should be unnecessary. For healthy growth, ensure a consistent watering schedule and side-dress with balanced fertilizer in midsummer.

Pests: Squash bugs, whitefly.

Diseases: Downy mildew, powdery mildew, black rot.

Container suitability: May be possible, but not recommended.

When and how to harvest: Harvest once fruit is full sized and properly colored and has a tough skin. The fruit can be left to cure on the vine as the plant dies back. Cut it from the vine once the stem is easy to break, and make sure to leave 5–6 in. of stem on the top of the fruit.

Storage and preservation:

DRIED: Winter squash can store up to 6 months in a cool, dry location. Make sure to harvest it only when properly cured, or it may rot more quickly.

COUNTER: When cured, winter squash will keep well on the counter for a month or so.

FREEZER: Fully cook squash, remove the skin, and freeze.

What Winter Squash Can Teach You: How to Shade Out Weeds

Why you do it: Many gardeners use the spreading habit of winter squash to their advantage. Because the plants get so large and have such huge leaves, they can be used to shade out the ground surrounding them, which might otherwise produce a crop of unruly weeds. Otherwise, it is best to trellis the plants up a structure or fence to keep them from overtaking the garden. Each solution has its place.

How you do it: Plant winter squash as directed (2–3 ft. apart), and let the plants sprawl into an area that has been weedy in past years, or that you intend to incorporate into the garden in the future but don't want to keep up this season. You can also let your plants sprawl into the lawn adjacent to the garden. It may be hard to mow near them, but it is a good way to save valuable garden real estate.

Also useful for: Although summer squash is smaller than winter squash, you can use it in the same way.

OPPOSITE: Winter squash is ready to harvest when the stem above each fruit is dried and the plant has begun to die back.

17

PERENNIAL VEGETABLES

THE VAST MAJORITY of vegetable crops are annuals, and as we've said, we strongly recommend planting your perennial vegetables in a bed separate from that of your annual crops. For one thing, you don't want to dig up the roots of the perennial crops as you work the soil in your annual beds each season, turning in compost and/or cover crops.

The perennials will be planted, watered, weeded around, pruned, and top-dressed with compost and fertilizers, but left in place year after year.

Perennial crops are nice because they generally require less maintenance than annuals. And once they are established, they will produce for years with little maintenance. The other side of the coin is that it may take several seasons before you can start harvesting from your perennials. We've included some seed information here, but starting perennials from seed can be a finicky, lengthy process. We recommend buying perennials as plants in 4 in. or larger pots, to give you a jump on the time between planting and harvesting.

You'll find that the perennial vegetables we've listed here are great for first-time gardeners, because they're easy to grow, tasty to eat, and they look great!

OPPOSITE: A bird's-eye view of an artichoke bud.

ARTICHOKES
Perennial Crop, Tall Crop

Cynara cardunculus

Originally a Mediterranean crop, artichokes can be grown from seed, from cuttings, or from dormant roots. The first-time farmer should consider buying these as transplants if possible. They should become available in the spring and can be planted outside after the danger of frost is past.

Artichokes can be grown as an annual crop, and in colder regions, they are always grown that way. But many varieties take 90–100 days to reach maturity, so it is possible that they will not flower their first year. In moderate climates it is possible to keep them as perennials.

What you eat: The unopened flower head.

Recommended varieties: Green Globe can be grown as a perennial or as an annual; Imperial Star is a better choice if grown as an annual.

Hardiness: Artichokes have limited frost tolerance. Apply heavy mulch in the fall in colder regions, and grow as annuals if necessary. Survives the winter reliably in zone 8 and warmer.

Seed information: Germination temp. 60°–80°F, optimal 70°; germination time 12 days at 60°, 9 days at 70°. Seed viability 3 years.

Mature plant size: Up to 6 ft. tall and 6 ft. wide.

How to plant: Plant in a well-prepared garden bed. Space 4 ft. apart, with the rows also 4 ft. apart. If transplanting, set them in the ground as with any other transplant. If planting roots, set the roots just below the surface of the soil.

When to plant: Seeds need to be sown indoors 6 weeks before the last frost. Plant out roots or young plants after danger of frost has passed.

How much to plant: Artichoke plants can be incredibly productive: A healthy plant may produce 10 heads or more each season. Consider planting 2 or 3 plants to start.

When to fertilize: Apply balanced fertilizer at planting time and again each spring. Artichokes benefit from rich, well-drained soil.

How it grows: Artichoke starts out as a short, leafy plant. As it grows, the leaves will get larger and larger, and by midsummer it will start sending up thick flower stalks. A bud will begin to develop at the top of each stalk, and eventually you will recognize that bud as an artichoke.

General care: Keep plants well watered through the summer for the best-tasting buds. If growing as a perennial, apply heavy mulch around the plant base in fall to protect it from hard frost. To mulch, cover the base of the plant with 4 in. of soil and then 4 in. of straw or leaves. Remove the straw or leaves in the spring. If the plants are grown successfully as perennials, you can dig up and divide the base of the plant each spring to produce more plants.

Pests: Aphids.

Diseases: Root rot (especially in poorly drained soils).

Container suitability: Not recommended.

When and how to harvest: You will be harvesting the immature flower of your artichoke plant. It is important not to let the flower remain on the stem for too long, or it will become tough and stringy. If it's not harvested when young, it will fully develop into a large, purple, thistlelike flower. (This will no longer be good for eating, but it looks beautiful in your landscape.) Keep an eye on developing

ABOVE: Harvest artichoke buds when they are still tight and compact. Cut just below the bud with a knife or hand pruners.

buds and cut them when they are still compact and tight. Use pruners or a sharp knife to cut the stalk 1–2 in. below the base of the bud. To maximize your harvest, cut even the overly mature flowers from the plant (similar to dead-heading ornamental flowers).

Storage and preservation:

FRIDGE: Artichokes keep for about 1 week in a sealed plastic container or bag in the fridge.

What Artichokes Can Teach You: Vegetable Plants Look Amazing!

Why you do it: Artichokes' large, spiky leaves and tall vertical presence make them a striking addition to your garden. While they do die back in the winter unless you live in a very warm climate, they can be used to add edible visual interest to any part of your landscape.

How you do it: Plant artichokes! If you live in zone 8 or warmer, they'll grow back every year. If you live in zone 7 or colder, you'll need to replant them each year.

Also useful for: We think all vegetables are striking in their appearance!

ASPARAGUS

Tall Crop, Perennial Crop

Asparagus officinalis

A native of the Eurasian land mass, this vegetable seems to accentuate the difference between fresh produce and grocery-store produce more than any other. Even if you already like asparagus, once you have harvested it from the garden, you will fully understand all the hype about fresh, local produce.

Asparagus can be grown from seed or from dormant roots called crowns. We recommend buy-ing crowns to start your asparagus. They should become available in the early spring from nurseries and mail-order seed companies.

What you eat: The new shoots.

Recommended varieties: Jersey Knight, Sweet Purple.

Hardiness: Asparagus has good frost tolerance. Apply compost and mulch in the fall. Asparagus can be grown in all hardiness zones.

Seed information: Germination temp. 50°–80°F,

ABOVE: Cut asparagus at ground level with a knife.

optimal 77°; germination time 50 days at 50°, 9 days at 77°. Seed viability 3 years.

Mature plant size: Up to 6 ft. tall and 2–3 ft. wide.

How to plant: Dig an 8 in. deep trench in a prepared garden bed. Spread out the roots of the asparagus crown in the bottom of the trench, spaced 18 in. apart. Cover with 3–4 in. of garden soil. Continue to fill in the trench by adding an additional 2–3 in. of soil every 2 weeks, until the trench is full and slightly mounded (see photo).

When to plant: Up to 6 weeks before your last frost date, but any time in the spring is fine.

How much to plant: Plan to set aside a separate area for your asparagus. The plants will spread over time to fill in the bed, but consider planting 3 or 4 crowns to start.

When to fertilize: Apply a balanced fertilizer at planting time and again each spring.

How it grows: Individual spears of asparagus will emerge from the ground in the early

ABOVE: Plant asparagus crowns 6-12 inches deep. ABOVE RIGHT: Allow some asparagus spears to grow into fronds each year so the roots can replenish themselves and send up shoots again next year. You can cut down the fronds in the fall when they turn yellow.

spring and will look just like the asparagus you are used to eating. Unharvested spears will continue to grow until they reach 3–4 ft. in height and branch out with fernlike fronds (see photo). The spears will stay this height for the remainder of the summer and then, in the fall, turn brown and fall over. Once they start to turn yellow or brown, it is OK to cut them down to ground level.

It is possible to grow male or female plants. Generally the males are considered more productive, but both put up edible spears. You will know you have female plants if the mature spears develop small red fruits late in the summer. These little fruits are not eaten, but they are full of asparagus seeds and can be left on the plant until they die back in the fall.

General care: Keep plants well watered through the summer. Apply 2–3 in. of compost to the bed each fall, and cover with 3 in. of straw or leaves.

Pests: Asparagus beetles.

Diseases: Root rot (especially in poorly drained soils).

Container suitability: Not recommended.

When and how to harvest: The most difficult thing about growing asparagus is waiting until it is mature enough to harvest. In order for the plant to become established, it needs to keep its spears all summer, so they can photosynthesize and send energy down into the roots. The plant needs two seasons to get established, so do not harvest any spears until the third season; in other words, if you plant asparagus this spring, don't harvest any this year or next year. It may be tempting to harvest a few spears prematurely, but be patient and you will be rewarded with years and years of high-quality asparagus.

In the spring of the third year (and each year thereafter), your asparagus plants should start sending up spears in the early spring. Once a spear has reached 8–10 in. in height, cut it off at ground level with a sharp knife (see photo). Continue to harvest spears for 3–4 weeks, checking on the plant each day to make sure the spears don't overmature and get tough. After 3–4 weeks you will notice the spears starting to get thinner and thinner, and this is a good time to stop harvesting. Just as in the first 2 years, you need to leave some spears to photosynthesize and replenish the roots with energy for the following season.

Storage and preservation:

FRIDGE: Asparagus will keep well for about 1 week in a sealed plastic container or bag in the fridge.

FREEZER: Freeze in plastic bags. Optional: Blanch 1–2 min. before freezing.

CANNED: Pickled asparagus!

What Asparagus Can Teach You: Frequent Harvesting Makes for Top-Quality Vegetables

Why you do it: An asparagus spear can go from tender and delicious to woody and unappetizing in a matter of 48 hours. Frequent harvesting ensures that you get to eat your asparagus when it's at its best.

How you do it: As harvest time approaches, check your asparagus every day (or at least every other day), and harvest as necessary.

Also useful for: Cucumbers, salad greens, snap peas, summer squash.

RHUBARB
Medium Height Crop, Perennial Crop

Rheum rhabarbarum

Rhubarb originated in China and has long been used as a food and medicine in Asian cultures. It grows in almost any climate and overall is one of the easiest edible plants to raise. Typically, if you can get a rhubarb plant established, it will require little to no care going forward (however, additional care will improve your harvest). Rhubarb is not an invasive plant in the garden, but it is hardy enough that it can take several attempts to remove it once it is established.

Rhubarb can be grown from seed but is easiest grown from root cuttings (rhizomes) or small potted plants. There are many varieties, but likely only a few available in your area. Some will have red stems, some will have green stems, and others will have pink or speckled stems—and most should be delicious.

What you eat: The stem.

Recommended varieties: Victoria.

Hardiness: Rhubarb has good frost tolerance. Apply compost and mulch in the fall. Rhubarb grows well in zones 3–8; you can grow it as an annual if you live in zones 9 and up.

Seed information: Germination temp. 50°–80°F, optimal 70°; germination time 20 days at 50°, 10 days at 70°. Seed viability 3 years.

Mature plant size: Up to 4 ft. tall and 3 ft. wide.

How to plant: Plant a rhizome with a distinguishable topside or crown (see photo). Dig a hole deep enough to cover the crown of the rhubarb, 2–3 in. Add ½ cup of balanced fertilizer when planting. Water the area until the soil is saturated. Space the plants 3–4 ft. apart.

When to plant: Up to 6 weeks before your last frost date. Rhubarb can be planted any time during the spring or fall.

ABOVE: Harvest rhubarb by pulling stalks off the plant near the base.

How much to plant: Plan to set aside a separate area for your rhubarb. The plants will spread over time to fill in the bed, but consider 1 or 2 plants to start.

When to fertilize: Apply a balanced fertilizer at planting time and again each spring.

How it grows: Rhubarb is an early-season crop, so it should start producing new leaves in the spring and continue until early summer. In midsummer, when temperatures rise, most varieties will start to send up spindly leaves that tend to wilt in the heat. Some types will send up tall stalks that flower, set seed, and then die back. It is best to cut down the flower stalks as soon as they emerge. This enhances the vigor of your plant. If you like the idea or are curious to see what the flower stalks will look like, you can leave them up until they die back on their own—this will not unduly damage the plant. Often, rhubarb plants put out a second flush of good leaves in the late summer or early fall, once temperatures begin to cool back down, so it's possible to get two crops from the plant each year.

Rhubarb will grow larger stems and leaves in full sun, but it can be a very productive plant even in partial shade.

General care: Keep plants well watered through the first summer. Apply 2–3 in. of compost to the bed each fall, and cover with 3 in. of straw or leaves. Eventually the plant will start to spread out, as the rhizomes you planted slowly expand over time. A large root mass will form, and eventually it may be necessary to prune back the roots to prevent the plant from taking over a larger area than you want. Simply dig around the base of the plant and chop back sections of the root mass. Make sure to remove divided sections from the garden, or they will become new rhubarb plants. When pruning the roots, try to remove older-looking sections and any unusually soft or rotten parts. If the root mass is pruned back every 5 years or so and the newest, healthiest parts of the plant are kept, your rhubarb should live for a long time.

Pests: Slugs and snails.

Diseases: Downy mildew and other fungal diseases may show up in poorly drained soil.

Container suitability: Not recommended.

When and how to harvest: When the leaves start to fill out in the spring, simply grab a stem near its base and pull it from the plant. The stem should easily come off the plant. Cut off the leaf—*do not eat rhubarb leaves!* Compost the leaves and eat the red and/or green stems. After several weeks, the stems may lose much of their flavor and become less tender. This is a good time to stop harvesting.

Storage and preservation:

FRIDGE: Rhubarb will keep for a few weeks in the fridge in a sealed plastic container or bag.

FREEZER: Chop and freeze in bags. Optional: Blanch for 1–2 min.

What Rhubarb Can Teach You: Know Which Parts of Your Vegetables Are Edible And Which Are Not!

Why you do it: The stems of rhubarb are great for making pies and crisps, but the leaves contain a significant amount of oxalic acid, which is toxic to humans.

How you do it: Eat the stems, not the leaves!

Also useful for: Eggplant, peppers, potatoes, tomatoes—the foliage of these crops is mildly toxic if ingested.

18

HERBS

IN ADDITION TO VEGETABLE crops, many gardeners love to grow their own herbs. Some herbs are eaten fresh, and some are dried for long-term storage (and some can be used both ways!). Often, just one or two plants of each herb will supply your kitchen with an almost overwhelming bounty.

Some herbs are grown as annuals and others are perennials. We recommend mixing annual herbs into your vegetable beds but planting your perennial herbs either at the outer edges of your garden beds or in a separate herb-only bed, or in containers.

ANNUAL HERBS

BASIL
Short Crop, Half Season Crop

Ocimum basilicum

Basil is an ancient and storied culinary herb thought to have originated in India. The name is linked to a mythological beast known as the Basilisk. The Basilisk is a fearsome dragon that can be kept at bay only by regular consumption of the

OPPOSITE: Fennel flowers.

herb ... just in case you needed one more reason to grow this delectable herb.

Of all the common annual garden crops, basil may be the most sensitive to cold. Any temperature below 50°F can result in damage to the plant (usually seen as brown, golden, or black areas on your leaves or stems). One of the great things about basil is that, as long as you harvest it regularly, it will produce new leaves for months.

What you eat: The leaves.

Recommended varieties: Genovese, Lime Basil, Lemon Basil. Purple varieties such as Red Rubin may be less hardy but are beautiful.

Hardiness: No frost tolerance.

Seed information: Germination temp. 70°–90°F, optimal 80°; germination time 5–10 days. Seed viability 8 years.

Mature plant size: Up to 24 in. tall.

How to plant: Since basil needs an early start, plan to grow or buy it as a transplant. If growing at home, seed basil 6 weeks before the last frost date. Space plants 6 in. apart.

When to plant: Transplant seedlings once the temperature is consistently above 50°F. Wait a week or two after your last frost day before planting outside. If you buy the plants early, keep them in a sunny window until ready to plant outside.

How much to plant: 6–8 plants will give you enough basil to use in summer cooking, dry some out for winter use, and make a few batches of pesto. If you want to put up a lot of frozen pesto or dried basil, plant twice as much.

When to fertilize: Before planting.

General care: Watch for cold damage in young plants.

Pests: Slugs, snails, aphids, whitefly.

Diseases: Susceptible to stem rot if the roots are too moist. Properly drained soil is essential, but don't let it dry out too much or the basil may flower prematurely.

Container suitability: Good. Basil grows very well in a container. 1 plant per gal. of pot size.

When and how to harvest: Harvest by pinching off leaf sets. If plants seem prone to early flowering, cut them back to the lowest set of leaves and let them regrow from the base up. See "What Basil Can Teach You" for more information.

Storage and preservation:

COUNTER: Fresh basil doesn't store well, so use it quickly. If necessary, keep it in a paper bag on the counter. Basil will turn black and slimy if stored in the fridge.

FREEZER: Make pesto and freeze it in ice cube trays (store the cubes in freezer bags once they're frozen solid) for small servings throughout the winter.

DRIED: Air-dry or use a dehydrator to preserve basil for use during the winter.

TOP LEFT: Cutting back each basil shoot to a lower section of leaves will allow the plant to bush out. LEFT: Stressed or unharvested basil will start to flower, leading to smaller, more bitter leaves.

What Basil Can Teach You:
How to Pinch Stems to Shape Your Plants

Why you do it: Each time you pinch back the stems on your basil, it will branch out, effectively giving you two branches where you had only one. So, the more often you pinch the plant back (and harvest the leaves), the more branches you will get. Eventually you will have a stout, bushy plant that allows you to make pesto ad nauseam.

How you do it: Simply use your fingers or a pair of scissors and cut back the top part of any stem that becomes elongated. You can pinch the top leaf set from your basil once the plant is 6 in. tall. Pinch it back to the next set of leaves. After this, your basil plant will grow outward as a bush, as opposed to upward. Continue to pinch off leaf sets from the whole plant as the leaves size up. If any branch seems excessively long, pinch it back 2 or even 3 sets of leaves. Repeat as needed, usually once or twice a week. If the plant begins to flower, redouble your efforts to keep it pinched back to extend your harvest. Once it begins to flower, the leaves will be much smaller and more bitter tasting.

Also useful for: Pinching basil is a skill unto itself, but the technique is similar to that for pruning tomatoes.

CILANTRO
Short Crop, Short Season Crop

Coriandrum sativum

In our humble opinion, cilantro is the finest of all herbs (although many people seem to think it tastes like soap!). The spice called coriander is actually the dried seed of the cilantro plant.

Growing cilantro can be frustrating for first-time gardeners, but a few simple strategies will allow you to eat this herb through most of the year. The key is to harvest it often and direct-seed it just as often.

What you eat: The leaves.

Recommended varieties: Santo, Calypso.

Hardiness: Some frost tolerance. Established plants may even live through the winter in moderate climates.

Seed information: Germination temp. 50°–80°F, optimal 70°; germination time 15 days at 50°, 7 days at 80°. Seed viability 8 years.

Mature plant size: Up to 18 in. tall.

How to plant: Direct-seed. Cilantro can be transplanted, but since it grows so readily in mild weather, there is usually little reason to grow as a transplant. Aim for 1 plant per in. Space rows 6 in. apart.

ABOVE: Cut cilantro an inch above the ground when the stems are 6-8 inches tall.

When to plant: Start sowing cilantro once the soil can be worked. It will germinate more slowly in cold soil but should grow even in mild spring and fall conditions.

How much to plant: Sow a 6–12 in. row of cilantro frequently.

When to fertilize: Before planting.

General care: The most important tasks are frequent sowings and timely harvesting.

Pests: Slugs, snails, aphids.

Diseases: Cilantro is generally a disease-free crop.

Container suitability: Good. Cilantro grows very well in a container. Sow into any size pot.

When and how to harvest: Once the plants are 6–8 in. tall, cut them back to 1 in. above the soil level. Harvest as needed. It is important to cut cilantro when it is at its best, so watch the plants to make sure you don't miss the narrow window before they start to flower. It is better to cut extra cilantro, even if you won't use it right away, than to let it flower in the garden. If cut before flowering, the plants should put on a second flush of leaves. Pull plants after the second cutting to make room for other crops.

Storage and preservation: Cilantro is best when used fresh.

FRIDGE: It will keep in the refrigerator for several days.

FREEZER: Cilantro pesto.

DRIED: If allowed to flower and set seed, the seeds can be harvested for cooking (the seed is coriander).

CANNED: Cilantro can be added to salsas.

What Cilantro Can Teach You: How to Manage Frequent Plantings

Why you do it: Cilantro bolts more quickly than perhaps any other crop. Once your plants reach maturity (ready to harvest), they will last only a week or two (even under ideal conditions) before they start to flower. That's why you should sow short rows of cilantro as often as possible (every week or two).

How you do it: For a consistent supply of cilantro during the season, plan to sow only a 6–12 in. row at each planting. It can be difficult to stop at such a short row, but that's the best idea: Extra-long rows of cilantro inevitably end up as flower stalks. Get in the habit of sowing a few inches of cilantro in the garden once a week or every other week.

Also useful for: Radishes, salad greens.

DILL
Medium Height Crop, Half Season Crop

Anethum graveolens

Dill: It's not just for pickles anymore … although it is still primarily for pickles. A Mediterranean herb, dill is beautiful and very attractive to the type of beneficial insects that you want in your garden. Like seeing a neon sign for your favorite beer in a bar window, when beneficial insects see dill, they say, "That must be a good place to hang out!" "Dill weed" is the culinary name for dill leaf fronds, and "dill seed" refers to the dried seed heads that are also used in cooking and canning.

What you eat: The leaves (dill weed) and the seed heads (dill seed).

Recommended varieties: Often just labeled "dill" or "dill weed."

Hardiness: Some frost tolerance.

Seed information: Germination temp. 50°–80°F, optimal 70°; germination time 14–20 days. Seed viability 3 years.

Mature plant size: Up to 36 in. tall.

How to plant: Direct-seed after danger of frost is past. Dill is easy to raise but does not grow as well from a transplant. For dill weed, space plants 2–3 in. apart. For seed, space plants 12 in. apart.

When to plant: Sow once the soil can be worked. It will germinate more slowly in cold soil but can be sown in early spring or even in the fall for spring emergence.

How much to plant: For dill weed, start with a 1 ft. row. For seed, start with a 2–3 ft. row and thin plants to 12 in. apart.

When to fertilize: Before planting.

General care: Dill usually requires little to no maintenance after planting.

Pests: Slugs, aphids.

Diseases: Generally disease free.

Container suitability: Good. Dill grows very well in a container. 1 plant per gal. of pot size.

When and how to harvest: Harvest young dill fronds as needed. To harvest the seed, cut the seed heads when they are still soft, and allow them to dry out in a paper bag in a dry location.

Storage and preservation:

DRIED: Air-dry for winter storage, or use in canning recipes (pickles).

FRIDGE: Fresh dill can be kept in a plastic bag in the fridge for about 1 week.

Recommended insult: Call your friends "dill weed" whenever appropriate.

What Dill Can Teach You: How to Attract Beneficial Insects

Why you do it: As we have mentioned throughout this book, at some point a few damaging insects will likely show up in your garden and do their best to wreak havoc. One way to help mitigate this problem is to invite other insects to the garden to prey on the pest insects.

How you do it: Just plant dill in your garden! Many predatory garden insects are attracted to dill and other flowering plants. Adult insects will come to your garden for the dill flower pollen and stay to lay their eggs. When the eggs hatch, the insect larvae will feed on many common garden pests.

Also useful for: Edible flowers.

ABOVE: Dill is a tall, thin plant that grows 3–4 ft. high.

PARSLEY
Short Crop, Long Season Crop

Petroselinum crispum

There was a time when parsley was thought of as merely a garnish for a dinner plate, to be disposed of before you dug into the *real* food. These days, fresh parsley is a popular ingredient in a wide range of dishes. There are several varieties, including curly leaf, flat leaf (Italian), and even some grown for their roots. Most home gardeners prefer the taste of flat-leaf parsley for cooking.

What you eat: The leaves.

Recommended varieties: Italian flat leaf, curly leaf.

ABOVE: Harvest parsley leaves from this vigorous plant throughout the season.

Hardiness: Frost tolerant. In moderate climates, parsley will often overwinter and put on new growth (and seed stalks) the next spring.

Seed information: Germination temp. 50°–80°F, optimal 60°; germination time 21–28 days. Seed viability 3 years.

Mature plant size: Up to 18 in. tall.

How to plant: Direct-seed or plant as a transplant. Space plants 8 in. apart. If direct-seeding, thin to 8 in. once seedlings emerge.

When to plant: If growing as a transplant, start up to 6 weeks before the last frost date. If direct-seeding, sow after the last frost date.

How much to plant: Parsley plants are prolific, and 2 or 3 plants should be adequate for most gardeners.

When to fertilize: Fertilize the area before planting with a balanced fertilizer.

General care: If your parsley resprouts on its own the next spring, cut back the flower stalks the second season to encourage further leaf growth. It's a good idea to seed new plants each year, so that you can transition to younger, leafier plants in the summer rather than continue fighting the flowering instinct of last year's plants. Remove the year-old plants once the new ones have grown to harvestable size.

Pests: Aphids, whitefly.

Diseases: Generally disease free.

Container suitability: Good. Parsley grows very well in a container. 1 plant per gal. of pot size. Parsley has a long taproot, so a pot 12 in. or deeper is ideal.

When and how to harvest: Cut leaves as needed.

Storage and preservation:

DRIED: Air-dry for winter storage.

FRIDGE: Fresh parsley can be kept in a plastic bag in the fridge for about 1 week.

What Parsley Can Teach You: How to Soak Seeds to Speed Up Germination

Why you do it: Some plants germinate quickly, others' germination rate varies depending on the weather, and some seem to germinate slowly no matter what. Parsley is notorious for slow germination. Soaking parsley seeds in water overnight allows them to absorb water, which will trigger the germination process. Just don't forget to plant them the next day!

How you do it: Simply place the parsley seeds in a bowl of cold water and let them sit overnight. The next day, drain the water and sow your parsley.

Also useful for: Soaking will speed the germination of almost any vegetable seed.

PERENNIAL HERBS

We recommend that you purchase perennial herbs as transplants in 4 in. pots or larger. You can propagate most perennial herbs from seed and/or soft- or hardwood cuttings, but these skills are slightly more advanced, something you may want to put off for a little while (check the Resources section for further reading).

The main thing to know about preparing an area for an herb garden as opposed to a vegetable garden is that the soil should not be as nutrient dense. Adding a lot of compost to a vegetable bed is always advisable, but too much compost or fertilizer in an herb garden can lead to rapid, unhealthy growth. Herbs prefer somewhat sandy soil, and proper drainage is essential.

If you fertilize appropriately and keep your herbs watered for the first few seasons, they should become firmly established and need very little care besides yearly pruning and cold protection. Plan to mulch around the base of your herbs with bark or wood chips to help retain moisture in the soil and reduce problems with weeds.

In cold climates, plan to grow your perennial herbs in containers and bring them indoors during the winter. Most herbs have limited frost tolerance and may not survive extended cold weather.

It's important to prune certain perennial herbs (oregano, mint, thyme) each season just as they bloom. If herbs are not pruned each year, the long branches will break and the center of the plant will die. A well-pruned herb should keep its shape and grow slightly larger each year from the base. To do this, shear off some of the new growth and dead blossoms as they begin to flower or just after they have finished flowering.

BAY
Tall Crop, Perennial Crop

Laurus nobilis

Unlike the other herbs listed here, bay grows like a tree. An evergreen Mediterranean plant, it can be kept small and raised in a container, or it can grow as large as 30 ft. out in the landscape. Traditionally, bay leaves have been associated with honor, good health, and just about everything else you might aspire to. If you win an Olympic marathon you'll be given a wreath of bay leaves, but you can always make one for yourself if you think you deserve it. One thing is for sure: You will never need to buy bay leaves again.

What you eat: The leaves.

Recommended varieties: Often labeled "sweet bay."

Hardiness: Somewhat frost tolerant, bay will sustain frost damage or die in very cold winters.

Survives the winter in zones 8 and up. In colder climates, train as a lower, bush shape (rather than a single trunk) to increase hardiness.

Mature plant size: Up to 40 ft. tall in warm climates. Usually maintained as a 5–6 ft. tall bush.

How to plant: Transplant.

When to plant: Transplanting should be done in early spring, or in the fall while temperatures are cool and rain is periodic.

ABOVE: Bay trees can grow 20–30 ft. tall, or can be regularly pruned and kept small, even in a container.

How much to plant: 1 plant.

When to fertilize: Fertilize the area before planting with a balanced fertilizer.

How it grows: Bay takes the form of a bush, or a large tree if grown in the ground in warm climates. You can prune it to maintain whatever size or shape you desire.

General care: Watch for cold damage in young plants. Plan to bring potted bays indoors during winter if possible. If planted in the landscape, consider mulching the base of the plant in the fall. Prune off any dead or winter-damaged wood in the spring. Bay responds very well to pruning; prune to maintain the shape and size that you prefer.

Pests: Bay sucker, scale, aphids.

Diseases: Mostly disease free.

Container suitability: Good. Bay grows well in a container. Plant in a 5 gal. pot or larger, and plan to prune each year. The plant will need root pruning every 1–2 years.

When and how to harvest: Harvest leaves as needed. Once established, bays grow rather quickly, so spring pruning will often provide a year's supply of bay leaves. The leaves develop a stronger aroma and taste when dried.

Storage and preservation:

DRIED: Air-dry or use a dehydrator to preserve bay leaves for year-round use.

What Bay Can Teach You:
Edible Perennials Can Make Great Hedges

Why you do it: If you need visual screening from a road, sidewalk, or neighbor's yard, consider using a row of bay laurels (if you live in a warm climate).

How you do it: Plant bay in a row where you want your hedge. Amend the soil as necessary, and space plants 2 ft. apart.

CHIVES
Short Crop, Perennial Crop

Allium schoenoprasum

The value of chives in the home garden should not be overlooked. Chives are a reliable source whenever onion flavor is needed. They start growing early in the spring, so you can get your onion fix as you wait for the scallions and larger onions to size up. Chive flowers are beautiful, delicious, and a great way to attract pollinating insects to the garden.

What you eat: The leaves and flowers.

Recommended varieties: May simply be labeled "chives."

Hardiness: Frost tolerant. Survives winter in zones 3 and up.

Seed information: Germination temp. 50°–90°F, optimal 60°; germination time 5–10 days. Seed viability 1–2 years.

Mature plant size: About 12–18 in. tall.

How to plant: This is one perennial herb that you may be able to direct-seed as well as grow from transplants. If direct-seeding, sow 15–20 seeds in a circle. These 15–20 seeds will grow as a clump and basically become one chive "plant."

When to plant: If direct-seeding, sow once the soil can be worked in the early spring. Chives take a while to germinate and grow to maturity, so early planting will be rewarded. Transplant them outdoors as soon as they become available in the spring. Space clumps 8 in. or more apart.

How much to plant: 1–3 plants/clumps.

When to fertilize: Fertilize the area before planting with a balanced fertilizer.

How it grows: Generally, you'll buy chives in a 4 in. pot. As they grow, they look like a clump of small onion plants close together. Eventually, you'll see purple flowers appear (these are edible), and the once-tender leaves will become tough. At this point you can cut the chives back to the ground if you'd like a second harvest, or leave them in flower for beauty and to attract pollinators. In winter in most climates, the chives will die back to the ground, but they will reemerge the following spring.

General care: Chives are easy to care for. Plant in a well-prepared garden bed. Cut as needed, and chop down excess growth in the fall to prepare for new spring growth.

Pests: Aphids, but generally pest free.

Diseases: Generally disease free.

Container suitability: Chives grow very well in any size of container.

When and how to harvest: Cut leaves as needed before flowering occurs. They can be cut halfway down or all the way to the ground. To harvest flowers for eating, just pluck them off the plant.

Storage and preservation:

FRIDGE: Chives store in the fridge for only a few days before turning slimy. Plan to cut as needed during the spring, summer, and fall.

ABOVE: Chives take care of themselves and can be cut repeatedly through the season.

What Chives Can Teach You: How to Cut Back Herbs to Encourage New Growth

Why you do it: When chives start to flower, the flower stalks become tough and make it difficult to harvest the leaves. If you want to harvest more leaves, you can cut the plant back to the ground to encourage the growth of new, tender leaves. Note, though, that you don't have to do this: Flowering chives are beautiful in the garden, and the flowers are edible.

How you do it: When you're ready for new leaves, simply cut the plant back to 1 or 2 in. above the soil. New leaves will soon follow.

Also useful for: Oregano, thyme.

FENNEL (PERENNIAL)
Tall Crop, Perennial Crop

Foeniculum vulgare

Perennial fennel is an invasive weed in many areas. It can take over a garden, an overgrown backyard, or even a parking lot, so plant with care. However, if planted properly (see "What Perennial Fennel Can Teach You"), fennel is a beautiful, tall herb that will make your garden more dynamic and attract beneficial insects as well.

NOTE: Don't confuse this plant, *Foeniculum vulgare*, a source of fennel seeds and fronds, with Florence fennel or *finnochio*, which is eaten as a vegetable.

What you eat: The leaves and seeds.

Recommended varieties: Sweet Fennel, Bronze Fennel.

Hardiness: Frost tolerant. Survives the winter in zones 9 and up.

Mature plant size: Up to 7 ft. tall.

How to plant: Transplant from a container or dig up and replant an existing fennel. Space plants 3 ft. apart. See "What Perennial Fennel Can Teach You" to learn how to plant it in a buried container.

When to plant: Transplanting should be done in early spring or in the fall, while temperatures are cool and rain is periodic.

How much to plant: 1 or 2 plants. Plants can become quite large (up to 6–8 ft. tall) and will spread out if not carefully contained.

When to fertilize: Before planting.

How it grows: Fennel starts off as a short plant

LEFT: Harvest fennel fronds and seed heads throughout summer and fall.

but quickly grows into a tall, narrow shrub with thick stalks. Depending on your climate, it may die back to the ground or die back completely in winter.

General care: Once established, fennel needs little care. If you've decided not to plant in a buried container, you'll want to remove new fennel plants as they emerge around your original plant to keep it from spreading.

Pests: Slugs, aphids.

Diseases: Powdery mildew.

Container suitability: Good. Perennial fennel grows very well in a container. 1 plant per gal. of pot size.

When and how to harvest: Cut fronds and flower heads from the plant as needed.

Storage and preservation: Fennel fronds are generally best used fresh.

DRIED: Try cutting seed heads and air-drying (place a container under the heads to catch falling seeds) for winter use.

What Perennial Fennel Can Teach You: Planting Herbs in Buried Containers to Prevent Them from Taking Over Your Garden

Why you do it: Fennel roots spread aggressively and can quickly fill your garden with unwanted volunteer plants. By using a buried container as a barrier, you can slow the spread and make fennel a more easily managed plant.

How you do it: Cut the bottom out of a 12 in. deep (or larger) container. Bury it in the garden where you want to site your perennial fennel. Make sure to leave the top 2 in. of the pot above the surface of the soil. Fill the container with soil from the garden, and plant the fennel in it.

Also useful for: Mint, oregano, thyme.

LAVENDER
Medium Height Crop, Perennial Crop

Lavandula angustifolia

Lavender is a beautiful and aromatic herb. It has been valued since antiquity for its strong fragrance and medicinal qualities, as well as for its usefulness in cooking. There are many varieties of lavender, with different bloom times and colors. The blossoms attract pollinators (especially bumblebees) to the garden and can be dried for use in cooking, beverages, ice cream, or to make potpourris.

What you eat: The flowers.

Recommended varieties: Hidcote, Munstead.

Hardiness: Somewhat frost tolerant. Consider mulching if very cold temperatures are expected. Survives winter in zones 5 and up.

Mature plant size: Up to 3–4 ft. tall.

How to plant: Transplant. Space plants 2–3 ft. apart.

When to plant: Transplanting should be done in early spring or in the fall, while temperatures are cool and rain is periodic.

How much to plant: 3 or 4 lavender plants add a great accent to the landscape. Plants generally grow to 2–3 ft. tall and wide but can be pruned for a much smaller size (1–2 ft. tall and wide).

When to fertilize: Before planting.

How it grows: Lavender grows from a single stem into a large, bushy plant with woody stems.

General care: Shear back blooms and the ends of all branches after the blossoms die back. Prune *every year* to keep the plant compact and healthy.

Pests: Aphids.

Diseases: Generally disease free, but potentially susceptible to powdery mildew.

Container suitability: Lavender grows very well in a container. 1 plant per gal. of pot size.

When and how to harvest: Cut flowers while in bloom. You can also cut branches, since the leaves are aromatic as well.

Storage and preservation:

DRIED: Tie lavender in bundles and air-dry.

ABOVE: Flowering lavender always attracts pollinating insects.

What Lavender Can Teach You: How to Prune Your Bushy Perennials to Maintain an Attractive Shape

Why you do it: If left on its own, lavender will grow into an odd-shaped blob that will probably overwhelm nearby crops. However, if you prune it each year, you can maintain the size and shape you desire.

How you do it: Using pruning shears, shave off the branches to create a shape and size you like. If the lavender is at the corner of a small raised bed, you may want to maintain it as a small bush with a 1 ft. diameter. If you're using it as a landscaping plant, you can prune it into a large bush or box shape. Or, if you're feeling inspired, you might try to sculpt it into a likeness of George Washington.

Also useful for: Rosemary, sage.

MINT: SPEARMINT, PEPPERMINT, PINEAPPLE MINT, CHOCOLATE MINT, LEMON BALM, ETC.
Short Crop, Perennial Crop

Mentha spicata

Mint is great for making teas, cocktails, chewing gum, toothpaste, and desserts. All members of the mint family are easily identified by their square stems. Take a look at a mint plant and feel one of the stems between your fingers—unlike those of most plants in your garden, it will have four distinct sides!

Mint is one garden plant that knows how to take care of itself. In fact, it usually treats itself a little too well, spreading out and taking over any space it can find. So decide on a way to contain the plant before you put it in the garden.

What you eat: The leaves.

Recommended varieties: Spearmint, Peppermint, Chocolate Mint, Lemon Balm.

Hardiness: Frost tolerant. Survives winter in zones 5 and up.

Mature plant size: Up to 12 in. tall.

How to plant: Even if you plant mint in your garden, it is important to keep it in a buried container. See "What Perennial Fennel Can Teach You" for instructions on how to do this. Otherwise, raise mint in a container on the patio or near the garden. Space plants 18 in. or more apart.

When to plant: Transplanting should be done in early spring or in the fall, while temperatures are cool and rain is periodic.

How much to plant: 1 plant of each variety you would like to have on hand.

When to fertilize: Fertilize the area before planting with a balanced fertilizer.

How it grows: Mint starts off as a single stem, then spreads into a low-growing, sprawling ground cover.

General care: Cut branches in spring, summer, and fall. If you wish to keep harvesting leaves, prune off flowers as they appear. Since bees are attracted to the flowers, consider letting the plants flower and then shearing the plant back when the flowering is finished. Plan to root prune contained plants every 1 or 2 years.

Pests: Slugs, snails, aphids.

Diseases: Rust is possible, but mint is generally disease free.

ABOVE: Mint is a very hardy plant that can spread through the garden if not properly contained.

Container suitability: Good. Mint grows very well in a container. 1 plant per gal. of pot size.

When and how to harvest: Cut mint branches and pinch leaves as needed during the summer.

Storage and preservation:

FRIDGE: Mint will keep for about 1 week in a plastic container or bag in the fridge.

DRIED: Tie stems in bundles and air-dry for winter use. When the leaves are fully dry, remove them from the stem and store them in a glass jar or plastic bag.

What Mint Can Teach You:
How to Divide Herbs to Get More Plants

Why you do it: Mint roots are survivors! Even a single small piece of root can produce a whole new plant (as you may have noticed if mint has ever gotten out of control in your yard or garden). You can use this to your advantage if you want to expand the number of mint plants in your garden or give plants to your friends.

How you do it: Dividing herbs is best done in the early spring, before the plants begin to grow new leaves. Dig up the roots of the plant, and cut the root mass into separate chunks (called divisions) with your pruning shears or a spade shovel. The size of the divisions isn't crucial, as most herbs will grow back from a small piece. You might start by cutting a single mint root structure into quarters or eighths. Replant each division where you want a new plant, and water it well. If you want to give divisions to friends, keep the roots moist with a damp towel until they can be planted.

Also useful for: Chives, oregano, rhubarb, thyme.

OREGANO
Short Crop, Sprawling Crop, Perennial Crop

Origanum vulgare

This Mediterranean herb is perhaps most closely linked to the addictive properties of pizza. Oregano can be used fresh but is most flavorful after drying. Although they are different plants, oregano and marjoram are very similar in taste and appearance and are often used interchangeably.

The name oregano translates as "joy of the mountain," which seems apt. It has been said that oregano is helpful if you are suffering from a scorpion sting, but we're not sure if that works—maybe you should just offer the victim a slice of pizza on the way to the doctor.

What you eat: The leaves.

Recommended varieties: Greek, Italian.

Hardiness: Frost tolerant. Survives winter in zones 4 and up.

Mature plant size: 12–18 in. tall.

How to plant: Transplant. Space plants 12 in. or more apart.

When to plant: Transplanting should be done in early spring or in the fall, while temperatures are cool and rain is still periodic.

How much to plant: 1 or 2 plants. These will slowly spread and can become quite large over time. Cut back branches and roots each year to limit the plant's size, if desired.

When to fertilize: Fertilize the area before planting with a balanced fertilizer.

How it grows: Oregano starts off as a small clump of stems, then spreads to become a low-growing ground cover. It will start to grow more vertically as it flowers. The top growth may die back in the winter, depending on your climate.

General care: You can cut the plant back to the ground when it begins to flower if you want a second harvest. If you don't do this, prune *every year* to keep the plant compact.

Pests: Aphids and whitefly, but generally pest free.

Diseases: Generally disease free.

Container suitability: Good. Oregano grows very well in a container. 1 plant per gal. of pot size.

When and how to harvest: Cut stems off at the base in spring, summer, and fall. If you wish to keep harvesting leaves, prune off flowers when they appear. Since bees are attracted to the flowers, consider letting the plants flower and then shearing the plant back when flowering is finished.

Storage and preservation:

COUNTER: Store oregano on the counter by placing the stems in a jar of water.

FRIDGE: Oregano will keep for a few days in the fridge in a plastic bag.

DRIED: Tie in bundles and air-dry for winter use. When the leaves are fully dry, remove them from the stem and store them in a glass jar or plastic bag. Oregano gains potency in taste and aroma after drying.

What Oregano Can Teach You: Dried Herbs Are Much More Potent Than Fresh Ones

Why you do it: For some herbs, drying is not only a good way to store them, but it also increases the potency of their taste and aroma. When cooking with fresh oregano, you need to use a huge amount, but a pinch of the dried stuff is often all you need for your dish to reach culinary perfection.

How you do it: Dry your herbs!

Also useful for: Rosemary, sage, thyme.

ABOVE: Cut down stems and dry oregano when the leaves are full and vibrant.

ROSEMARY
Medium Height Crop, Perennial Crop

Rosmarinus officinalis

Named after the Latin for "dew of the sea," rosemary is a beautiful, woody, evergreen shrub. It is very versatile, grows prolifically in warm climates, and stores well. Rosemary has long been thought to improve memory; try surrounding yourself with sprigs of this herb next time you are studying for a standardized test, or if you lose your house keys.

What you eat: The leaves.

Recommended varieties: Tuscan Blue, Arp, and Hill's Hardy are preferable in colder regions.

Hardiness: Somewhat frost tolerant. Consider mulching around the plant if unusually cold weather is expected, since rosemary will die in an extended freeze. Survives winter in zones 8 and up.

Mature plant size: 3–4 ft. tall in warm climates.

How to plant: Transplant, 18–24 in. apart. In mild climates rosemary will grow into a large bush, in cooler ones it takes a smaller form.

When to plant: Transplanting should be done in early spring or in the fall, while temperatures are cool and rain is periodic.

How much to plant: 1 or 2 plants. Rosemary can grow very large (5–6 ft. wide and tall) but can be pruned to retain a much smaller shape (1–2 ft. wide and tall).

When to fertilize: Before planting.

How it grows: Rosemary starts off as a single stem with branches, then grows into a bush. It will set small purple flowers midway through the season.

General care: Cut branches in spring, summer, and fall. Watch for cold damage in young plants and after a severe winter. If you live in an area with very cold weather, plan to keep rosemary in a container and bring it indoors for the winter. Plan on one substantial pruning each year after the plant flowers. Regular pruning will keep the plant from growing too large.

ABOVE: Harvest rosemary by snipping off branches. Hang them to dry or use them fresh.

If not regularly pruned, it may grow into an odd shape and be more susceptible to broken branches, which can encourage rot and create disease issues.

Pests: Aphids.

Diseases: Generally disease free.

Container suitability: Good. Grows very well in a container. 1 plant per 5 gal. pot size.

When and how to harvest: Harvest by cutting branches as desired. If you harvest only new growth (with tender white stems), you can use the stems in cooking. But if you cut back into the woody part of a branch (during an annual pruning, for example), you'll want to discard the woody section. You can easily remove the leaves from the branch once they've dried.

Storage and preservation:

DRIED: Tie stems in bundles and air-dry for winter use. When the leaves are fully dry, remove them from the stem and store them in a glass jar or plastic bag.

What Rosemary Can Teach You:
How to Grow Tender Herbs in Containers
So You Can Protect Them in the Winter

Why you do it: If you live in zone 7 or colder, your rosemary probably won't survive outdoors during the winter. If you grow it in a container, you can bring it indoors to protect it.

How you do it: When temperatures dip into the mid-20s, bring the container indoors. If you're only protecting it for short periods, you can keep it in a garage, but if you'll be keeping it indoors for more than a week or so, keep it in the sunniest room of the house. Water it sparingly to prevent fungal diseases.

Also useful for: Depending on what zone you live in, this skill can be used for any perennial herb.

SAGE
Medium Height Crop, Perennial Crop

Salvia officinalis

Sage has been used for ages in cooking and as a medicinal herb. There are a wide variety of cultivars with different-sized leaves and different-colored flowers, but typically sage is known as an evergreen landscape plant with fuzzy leaves and beautiful blue or purple flowers. Traditionally, sage is often burned to ward off evil and banish bad spirits.

What you eat: The leaves.

Recommended varieties: Purple Garden Sage, Greek Sage.

Hardiness: Some varieties are frost/freeze tolerant and some are not. Consider mulching around the plant if unusually cold weather is expected. Survives winter in zones 4–8 (depending on the variety).

Mature plant size: 3–4 ft. tall.

How to plant: Transplant, 2–3 ft. apart.

When to plant: Transplanting should be done in early spring or in the fall, while temperatures are cool and rain is periodic.

How much to plant: 1 or 2 plants. Each plant can grow to 2–3 ft. tall and wide.

When to fertilize: Fertilize the area before planting with a balanced fertilizer.

How it grows: Sage grows into a midsize bush. It will set flowers (usually purple) partway through the growing season.

General care: Cut branches in spring, summer, and fall. If you wish to keep harvesting leaves, prune off flowers when they appear. Since bees are attracted to the flowers, consider letting the plants flower and then shearing the plant back when flowering is finished. Watch for cold damage in young plants.

Pests: Aphids.

Diseases: Mildew, but generally disease free.

Container suitability: Good. Sage grows very well in a container. 1 plant per 5 gal. pot size.

When and how to harvest: Harvest as needed. Plan on one substantial pruning each spring to keep the plant from growing too large. If it gets too large it can become susceptible to broken branches, which may rot and create disease issues.

Storage and preservation:

DRIED: Tie stems in bundles and air-dry for winter use. When the leaves are fully dry, remove them from the stem and store them in a glass jar or plastic bag.

What Sage Can Teach You: Let Your Perennial Herbs Flower to Attract Pollinators

Why you do it: Increasing the number of pollinating insects in your garden is a great thing for all of your fruiting crops. Sage flowers are particularly good at attracting bees.

How you do it: Let some or all of your sage plant (or plants) flower before harvesting or pruning them.

Also useful for: Chives, lavender.

ABOVE: Snip off individual leaves or short sprigs of sage to dry or use fresh.

THYME
Short Crop, Perennial Crop

Thymus vulgaris

Thyme is one of the most versatile of garden herbs. This Mediterranean herb can be used fresh or dried in almost any savory dish. If you are getting ready for a presentation at school or at work, add thyme leaves to your bath: They are thought to impart courage.

What you eat: The leaves.

Recommended varieties: French Thyme, Lemon Thyme, Creeping Thyme.

Hardiness: Frost tolerant. Survives winter in zones 4 and up.

Mature plant size: 12–18 in. tall.

How to plant: Transplant, 18–24 in. apart.

When to plant: Transplanting should be done in early spring or in the fall, while temperatures are cool and rain is periodic.

How much to plant: 1 or 2 plants. Plants will slowly spread out over time and can extend to cover several feet of ground space. In fact, creeping thyme is often used in pathways to soften the edges around stone pavers (see photo). You can cut plants back each year to keep them from spreading.

When to fertilize: Fertilize the area before planting with a balanced fertilizer.

How it grows: Like oregano, thyme starts off as a small clump of stems, then spreads to become a low-growing ground cover. It will set small flowers midway through the season but does not send up vertical flower stalks. The top growth may die back in the winter, depending on your climate.

General care: Thyme should be cut back completely to the ground at least once a year to encourage new, tender growth and maintain a manageable size and shape. Since bees are attracted to the flowers, consider letting the plants flower and then shearing the plant back when flowering is finished. Watch for cold damage in young plants.

Pests: Generally pest free.

Diseases: Generally disease free.

Container suitability: Good. Thyme grows very well in a container. 1 plant per gal. of pot size.

When and how to harvest: Cut branches off just above soil level in spring, summer, and fall.

Storage and preservation:

COUNTER: Store thyme on the counter by placing the stems in a jar of water.

FRIDGE: Thyme will keep for a few days in the fridge in a plastic bag.

DRIED: Tie stems in bundles and air-dry for winter use. When the leaves are fully dry, remove them from the stem and store them in a glass jar or plastic bag.

What Thyme Can Teach You:
How to Use Herbs for Landscaping Accents

Why you do it: Thyme's low-growing form makes it a great choice for adding edible flair to rockeries, rock walls, the edges of paths, cracks in stone walkways, and open spaces in ornamental beds. Creeping thyme is a great variety for this, but any variety will work.

How you do it: Plant thyme as desired in your landscape.

Also useful for: Oregano.

ABOVE: Cut back thyme stems when the leaves are full and use them fresh or dried in a variety of dishes.

19

FLOWERS IN THE VEGETABLE GARDEN

FLOWERS ARE A GREAT ADDITION to a vegetable garden for many reasons. They attract pollinating insects, they attract other types of beneficial insects, they smell good, they look beautiful, and that's not all—many are also edible! There's no reason you can't incorporate flowers into your vegetable garden to serve any or all of these purposes.

To begin with, many of the vegetables and herbs profiled in this book produce flowers that can be eaten fresh or incorporated into cooked dishes. You may work hard to prevent those crops from flowering during the season, but once they start to produce flowers, you can eat those too! The following vegetables and herbs produce commonly eaten flowers:

- Arugula
- Broccoli
- Chives
- Cilantro
- Dill
- Fennel
- Kale
- Lettuce
- Mint
- Parsley
- Radish
- Rosemary
- Summer squash/zucchini
- Thyme

All of the vegetable flowers in this list will attract beneficial insects (or "beneficials" for short). These insects include ladybugs, green lacewings, praying mantises, beetles, and even some species of spiders and wasps. They're called beneficials because they prey on common garden insect pests. Typically, the adult form of the beneficial will feed on the nectar of the flower, while the immature form (larva or pupa) feeds on the pests.

There are many other flowers that are particularly good at attracting beneficials (as noted, some are edible and some aren't). Some favorites include the following:

OPPOSITE: Bees are strongly attracted to purple and blue flowers such as this Echinacea.

ANNUALS

Alyssum: Short height, long season. Not edible.

Bachelor's button: Medium height, short season. Petals are edible.

Borage: Medium height, short season. Flowers are edible.

Calendula: Medium height, short season. Flowers are edible.

Cosmos: Medium to tall, long season. Not edible.

Marigold: Short crop, half season. Not edible.

Sunflower: Tall, half season. Seeds are edible.

PERENNIALS

Bee balm: Tall. Leaves and flowers are edible.

Echinacea: Medium height. Leaves and roots are edible.

Hyssop: Medium height. Leaves and flowers are edible.

NOTE: Marigolds are often planted because they are thought to deter insect pests from entering the garden!

EDIBLE FLOWERS

Some plants are grown in the home garden primarily for their edible flowers (they all also attract beneficial insects). Plant them in the garden like any vegetable crop. Mix them in among your vegetable plantings or in the far corners of the garden, or make a flower border along the edges of your beds (see the "Crop Size, Spacing, and Scheduling" chart for flower spacing). Here are their profiles.

ABOVE TOP: An array of flower shapes and colors will help attract a diversity of insect species.
ABOVE: All types of flying insects can help pollinate crops.

BORAGE
Medium Height Crop, Short Season Crop

Borago officinalis

Sometimes known as starflower, borage is an easy-to-grow, tall edible flower with beautiful small pink, purple, or blue flowers. Eaten fresh, the flowers have a taste that is amazingly similar to that of cucumbers. The plant will bloom for months on end and is thought to deter some garden pest insects. And one other thing: Traditionally, borage flowers are thought to induce lactation in women! (Note that this plant self-seeds so proficiently that it may develop into a garden weed over time.)

What you eat: The flowers.

Recommended varieties: Often simply labeled "borage."

Hardiness: Some frost tolerance.

Seed information: Germination temp. 60°–80°F, optimal 70°; germination time 12 days at 70°. Seed viability 3 years.

Mature plant size: 24 in. tall and wide.

How to plant: Direct-seed at the edges of your garden. Space plants 18 in. apart.

When to plant: After danger of frost has passed.

How much to plant: Plant clusters of 3 or 4 plants in one spot or at a few different edges of your garden space.

When to fertilize: At planting.

General care: Borage is a vigorous, indeterminate plant. Trim off excess branches as the plants grow too wide and too tall. Weed out volunteer plants as needed.

Pests: Aphid, whitefly.

Diseases: Usually disease free.

Container suitability: Good. 1 gal. pot or larger.

When and how to harvest: Pick flowers as needed.

Storage and preservation:

FRIDGE: Borage will keep for a few days in a plastic bag in the fridge.

DRIED: The flowers can be dried for winter use but will lose potency.

FREEZER: Try freezing the flowers inside ice cubes. Great for adding flair to chilled summer drinks!

ABOVE: Borage flowers ready for harvest.

CALENDULA
Medium Height Crop, Short Season Crop

Calendula officinalis

Although it is often referred to as "pot marigold," calendula is not related to the common marigold flower. This is one of the easiest garden plants to grow: It blooms quickly and persistently and often self-seeds or "volunteers" in subsequent years. The flowers come in a variety of colors; most are a shade of yellow or orange.

What you eat: The flowers.

Recommended varieties: Flashback, Solar Flashback, Red Heart.

Hardiness: Calendula tolerates frost well, and their blooms often add color to the garden well into the fall.

Seed information: Germination temp. 50°–90°F, optimal 70°; germination time 7 days at 70°. Seed viability 3 years.

Mature plant size: 24 in. tall and wide.

How to plant: Direct-seed at the edges of your garden. Calendula is a vigorous plant and is best planted in areas where it will not interfere with crop production. Plant in clumps or space 9 in. apart.

When to plant: After danger of frost has passed. Calendula can be seeded in late summer or early fall in areas with mild winters.

How much to plant: Plant clusters of 3 or 4 plants in one spot or at a few different edges of your garden space.

When to fertilize: At planting.

General care: These plants generally take care of themselves. To keep them flowering, trim off any flower that is drying out and going to seed. Trim excess branches if the plants grow too wide or into your beds or pathways.

Pests: Aphid, whitefly.

Diseases: Powdery mildew, downy mildew.

Container suitability: Good. 1 gal. size pot or larger.

When and how to harvest: Pick blooming flowers as needed.

Storage and preservation:

FRIDGE: Calendula will keep for a few days in a plastic bag in the fridge.

DRIED: The flowers can be dried for winter use.

ABOVE: Snipping or pulling off spent blossoms helps keep plants producing new flowers. Shown here: calendula.

CARNATION
Medium Height Crop, Half Season Crop

Dianthus caryophyllus

There are perennial and annual varieties of carnation. If you are planting perennial types, be sure to set aside a separate space in your garden so they don't interfere with your seasonal soil work in the annual garden. Often called "pinks" or "Sweet William," or referred to by their Latin name, carnations are beautiful and easy to grow and will add quite an elegant look to your salads.

What you eat: The flowers.

Recommended varieties: Hollandia Mix, Rainbow Loveliness Mix.

Hardiness: Some frost tolerance. Some varieties can be sown in the fall for the following season.

Seed information: Germination temp. 60°–80°F, optimal 70°; germination time 14–20 days at 70°. Seed viability 3 years.

Mature plant size: 24 in. tall and wide.

How to plant: Carnations are easiest to grow when transplanted. Look for plants in the early spring. Space them 12 in. apart.

When to plant: Transplant or direct-seed after danger of frost has passed.

How much to plant: Try planting 3–6 plants.

When to fertilize: Fertilize once with a balanced fertilizer just prior to planting.

General care: Prune when young to create a bushy plant with numerous stems. Deadhead as needed to keep the plants in bloom.

Pests: Generally pest free.

Diseases: Powdery mildew, but fairly disease resistant.

Container suitability: Good. 1 gal. size or larger.

When and how to harvest: Pick flowers as needed.

Storage and preservation:

FRIDGE: Carnations will keep for a few days in a plastic bag in the fridge.

ABOVE: Carnations are beautiful and edible.

NASTURTIUM
Sprawling Crop or Climbing Crop,
Short Season Crop

Tropaeolum majus

The nasturtium is a wildly prolific, easy-to-grow garden flower. There are many varieties of the plant with an assortment of flower colors from yellow to orange to bright red. Nasturtiums will often self-seed in the garden and volunteer year after year.

In the world of plant taxonomy, nasturtium flowers are often confused with the Nasturtium plant family, which includes watercress. Although this flower and watercress are unrelated, they share a name due to the similarity of their taste. The flower and leaves have a strong, peppery flavor and are great additions to brighten up a summer-time salad. A word of caution: Nasturtiums are notorious attracters of aphids and may be overrun with these pests by midsummer.

What you eat: The flowers, the leaves.

Recommended varieties: These often come in packets containing a few different varieties in a spectrum of colors.

Hardiness: Most varieties have limited frost tolerance.

Seed information: Germination temp. 50°–90°F, optimal 70°; germination time 7–12 days at 70°. Seed viability 3–4 years.

Mature plant size: These sprawling or climbing plants can spread 3–4 ft.

How to plant: Direct-seeding is the most common way to plant nasturtiums. Transplants may be available in the spring. Spacing is variable: Plant at 12 in. apart for a solid border, otherwise 2–3 ft. apart.

When to plant: As soon as danger of frost has passed. Because they grow quickly, nasturtiums can be seeded until midsummer.

How much to plant: Try planting 4 or 5 plants at the edge of the garden, overhanging the edge of a bed, or let a climbing variety grow up a trellis or fence.

When to fertilize: At planting.

General care: Nasturtiums are planted by some gardeners as "trap crops," to lure aphids away from the more important vegetable crops. Nasturtiums certainly attract aphids; the problem is, if left in the garden once infested, they can provide a launching pad for a full-garden aphid attack. If plants become overrun with aphids, remove and burn the plants immediately.

Pests: Aphid, whitefly, cabbage moth.

Diseases: Powdery mildew, downy mildew.

ABOVE: Nasturtiums come in a variety of bright colors.

Container suitability: Good—in fact, very good!

When and how to harvest: Pick blooming flowers as needed. Pick leaves if you desire a slightly milder taste.

Storage and preservation:

FRIDGE: Nasturtium flowers and leaves will keep for a few days in a plastic bag in the fridge.

PANSY, VIOLA
Short Crop, Long Season Crop

Viola × wittrockiana or *Viola tricolor*

The low-growing pansy is an amazing long-blooming and great-tasting flower. Pansies are easy to grow and will bloom year-round in warmer climates.

What you eat: The flowers.

Recommended varieties: Try a mixture of pansy varieties.

Hardiness: Good frost tolerance. Can grow year-round in areas with mild winter weather.

Seed information: Germination temp. 60°–80°F, optimal 65°; germination time 4–7 days at 65°. Seed viability 3 years.

Mature plant size: 12 in. tall and wide

How to plant: Transplant. Pansies are known to germinate poorly. Space plants 4 in. apart.

When to plant: In early spring, or any time temperatures are above freezing.

How much to plant: Try 6–10 plants along a border or at the edges of garden beds.

When to fertilize: Fertilize once with a balanced fertilizer just prior to planting.

General care: Keep plants deadheaded for continual blooming.

Pests: Aphid, whitefly.

Diseases: Mildews, stem rot.

Container suitability: Good.

When and how to harvest: Pick flowers as needed.

Storage and preservation:

FRIDGE: The flowers will keep for a few days in a plastic bag in the fridge.

ABOVE: Pansies can bloom through the whole season.

SUNFLOWER
Tall Crop or Medium Height Crop, Half Season Crop

Helianthus annuus

The sunflower is one of the most iconic home garden crops. The sight of sunflowers can put just about anybody in a good mood. Fortunately, they are easy to grow and can self-seed in your garden. Since many varieties are tall, plant these flowers on the very north side of your garden, or in another location where they will not block the sun from other crops!

What you eat: The seeds.

Recommended varieties: Soraya, Mammoth, Teddy Bear.

Hardiness: No frost tolerance.

Seed information: Germination temp. 60°–90°F, optimal 70°; germination time 7–10 days at 70°. Seed viability 3 years.

Mature plant size: Variable depending on type. Some giant sunflowers can grow as tall as 15 ft., dwarf types are 3–4 ft.

How to plant: Direct-seeding is the best way to plant sunflowers. Plant 3 or 4 seeds in a hole 1 in. deep. Space holes 12–18 in. apart and thin the seedlings down to 1 plant once they have emerged.

When to plant: As soon as danger of frost has passed. Sunflowers grow quickly in warm soil, so they can be seeded through the early summer into July.

How much to plant: As many as you have space for; 4–8 plants will make a nice sunflower display.

When to fertilize: Fertilize once with a balanced fertilizer just prior to planting.

General care: Watch for slug damage in young plants. Strip dying leaves from the base of the stalks as necessary.

Pests: Slugs, snails, aphids, birds, squirrels.

Diseases: Downy mildew, powdery mildew.

Container suitability: OK. Sunflowers will grow in a container but will remain small and have thin stems.

When and how to harvest: Cut the heads of your sunflowers as they start to drop petals. If harvested too early, the seeds may be very small; if left too long, they will fall out of the seed head into the garden. Hang flower heads in a dry, warm location until the seeds are completely dry and easily fall out of the head. Then collect and roast them.

Storage and preservation:

DRIED: Hang flower heads in a dry, warm location until the seeds are completely dry and easily fall out. Collect and roast them.

OPPOSITE: Sunflowers come in all sizes, from 1 ft. tall to 12 ft. tall.

20

BERRIES

EVERYBODY LIKES BERRIES. It's hard to resist the notion of picking fresh berries in your own yard, but different berries have different growing habits and management needs, and some may suit your gardening situation while others don't. Fortunately, a lot of berries are fairly easy to grow in most regions of the country.

Unlike the majority of vegetable crops, berries are perennials. Like other perennial plants, they will provide you with a harvest year after year, but it may take a few years before they start to produce a reliable crop. Some produce more quickly than others.

Let's survey the berries available to the home gardener:

BLUEBERRIES

Medium Height Crop to Tall Crop,
Perennial Crop

Vaccinium corymbosum

Blueberries are a very popular choice in the home garden. The plants are beautiful year-round. Most are deciduous, with leaves that turn brilliant red or

OPPOSITE: A fresh blueberry harvest.

yellow in the fall, and a few varieties are evergreen.

If you decide to order blueberry plants through the mail, you'll have many varieties to choose from. Some will produce bigger berries and some will produce smaller, tastier ones; some will produce many berries in a short time, and others will produce over a long season. There are advantages to each, and personal preference plays a big part in selecting the right variety.

If you purchase plants from a nearby nursery, your options will be more limited, but the plants will be more mature and will likely produce a crop sooner than a mail-order plant. Hopefully, your local nursery has chosen varieties that do well in your region. Each plant should have a tag that provides the variety name and a brief description of its characteristics.

What you eat: The fruit.

Recommended varieties: One characteristic to note when selecting a blueberry variety is the mature size of the plant. Some varieties grow only 2 ft. tall, while others reach 4, 5, or even 6 ft. This should be listed on the plant tag and/or in the online or catalog description. Generally, blueberry plants will be about the same width as height, so spacing in your landscape should be determined by their mature size. As with vegetables, it is easy to plant your berries too close together, because it seems hard to believe how

big they will get. Any blueberry you choose will probably be a good one, but it's worth asking at the local nursery for particularly good selections. Our favorite types are Bluegold, Jersey, and Sunshine Blue (Sunshine Blue is an evergreen variety).

Hardiness: Survives the winter in zones 4 and up. Some varieties are evergreen through the winter in mild climates.

How to plant: Blueberries need full sun, lots and lots of water, and particularly acidic soil. Even if your soil is slightly acidic to begin with, it is very likely you will need to add elemental sulfur (available at local garden stores or online) when planting blueberries.

When planting, check for broken or dead branches and prune these off. Dead branches will lack the color and flexibility of live branches. Young, healthy blueberry branches will be red or yellow and somewhat flexible. If you are not sure if a branch is dead, use your pruners to scrape off a

little bark; a live branch will be green underneath the bark, and a dead branch will be completely brown.

When to plant: Blueberries can be planted any time in the spring, and in the fall in zones 8 and up.

How much to plant: Try starting with a plant or two. Blueberries are relatively low maintenance, so don't be scared to plant more if you have space. A fully mature plant will yield up to 8 pounds of berries, but it will take 8 or 9 years to reach this production level.

When to fertilize: Plan to add a balanced fertilizer and 1 in. of compost to your plants each spring.

General care: Your blueberries will need to be pruned each year to improve air circulation and sunlight penetration through the plant. The first year, use your pruners to cut off all the flower buds when they emerge in the spring. This may be hard to do, but it will allow the plant to use its energy to set a healthy root system, which will repay you with a bigger harvest the following year. It is important to get the plant off to a healthy start in this way, to ensure long-term productivity.

For the first 5 or 6 years of the plant's life, all the pruning you'll need to do is to remove dead branches and those that are rubbing against each other. This is best done in the late winter. The idea is to promote new, healthy branches and allow air circulation through the bush. When the plant is 7 or 8 years old, you can begin to selectively remove 1 or 2 of the oldest main branches each year to open up space for new shoots.

Keep the ground below the berries clear of dropped fruit and foliage to minimize disease problems.

ABOVE: A row of blueberry bushes makes a beautiful hedge.

Pests: Slugs, blueberry maggots.

Diseases: Watch out for mummy berry, a fungal disease specific to blueberries that results in shriveled, inedible fruit. If it shows up, make sure to clean up any dropped fruit, and try spraying an organic fungicide such as Serenade.

Container suitability: Good, if you use dwarf varieties. Use a 16–20 in. pot.

When and how to harvest: Pluck berries from the plant when they have fully ripened to a dark blue color.

Storage and preservation:

FRIDGE: Blueberries keep well for a few weeks in the fridge. Store them in a container covered with a dish towel rather than sealing them completely in plastic.

FREEZER: Tray-freeze and then pack in freezer bags.

CANNED: Blueberry preserves and jam.

RASPBERRIES, BLACKBERRIES

Tall Crop, Perennial Crop

Rubus idaeus, Rubus allegheniensis

Raspberries and blackberries grow like weeds, literally. These plants are generally referred to as "brambles," which is a term indicating a thorny bush.

There are two basic types of raspberries: June-bearing (also called summer-bearing) and everbearing (also called fall-bearing). Which you choose is a matter of personal preference. If you really like raspberries and/or you have a lot of room, consider growing a row of each.

JUNE-BEARING plants set a lot of fruit at one time, usually in the early summer. The berries are typically very large and sweet, and the bulk of the harvest lasts two or three weeks. All fruit is set on 2-year-old canes. This is a good type to grow if you like the idea of freezing raspberries or making jam, because you will have a lot of raspberries at once.

EVERBEARING raspberries are so called because they can produce two crops of raspberries each season. The plants will set fruit at the tops of 1-year-old canes in the late summer/early fall, and then lower down on the canes the following early summer. The early summer harvest is typically smaller than what you would get from a June-bearing plant. The fruit is often smaller too, but it often tastes as good as or even better than that of June-bearing plants. The fall harvest is usually bigger than the spring harvest.

ABOVE: A trellis containing tall, fruiting raspberry plants.

Blackberries are very similar to raspberries in their cultural requirements and in the way that they grow and produce fruit. Most produce fruit only on the 2-year-old canes, but some new varieties produce fruit on the first-year canes. Blackberries are also divided into "erect-growing" and "trailing" types. For simplicity's sake, we only discuss erect blackberries here.

When you buy blackberry or raspberry plants, you should be getting short canes with well-developed root systems. Since the plants will be dormant when you buy them, it will be somewhat difficult to tell which are the healthiest, so look for pots without broken, too-thin, or off-colored canes (a rotting cane will be darker and softer than the other canes). You want a pot that has a group of firm, thick, light-brown canes. You may also be able to find blackberries or raspberries rooted into a 4 in. or larger pot at some nurseries.

What you eat: The fruit.

Recommended varieties: Generally speaking, most raspberries have slightly thorny stems but are not too hazardous. There are both thornless and very thorny varieties of blackberry. NOTE: In some areas, the Himalayan blackberry is an invasive species that is taking over many natural areas and has very sharp thorns. *Whatever you do, don't grow Himalayan blackberries!*

JUNE-BEARING RASPBERRIES: Tulameen, Meeker.

EVERBEARING: Autumn Britten, Caroline.

ERECT BLACKBERRIES: Arapahoe Thornless, Prime Jan, Prime Jim.

Hardiness: Raspberries survive the winter in zone 2 and warmer. Blackberries grow well in zones 5–10.

How to plant: Most types of raspberry and erect blackberry need a trellis to keep them upright. Raspberries and blackberries send up a large number of canes each year that are of varying sturdiness. They grow pretty quickly (up to 8 ft. in a season) and will flop all over the place if there is nothing to discipline them a little. This can be as simple as stringing lightweight wire between wooden or metal posts. Some people prefer to plant their berries up against a fence or wall, which makes trellising them easier.

Most brambles can handle nearly any soil condition. They can get by with a little less sun than other berries and still provide bountiful harvests. Raspberries grow in many different soil types, but if you hope to get a great harvest out of them year after year, give them what they really want: well-drained soil, sandy as opposed to clayey, with a lot of compost.

Blackberries and raspberries are easiest to manage when planted in rows. Space everbearing raspberries 1 ft. apart and June-bearing raspberries and erect blackberries 2–3 ft. apart. Immediately after planting, cut the cane back to the ground.

When to plant: Raspberries and blackberries are best planted in the spring, but can be planted in the fall in mild climates (zones 8 and up).

How much to plant: Try starting with 3 or 4 plants to get a feel for growing raspberries and blackberries. Yields will range from a ½ pint to 2 pints of berries per plant.

When to fertilize: Fertilize the area with a balanced fertilizer before planting. Top-dress with compost and a balanced fertilizer every spring thereafter.

General care: Raspberries and blackberries can be hard to contain in a single area, because they spread by underground "runners" that will start popping up in the yard, in your other landscape beds, and in your bedroom closet. Keeping them under control is not hard, but it requires yearly root pruning. Plan to edge along the perimeter of the bed each spring and summer and remove escaping shoots. If you see any new shoots pop up in an unwanted area, weed them out as soon as possible.

Pruning: Pruning your brambles properly will depend very much on the type you have chosen.

HOW TO PRUNE EVERBEARING RASPBERRIES (AND ERECT BLACKBERRIES THAT PRODUCE ON 1-YEAR-OLD CANES):

The canes can be pruned to provide two crops per season (spring and fall) or a fall crop only. The first technique will provide you with a longer berry-picking season, while the second is less time-consuming and produces a larger, more concentrated set of berries.

FOR TWO CROPS: After planting, let the canes grow all summer, pruning out especially thin and weak canes. In the middle of summer, the tops of the canes will start to flower, and in the fall these flowers will turn to fruit. After the tops have finished fruiting, cut them off just below the lowest fruiting section. The next spring, the bottom of last year's canes will set fruit in the spring. As this is happening, new canes will be emerging and getting ready to fruit in the fall. It's easy to tell the difference between the new and old canes, as the 1-year canes have greenish stems and the 2-year canes are brown and woody. At this time, thin the new canes out to about 3 per sq. ft. When the 2-year-old canes have finished fruiting in midsummer, prune them out at soil level.

FOR ONE CROP: After planting, let the canes grow all summer, pruning out especially thin and weak canes. In the middle of summer, the tops of the canes will start to flower, and in the fall these flowers will turn to fruit. After the tops have finished fruiting, cut all canes down to 2 in. above the ground. In the spring new canes will emerge. Repeat.

HOW TO PRUNE JUNE-BEARING (SUMMER-BEARING) RASPBERRIES AND MOST ERECT BLACKBERRIES:

Let the canes grow all summer, pruning out especially thin and weak canes. Keep the canes thinned to about 3–5 per sq. ft. The next season, the previous year's canes will be stiff and brown. For blackberries, cut off the tip of these canes when they reach 4 ft. in height. Cut the tips of raspberries when they're about 5–6 ft. tall. That spring they will flower, and these flowers will develop into fruit in the summer. While they are starting to fruit, new green canes will be emerging from your plants. After the brown canes (last year's) finish fruiting, cut them all the way to the ground. Leave the new, green canes to grow all season (they will fruit the following year). Prune out especially thin and weak canes.

Pests: Aphids, cutworms, leaf rollers, mites, nematodes.

Diseases: Anthracnose, gray mold, powdery mildew, rust, and raspberry- and blackberry-specific viruses can cause problems. If your berries have foliar problems and are generally unhealthy for no apparent reason, do a little research online to see if viruses are a problem in your area.

Container suitability: Not recommended.

When and how to harvest: For blackberries, pluck the fruit when the berries have changed from shiny to a dull black color (the shiny ones aren't quite ripe yet). Raspberries are ready when they're fully red, soft, and easy to pull off the canes.

Storage and preservation:

FRIDGE: Raspberries and blackberries keep well for about 1 week in the fridge. Store them in a container covered with a dish towel rather than sealing them completely in plastic.

FREEZER: Tray-freeze and then pack in freezer bags.

CANNED: Preserves and jam.

STRAWBERRIES

Short Crop, Sprawling Crop, Perennial Crop

Fragaria × ananassa

Once you've tasted your own fresh strawberries, you'll likely never again buy those lame-looking ones in the grocery store that have been shipped from halfway around the world. In addition to being delicious, strawberries are easy to grow.

Each strawberry plant should be left in the ground for only two or three years. Fortunately, by the end of this time it will have sent off countless runners that will be its offspring for subsequent years, so you won't ever have to buy new strawberry plants. But you will have to spend a few minutes each season managing your plants.

Similar to raspberries, the two general categories of strawberries are June-bearing and everbearing. June-bearing plants generally produce a large fruit set over a period of a few weeks, usually in early summer. Everbearing plants set smaller-sized fruit over the course of an entire growing season.

As of the writing of this book, most everbearing varieties are technically "day-neutral types." Here's what that's about: The flowering cycle of most plants is determined by the hours of sunlight in the day. Along with temperature changes, increasing day length is the principal signal for plants to begin blooming each season, just as many plants cease blooming once the days start to shorten in late summer. Day-neutral strawberries don't work this way; they keep blooming and setting fruit until the cold temperatures of the fall really set in. The terms "day-neutral" and "everbearing" are often used interchangeably in plant catalogs and at nurseries. Make sure to choose everbearing varieties that are actually day-neutral.

Non-day-neutral everbearing varieties tend not to produce well.

(Whew, what a mouthful—unfortunately, pun intended!)

If you'd like a large amount of strawberries at one time for freezing or making jam, June-bearing types are your best option. If you'd like an extended harvest over the course of the season for fresh eating, then go for an everbearing type. The overall per-plant harvest is approximately the same for both types. Also, keep in mind that many day-neutral types don't produce as well in areas with very hot summers.

What you eat: The fruit.

Recommended varieties: Most strawberry varieties are particularly well suited to one part of the country, so it's best to buy or order your plants from a local supplier. Some of our favorite day-neutrals are Albion (widely adapted), Tri-Star (widely adapted), and Seascape (Northwest, California). Favorite June-bearers include Earliglo, Jewel (Northeastern and Midwestern) Shuksan, Puget Reliance (Northwest).

Hardiness: Depending on what varieties you choose, strawberries will grow well in zones 4–10. If you mulch over the plants in the winter, they can be grown down to zone 2. Make sure not to apply the mulch until the plants have been exposed to temperatures in the upper 20s, and be sure to pull the mulch off in early spring so the soil can warm back up again.

How to plant: Plan to buy plants "bare root" or in 4 in. pots. Plant in a well-prepared, fertilized garden bed. Strawberries will grow in a range of soils. They prefer a pH slightly more acidic than vegetable crops, but the main concern is proper drainage. Prepare a bed for strawberries just as you would prepare a vegetable bed. Dig a hole for each plant, and set it in the ground so that

half of the crown is under the soil. Space plants 12 in. apart.

When to plant: As soon as the soil can be worked in the spring, or after temperatures have cooled down in the early fall.

How much to plant: Try planting 10–12 plants to get started, or more if you want to make jam. Planting even one strawberry plant in a container is a satisfying experience. Each plant will yield about ½ to 1½ lb. of berries.

When to fertilize: Fertilize the area with a balanced fertilizer before planting. Top-dress with compost and a balanced fertilizer every spring thereafter.

ABOVE: Fruiting strawberry plants surrounded by burlap mulch.

General care:

JUNE-BEARING, YEAR 1: Be prepared to pinch off all flowers. You may be reluctant to do this, but the plants need their energy to set out a good root system in the first year instead of producing fruit. Sacrificing an early harvest the first year will result in much healthier plants and much better yields in future years. Your strawberry plants will produce "runners," which are baby plants sent off from a mother plant. Leave the runners attached to the mother plant until they have rooted and become established. These will develop into full-sized plants.

JUNE-BEARING, YEAR 2 AND BEYOND: Let the plants flower and fruit at will during their second spring; you'll be harvesting fresh berries early that summer. When the plants have finished producing fruit, renovate the patch by cutting off all the leaves with your pruning shears (you can use a lawn mower on a large planting). Avoid cutting into the crown, or top of the root structure. Fertilize each plant with ⅛ cup of organic fertilizer, and then let everything regrow in preparation for the next year. The plants will become less productive after the third year, and many growers simply plant a new patch every 3 years.

DAY-NEUTRAL, YEAR 1: Pluck off all flowers for the first 6 weeks after planting, then let the plants flower and fruit at will—berries will come along soon. Prune off runner plants to maintain about a 1 ft. spacing between plants.

DAY-NEUTRAL, YEAR 2: Let plants flower and fruit at will. Fertilize with about ⅛ cup of balanced fertilizer once a month. As with June bearers, you'll want to replant a new strawberry patch every 3 or 4 years.

Pests: Ripe strawberries are attractive to most animals; deer, rabbits, squirrels, and birds can all be a problem. Consider covering your strawberries with black poly bird netting or spun bonded polyester row cover (Reemay) as the fruits begin to ripen. Additionally, a host of insects may attack your strawberry plants, including aphids, spider mites, leaf rollers, and root weevils.

Diseases: Gray mold and a number of fungal diseases. If possible, plan to transplant your strawberries to a new bed every 3 or 4 years. When setting up a new strawberry bed, select the youngest, healthiest plants and compost the oldest, largest ones. It is these older plants that are most likely to develop disease problems as they age. Maintaining a younger stand of plants will keep your strawberry bed healthy indefinitely.

Container suitability: Good. Strawberries grow well in containers.

When and how to harvest: After your plants are established (year 2 for June bearers, early fall during the first year for day-neutrals), you should see a bountiful harvest. Pick berries when they are completely red (no white tips).

Storage and preservation:

FRIDGE: Strawberries keep well for about 1 week in the fridge. Store them in a container covered with a dish towel rather than sealing them completely in plastic.

FREEZER: Tray-freeze and then pack in freezer bags.

CANNED: Strawberry preserves, jam, or jelly.

part V
MORE GARDEN KNOWLEDGE

"All man has to do is cooperate with the big forces, the sun, the rain, the growing urge. Seeds sprout, stems grow, leaves spread in the sunlight. Man plants, weeds, cultivates and harvests. It sounds simple, and it is simple, with the simplicity of great truths."

~ *Hal Borland* ~

You now know how to get your crops into the ground and care for them, but there's still more to learn! In this section, we'll address some of the nagging gardening questions that may be lurking in the back of your mind, like "What do I do with my garden in the winter?" or "What's eating all my newly planted crops?" or "If a tree falls in the woods and no one's there to hear it, does it make a sound?" We provide a month-by-month breakdown of what happens in a garden over the course of a year, a section to help you prepare your garden for the winter, and information on how to deal with many common garden pests, diseases, and other problems.

21

MONTH BY MONTH

FOLLOWING IS A GENERAL overview of what your garden tasks may look like month by month over the course of a year. Each month's activities will vary depending on your local climate. For example, if your garden is still covered with snow in March, you probably won't be able to do any early-season weeding, or you may be able to start planting in January or February if you live in a really warm region. Regardless of your climate, this section will give you a feeling for the flow of garden work throughout the year.

The tasks that require your attention will change according to the time of year. Early in the season, you will focus mostly on garden preparation and taking extra care of young plants to ensure they get a healthy start. Later in the summer, you will spend more of your time harvesting crops and keeping weeds in check.

JANUARY

The early months of the year require very little (if any) time spent outside in the garden. Use this time to read about gardening, buy seeds, and start to envision this year's garden. Take an hour or two

to peruse seed catalogs and websites and create a list of plants you want to grow. While you will purchase some of these in advance as seeds, others will wait till spring, when you buy them from a nursery or farmers market as transplants. If you're shopping from a catalog, place your seed order as early in the year as you can. But don't expect seeds to arrive on seed racks at your local nursery or other store for another few months.

Weeding: As long as things were cleaned up properly the previous year, most weeds should still be dormant.

Seeding: If you want to try growing your own onions and leeks from seed, now is the time to start them indoors (under lights).

Transplanting: N/A

Watering: N/A

Harvesting: If you overwintered any vegetables outside in the garden (such as carrots, leeks, or kale), harvest them this month to start opening up space for spring crops.

FEBRUARY

This is still a quiet time in the garden. If the soil is relatively dry (not muddy) and not frozen, you can start to prepare new garden beds, adding compost and/or turning over your cover crop from last fall. If you planted a cover crop, make sure it does not

OPPOSITE: Young spring pea plants starting to grow up a net trellis.

resprout after it is turned into the soil: Check once a week after first tilling it in.

The very first crop of the season (peas) can be planted in late February, but keep an eye on it for early signs of pest damage (slugs, snails, etc.).

Weeding: Clear any weeds that may appear.

Seeding: Late February is a good time to start peas outdoors.

Transplanting: Start looking around for healthy berry bushes at nurseries (or order them online).

Watering: If you've transplanted any berry bushes (or vegetables if you live in a warm climate), water them in after planting.

Harvesting: If you overwintered any vegetables outside in the garden (such as carrots, leeks, or kale), harvest them this month to open up space for spring crops.

MARCH

This is a good time to get the garden into shape and ready for the upcoming planting season. Make sure it's very well weeded.

You can start planting potatoes and very cold-hardy salad greens now. And keep an eye on your peas.

Weeding: Make a clean sweep of early weeds. Diligent early-season weeding will repay you many times over during the real weeding season (summer).

Seeding: Arugula, lettuce, potatoes, spinach.

Transplanting: If the ground is not frozen: asparagus, blueberries, leeks, lettuce, onions, raspberries, rhubarb.

Watering: If applicable. Water right away when transplanting any crop.

Harvesting: Finish harvesting all overwintered crops.

APRIL

This is the month when you can finally start planting a wider variety of crops. Things may still be growing slowly, but not for much longer. Stay true to suggested crop spacing (even though the plants look small now) to avoid crowding problems later in the season.

Weeding: At least a few minutes a week.

Seeding: Beets, broccoli, cabbage, carrots, cauliflower, chard, collards, kale, radishes, salad greens.

Transplanting: Broccoli, cabbage, cauliflower, chard, collards, kale, lettuce.

If you haven't yet, plant asparagus, blueberries, leeks, onions, potatoes, raspberries, rhubarb, and perennial herbs.

Watering: It will likely be cool and wet enough that irrigation is not yet needed. Water in all plants and seeds when planting, and don't let the soil surface dry out. Now is a good time to test your irrigation system and fix any problems before the weather starts to heat up.

Harvesting: Any remaining fall crops or overwintered salad greens (mustard greens, spinach).

MAY

This is the time of year to start looking for transplants for summer crops: basil, peppers, squash, tomatoes, etc.

Many more crops will start to go into the garden, and the key is to make sure they get everything they need while they are still young. They should receive adequate and consistent moisture, and this is also a good time to dispense liquid fertilizers (every 2 or 3 weeks).

Start watching in earnest for insect and disease problems.

Weeding: At least a few minutes every week.

Seeding: Beans, carrots, radishes, salad greens, summer squash, winter squash.

Transplanting: To defend against cold damage, make sure temperatures have reached those suggested in this book's profiles for basil, corn, cucumbers, peppers, summer squash, and tomatoes.

Watering: Start watching the weather forecast closely for upcoming dry, hot weather, or for severe thunderstorms or windstorms.

Harvesting: Early-season crops like radishes and salad greens.

JUNE

Now is a good time to start thinking more about watering the garden. Spring rains may be slowing down, and you don't want to stress out young plants by letting the soil dry out while they are still getting established.

Rapid plant growth means that many more insects will be on the prowl for a meal. Spend a few minutes each week looking over your plants for potential pests or diseases. Common pests like caterpillars and aphids often start to show up this time of year.

Tie up vining plants that may need help staying on their trellises: beans, cucumbers, peas, squash, tomatoes.

Thin direct-seeded crops if necessary: beans, carrots, radishes.

Weeding: This is the beginning of the true weeding season. Spend a few minutes every week keeping them in check, making sure no weeds get large enough to flower and set seeds.

Seeding: If you haven't yet, plant beans, carrots, corn, and cucumbers. You can keep planting radishes, salad greens, and summer squash as well. Stop seeding salad greens until midsummer (when you will start to plant them for fall).

Transplanting: If you haven't already, there is still time to put in summer crops: basil, cucumber, corn, peppers, tomatoes.

Watering: If necessary, this is a good time to turn on your irrigation system.

Harvesting: Early spring crops: peas, radishes, salad greens.

JULY

Many crops are now established and should be growing rapidly each week. Some early, short-season crops (salad greens, radishes, etc.) will need to be removed from the garden to make room for new crops or the expansive growth of summer crops. Start thinking about and planting fall crops: Even though it is summer, this is the best time to plant them, so they are established before the cold weather.

Now is the time of year when you may need to start clearing out crops that you already harvested and that are either dead or exhausted (meaning they no longer produce food, or the food they produce is not good enough to eat—or you're just tired of eating it!). You may need to clear bush beans, broccoli, cabbage, cauliflower, chard, kale, peas, salad greens.

Prune tomatoes.

When you have cleared out a crop, amend the soil with compost and fertilizer in the newly opened spaces to prepare for the next crop.

Weeding: Keep after the small weeds that keep appearing.

Seeding: Continue seeding bush beans and radishes. Seed a second planting of summer squash. Start seeding fall crops: beets, broccoli, cabbage, carrots, cauliflower, chard, collards, kale, peas.

Transplanting: Stop transplanting long-season crops.

Watering: Check the soil each week to make sure it is moist (it should never be bone dry or soggy wet).

Harvesting: July is usually the month when serious harvesting starts. Look for basil, beans, broccoli, cabbage, carrots, cauliflower, chard, collards, kale, peas, potatoes, radishes, and salad greens. Harvest last year's garlic once half of the plant has turned brown.

AUGUST

This is often the hottest time of year. Mature crops are not as sensitive to water shortages, but they still require some water (from irrigation or rain)—you never want to see your plants wilting in the heat.

This can be a busy time for weeding, so stay on task removing small weeds as soon as they appear.

Continue to clear exhausted/harvested crops. Prune tomatoes.

Weeding: This is the thick of the weeding season. Try to weed once per week.

Seeding: There is still time for fall seeding: carrots, radishes, salad greens, turnips.

Transplanting: Transplant fall crops if available: broccoli, cabbage, cauliflower, chard, kale.

Watering: The garden will require regular watering (every day or every other day).

Harvesting: Basil, beans, broccoli, cabbage, carrots, cauliflower, chard, collards, corn, cucumbers, kale, onions, leeks, peas, peppers, potatoes, radishes, salad greens, summer squash, tomatoes.

SEPTEMBER

Continue to assess the garden's water needs. It can still be very hot this time of year, or it may start raining enough to eliminate the need for irrigation.

Inspect crops for signs of pest or disease damage and remove very damaged plants.

Continue to clear exhausted/harvested crops.

Weeding: Still very important, as fall weeds can come on strong.

Seeding: Finish seeding fall crops such as radishes and salad greens. Now is a good time to seed a cover crop.

Transplanting: Only short-season crops or overwintering greens: arugula, lettuce, spinach.

Watering: Watch the weather to see if irrigation should be adjusted.

Harvesting: Basil, beans, broccoli, cabbage, carrots, cauliflower, chard, collards, corn, cucumbers, kale, onions, leeks, peas, peppers, potatoes, radishes, salad greens, summer squash, tomatoes.

OCTOBER

Continue to assess the garden's water needs. It will be cooling down quite a bit now, and you may be able to turn the water off if you haven't already.

Inspect crops for signs of pest or disease damage, and remove very damaged plants.

Continue to clear exhausted/harvested crops.

Weeding: As needed. If you have stayed on top of the weeds during the summer, this work may start slowing down.

Seeding: Cover crop.

Transplanting: Garlic.

Watering: As needed.

Harvesting: In many regions, frosts can occur any time starting in October. Make sure to clear sensitive summer crops before it starts to frost: basil, beans, corn, cucumbers, peppers, summer squash, tomatoes. Also continue to harvest hardier crops: broccoli, cabbage, carrots, cauliflower, chard, collards, kale, leeks, onions, peas, potatoes, radishes, salad greens. Finally, it's time to harvest winter squash and pumpkins: Pick them once the vine has turned yellow/brown or mostly yellow/brown.

Transplanting: N/A
Watering: N/A
Harvesting: Any overwintering crops: carrots, kale, spinach, arugula.

NOVEMBER

Now is a good time to cover-crop your empty beds, or cover them with a couple of inches of compost for the winter.

Continue to clear exhausted/harvested crops.
Weeding: N/A
Seeding: N/A
Transplanting: If you haven't yet, transplant garlic.
Watering: Should not be necessary.
Harvesting: Many crops will now be finished producing. Clear the remaining harvest from beans, broccoli, cabbage, carrots, cauliflower, chard, collards, corn, cucumbers, kale, leeks, onions, peas, peppers, potatoes, radishes, salad greens, summer squash, tomatoes. If you haven't already, bring in all your winter squash.

DECEMBER

There is little to do in most gardens during December. If you have planted overwintering crops, make sure to check on them once a week. If you have any fall-planted crops that are ready, you can harvest them as desired.
Weeding: N/A
Seeding: N/A

Snapdragons in a July garden add beauty and attract beneficial insects.

22

YOUR GARDEN IN WINTER

IMAGINE IT'S OCTOBER. It's 38 degrees and pouring rain. Your tomatoes have stopped ripening. Your eggplant has died. You've harvested a lot of food over the past few months, and now the garden looks like a war zone. You've heard other gardeners talking about "fall crops," "floating row covers," and "cover cropping," and you're wondering if those phrases should mean anything to you.

Look at it this way: You already made it through your first summer as a gardener, and it might be nice to have a break for a few months, so you can really look forward to getting started again in the spring. Then again, maybe you just can't wait that long to start planting again, and you want to try growing some crops through the winter. Either way, you'll want to winterize your garden, which means cleaning it up and protecting your soil from the ravages of winter. If you're up for it, you can also grow a few crops through the winter to keep a little fresh food on the table. And if you like garlic, October is the month to plant your own.

WINTERIZING YOUR GARDEN

Winterizing your garden is really a simple process. You may live in an area where the ground will be snow covered all winter, or maybe the weather will only be cool and rainy. In either case, you want to protect the microorganisms in your soil through the cold winter months, and prevent the nutrients from leaching away.

CLEANING UP

First, get your garden cleaned up. Pull all the dead and dying summer crops out, and compost them. Take a soft rake and clear out all the dropped foliage lying on the ground. Getting the dying plant matter out minimizes the spread of insect pests and diseases from year to year.

PROTECTING YOUR SOIL

Next, get your soil protected. The easiest way to do this is to spread a thick (6–8 in.) layer of straw or leaves or a 1–2 in. layer of compost over the top of your garden beds. This mulch protects beneficial microorganisms below, and rain will wash nutrients from the compost into your garden soil. In the spring, turn in the compost prior to planting.

If you already have a layer of straw or other mulch on top of your garden beds, leave it in place through the winter. It will protect the soil and slowly decompose, adding additional organic matter to the soil. You can move the remaining mulch aside in the spring and add compost to your beds at that time.

OPPOSITE: Fall cabbages.

COVER CROPS

Cover crops are typically grown in the garden during the off-season. A variety of plants can be used as cover crops, including buckwheat, clover, fava beans, field peas, oats, rye grass, and vetch.

Planting cover crops will add organic matter and nutrients to your soil, protect it from erosion and leaching, and keep its beneficial microorganisms and fungi happy. If you plant leguminous cover crops such as peas, vetch, or fava beans, they will pull nitrogen out of the air and fix it in your soil, reducing the need for fertilizer the following year.

However, in a typical home garden, cover crops sometimes prove to be more trouble than they're worth. They can take a long time to break down and release nutrients, which means you may lose a month or two of your growing season waiting for the cover crop to decompose. Also, there may still be vegetables growing in your garden when it's time to sow cover crops (usually in late August). Because of these drawbacks, many gardeners find it preferable to forgo the cover crops in favor of mulching for winter protection. Still, if you're feeling ambitious and want to try cover cropping, it's a fairly simple process.

OPPOSITE: As the vine dies back, a large pumpkin emerges from a patch of overgrown grass at the end of the summer growing season. ABOVE: A cover crop of rye being turned into the soil at the end of winter.

Sowing and Managing Cover Crops

Timing is important with cover crops. If they are seeded too late in the fall, they'll have a hard time getting established. (If you will not be using portions of your garden during the growing season, you can also plant cover crops in the spring and let them grow in the garden bed all summer long, to improve your soil for future years.)

For late-fall planting, try a mixture of rye grass and vetch or rye grass and field peas. Rye, vetch, and/or field peas are the best cover crop options for fall planting because they grow fast and reliably germinate in cold weather. You can also try fava beans, oats, wheat, or a premixed blend of cover crops from a seed company. For early fall or spring planting, try clover. For a fast-growing cover in warm weather, try buckwheat.

Here are the steps in cover cropping:

1. After you've cleaned up your garden, rake the soil smooth. For larger cover-crop seeds, use a trowel to dig furrows about 1 in. deep and 6 in. apart (as if you were seeding beans).
2. Sow the seed. For larger seeds such as peas, rye, or oats, aim for about 1 seed per inch of furrow (sow fava beans at 1 seed per 4 in.). Rake soil over the furrows, and pat it in place for good seed-to-soil contact. For smaller seeds like clover, simply sprinkle them over the surface of the bed (imagine about 2 seeds per square inch), then rake over the bed to incorporate them into the soil.
3. Water the area. If planted in the fall, the seeds will sprout and grow slowly through the winter. Typically, when growing through the winter, irrigation is not necessary once the crops have germinated. Growth will start to speed up in early spring, depending on the weather.
4. About 3 weeks before you're ready to start planting vegetables in the spring (as soon as

the ground is workable), use a spade shovel to chop the cover crop down and hack it into small pieces.
5. Use a fork or shovel to turn the green matter into the soil. Ensuring that the top growth is buried will help it break down and keep it from resprouting. Note that the longer you wait to turn in the cover crops in the spring, the more green matter you will be able to add to the soil, but the harder it will be to chop it up and work it in.
6. Check the plot once a week. You may have to rechop and rebury any spots where the plants have started growing again.
7. After 3–4 weeks, when the plant material is mostly decomposed, start planting vegetables.

WINTER CROPS

If you need a break from the garden after your first season, don't worry about winter gardening. A lot of people find it nice to get the garden cleaned up and the soil protected in the fall, and then have a few months to look forward to starting over again.

If you do want to keep some edible crops going through the winter, here are some easy greens that we recommend:

Arugula, mustard greens: Seed August through September.

Claytonia (also called miner's lettuce): Seed in early September.

Kale and collards: Direct-seed in July, or transplant August through September.

Lettuce: Transplant or seed August through mid-September.

Spinach: Seed August through September.

These crops are good for winter growing because they can tolerate subfreezing temperatures without protection (although they will benefit from the addition of a hoop house with floating row cover or greenhouse plastic, described in chapter 12: Essential Garden Skills).

Sow your winter crops as directed in the list, and harvest them as long as your winter allows. A good snow cover will actually help protect these greens from the cold. Try digging down through the snow for a midwinter spinach harvest. Once temperatures get too cold (below 20 degrees), the plants may perish. There's nothing you can do about it—just clean them up and wait until spring to plant again!

ROW COVERS

Putting up row covers is a great means of keeping out garden pests, but you can also use them to improve growth in your winter crops. They serve as mini-greenhouses when the sun is shining, they add a few degrees of warmth at night, and, most important, they protect plants from the wind. Put them up after seeding or transplanting (see chapter 12: Essential Garden Skills for detailed instructions).

23

GARDEN PROBLEMS AND SOLUTIONS

WE'D LOVE TO TELL YOU that all your crops will grow to maturity with no problems, every year, but the truth is that you're likely to run into a few minor difficulties sooner or later.

Trouble in the garden is usually a result of severe weather, pests, or diseases, or insufficient water or nutrients. The good news is that with a little bit of preparation and attention, you can avoid most common gardening problems and resolve the ones that do arise before they do a lot of damage to your crops. Crop management isn't that hard, and it's a great excuse to stay in touch with your plants. If you watch out for a few key pests and diseases and take some preventive measures, your crops will be healthy and happy.

We recommend using only organic solutions to control pest and disease issues. Because even organic pesticides can injure or kill non-target species, they should be used only as a last resort option.

Start off with a troubleshooting chart (next

page) that you can consult if you notice a problem in the garden. This will refer you to more detailed information on possible solutions.

SEVERE WEATHER

FREEZING TEMPERATURES

Some garden crops can tolerate below-freezing temperatures, and others cannot. If crops are planted when the weather's still too cold, they will likely grow very slowly, and their growth may be permanently stunted (or they may die!).

At the end of the main growing season, many crops will perish in the first frost. You may be able to protect some crops in light frosts, but expect a quick decline in most summer crops once temperatures regularly dip below freezing. Follow the instructions in this book's crop profiles to avoid frost damage. Consider adding floating row covers if you want to extend your harvest at either end of the season.

EXTREME HEAT

Even when adequately watered, crops can suffer in very hot weather. Heat-sensitive crops have a

OPPOSITE: A blueberry bush with ripe fruit surrounded by bird netting.

TROUBLESHOOTING CHART

PLANT PART	PROBLEM	YOU SHOULD READ ABOUT:
Stems, Leaves	Plants appear wilted	Extreme heat, water and irrigation, root maggots, wilts (*Verticillium, Fusarium*), clubroot, root rot, white mold, squash vine borer, root aphids, parasitic nematodes, freezing temperatures, wireworms
Leaves	Leaves are yellow, plant not growing well	Lack of nitrogen, leaf miners
Leaves	Leaves are purple, plant not growing well	Lack of phosphorous
Leaves	Leaf edges are yellow, plant not growing well	Lack of potassium
Leaves	Leaf veins are yellow, plant not growing well	Lack of magnesium
Stems, Leaves	Plant stunted, weak, generally not growing well	Excess potassium, lack of calcium, excess magnesium, excess phosphorous and potassium, other nutrient deficiencies, wilts, clubroot, root rot, white mold, squash vine borer, parasitic nematodes, aphids, flea beetles, wireworms
Leaves	White powdery substance on leaves, plants not growing well	Powdery mildew, white mold
Leaves	Lesions on leaves, leaves dying, plant not growing well	Alternaria, anthracnose, downy mildew, squash bugs, spider mites
Stems	Gray, fuzzy growth on plant stems	Gray mold
Stems, Leaves	Brown lesions or other damage on stems; foliage yellow, black, and/or dying	Late blight, stem rot, anthracnose, freezing temperatures
Stems, Leaves	Orange specks and bumps on leaves or stems	Rust
Stems	Young plants are cut off at base	Cutworms, damping off, stem rot, crows and other birds
Leaves	Larger holes in leaves (½ in. or larger)	Slugs and snails, tobacco and tomato hornworm, squash bugs, corn borers, Colorado potato beetle, cabbage loopers, bean beetles, cucumber beetles, heavy rains and hail
Leaves	Tiny holes in leaves	Flea beetles, spider mites
Leaves	Leaves are stripped off or skel-etonized	Deer, Japanese beetles, Colorado potato beetles, cabbage loopers, bean beetles, cucumber beetles
Leaves	Leaves are yellow and damaged, squiggly lines in leaves	Leaf miners
Stems	Plants bolting or sending up seed heads prematurely	Extreme heat, nutritional deficiencies and excesses

PLANT PART	PROBLEM	YOU SHOULD READ ABOUT:
Fruit	Fruit has black, rotting tips	Lack of calcium
Fruit	Fruit generally small, stunted, unhealthy	Lack of potassium, lack of calcium, spider mites, stinkbugs
Fruit	Holes or bites in fruit	Moles and voles, slugs, tobacco and tomato hornworms, raccoons, crows and other birds, rats and mice, woodchucks (groundhogs)
Fruit	Rotting, discolored, dying fruit; lesions on fruit	Stinkbugs, late blight, Alternaria/early blight, black rot, anthracnose, gray mold
Roots	Holes or bites in root crops	Wireworms, root maggots, moles and voles, rats and mice, woodchucks (groundhogs)
Fruit	Fuzzy grayish mold on fruit	Gray mold
Roots	Corky, cracked lesions on root crops	Scab

tendency to bolt when exposed to high temperatures. The flower stalks of bolting crops can be cut back to keep the plants alive, but once the flowering instinct has been triggered, it is typically difficult or impossible for a plant to recover.

The best approach is to remove bolted crops and replace them with new half- or short-season crops. In addition to keeping the plants well watered, consider providing shade-cloth covers over heat-intolerant crops through the summer.

HIGH WINDS

Spring and summer storms can bring severe winds, which can damage your crops, especially taller ones like corn and tomatoes. Hoop houses with securely fashioned row covers can help protect plants. If persistent high winds are a problem in your area, consider planting a windbreak of tall shrubs or building a fence around the garden. Make sure the windbreak doesn't cast shade into the garden.

LEFT: Plants wilted from heat may become stunted and produce smaller quantities of food.

HEAVY RAINS AND HAIL

Very heavy rains and hail can damage crops, breaking stems and branches. If heavy rain or hail is expected, protect your plants by covering them with buckets, tubs, empty plant pots, garbage cans turned upside down—whatever you've got. It may not be fancy, but it works!

NUTRITIONAL DEFICIENCIES AND EXCESSES

LACK OF NITROGEN

In new garden soils, where soil organisms have not had adequate time to break down and release nutrients in compost and fertilizers, there may be a lack of available nitrogen. Mixing carbon materials such as sawdust, bark, or straw into your soil (rather than top-dressing) can also make nitrogen unavailable to your plants, since the soil microbes will use all of the available nitrogen to help decompose the carbon source.

Telltale signs: Plants will look stunted and will not grow; leaves of affected plants will be yellow or pale green.

Susceptible crops: Almost any garden plant, with the exception of nitrogen-fixing crops like peas and beans, can suffer from a lack of nitrogen.

What to do: Add a high-nitrogen fertilizer such as blood meal, feather meal, or bat guano to the soil. Water the crops with a liquid fertilizer that is high in nitrogen once per week while they start to recover. If crops are severely damaged, remove them, add nitrogen fertilizer to the bed, and plant new crops. In the long term, make sure to add compost and fertilizers at the start of each season. If it is available, add composted manure to your beds in the fall or early spring for an extra supply of nitrogen.

EXCESS NITROGEN

If organic fertilizer is applied too heavily or too frequently, the soil may end up with an overabundance of nitrogen.

Telltale signs: Plants grow very quickly, so quickly that they end up too thin and tall to support themselves. Quick, unhealthy growth can make plants more susceptible to pests (especially aphids). Fruiting plants may grow very large without flowering or setting fruit.

Susceptible crops: Although it is difficult to give Brassicas too much nitrogen, fruiting plants such as tomatoes, peppers, and eggplant should only be given nitrogen early in the season.

What to do: Stop adding fertilizers with nitrogen. The excess will eventually leach out of the soil. Remove severely damaged plants, and let the remaining crops use up the excess until they resume healthy growth habits.

LACK OF PHOSPHORUS

A less common problem for most gardens, phosphorus deficiency can occur in new garden soils that do not contain enough compost, or soils that have been planted for several years without receiving proper amendments.

Telltale signs: Plants will turn purplish and look stunted. Fruiting crops will not flower or set fruit.

Susceptible crops: Almost any garden plant, though especially plants such as beets, tomatoes, and cucumbers, which require high amounts of phosphorus to grow well and/or fruit.

What to do: Add a fertilizer such as bone meal or rock phosphate to the soil. Water the crops with a liquid fertilizer once per week while they start to recover. If crops are severely damaged, remove them, add bone meal or rock phosphate to the bed, and plant new crops. In the long term, make sure to add compost and fertilizers at the start of each season.

EXCESS PHOSPHORUS

If organic fertilizer is applied too heavily or too frequently, the soil can end up with an overabundance of phosphorus. Excess phosphorus prevents crops from absorbing essential micronutrients.

Telltale signs: Plants will be stunted and will not grow.

Susceptible crops: Almost any garden plant, although it is an uncommon problem in most gardens.

What to do: Stop fertilizing. The excess phosphorus will eventually leach out of the soil. Remove severely damaged plants, and let the remaining crops use up the excess until they resume healthy growth habits.

LACK OF POTASSIUM

An uncommon problem for most gardens, a lack of potassium can occur in new garden soils that do not contain enough compost, or soils that have been planted for several years without receiving proper amendments.

Telltale signs: The outer edges of older leaves will start to turn yellow and will eventually die. Fruit will be unhealthy looking and/or stunted.

Susceptible crops: Almost any garden plant.

What to do: Add a fertilizer such as greensand, kelp, or wood ashes to the soil. Water with a liquid fertilizer once per week while the crops start to recover. If crops are severely damaged, remove them, add greensand, kelp, or wood ashes to the bed, and plant new crops. In the long term, make sure to add compost and fertilizers at the start of each season.

EXCESS POTASSIUM

If organic fertilizer is applied too heavily or too frequently, the soil may end up with an overabundance of potassium. Excess potassium salts prevent plants from absorbing other essential nutrients like calcium and magnesium.

Telltale signs: Plants will seem stunted and take on a yellow, blue, or gray color. Fruit may develop blossom-end rot, wherein the tip turns black or brown and quickly rots the entire fruit.

Susceptible crops: Young plants are very prone to this problem, as are maturing fruiting crops like squash and tomatoes.

What to do: Stop fertilizing. Increase watering cycles to remove some of the potassium. Remove severely damaged plants, and let the remaining crops use up the excess until they resume healthy growth habits.

LACK OF CALCIUM

Calcium is vital for the development of strong cell walls in plants, and it is especially important to fruiting crops. Soils can be naturally low in calcium, but it's also possible for the calcium to be in good supply in the soil but unavailable to your crops because of insufficient water, a shortage of potassium, or an excess of magnesium.

Telltale signs: Fruit may develop blossom-end rot, wherein the tip turns black or brown and quickly rots the entire fruit. Growing tips may die, and the plant will appear generally unhealthy and stunted.

Susceptible crops: Almost any garden plant.

What to do: Balanced organic fertilizer that contains bone meal is a good source of calcium and will also correct potassium deficiencies. Proper liming in acidic soils or gypsum application in alkaline soils will ensure adequate soil calcium (see chapter 4: Preparing Your

Soil for more information). If your soil is alkaline, you can use gypsum to increase calcium levels. Make sure plants are getting enough water (see chapter 7: Watering and Irrigation). To prevent magnesium overdoses, avoid using dolomite lime.

EXCESS CALCIUM

Very uncommon in organically managed gardens, excess calcium can inhibit plants' absorption of potassium and magnesium.

Telltale signs: Slow, unhealthy growth.

Susceptible crops: Any garden crop.

What to do: Stop fertilizing. Remove severely damaged plants, and let the remaining crops use up the excess until they resume healthy growth habits.

LACK OF MAGNESIUM

A lack of magnesium can occur in new garden soils that do not contain enough compost, or soils that have been planted for several years without receiving proper amendments. Uncommon in most gardens.

Telltale signs: Yellow color in leaves, first appearing in between leaf veins.

Susceptible crops: Almost any garden plant.

What to do: Kelp meal is a good source of magnesium and other soil micronutrients. You can also correct a magnesium deficiency with an application of dolomite lime.

EXCESS MAGNESIUM

Very uncommon in organically managed gardens, excess magnesium can cause nutrient imbalances in your plants.

Telltale signs: Slow, unhealthy growth.

Susceptible crops: Any garden crop.

What to do: Stop fertilizing. Remove severely damaged plants, and let the remaining crops use up the excess until they resume healthy growth habits. Avoid using dolomite lime.

OTHER NUTRIENT EXCESSES OR DEFICIENCIES

Garden soil can be lacking in any vital micronutrient, including sulfur, iron, boron, and zinc.

Telltale signs: Slow, unhealthy growth.

Susceptible crops: Any garden crop.

What to do: Supplying your garden with well-made balanced fertilizer and regular additions of compost should prevent most of these problems. Kelp meal and greensand are great sources of a wide variety of micronutrients.

INSECT PESTS

APHIDS

Aphids are tiny (most are less than ⅛ in. long) pear-shaped insects that suck sap from a variety of garden vegetables. They can range in color from black to green to red to blue.

Telltale signs: Aphids usually cluster on the underside of crop leaves. If you catch them early on, you may see only a few. They reproduce fast, though, so it's more likely you'll see a lot of them. Watch for yellowing, crinkly, and otherwise stunted leaves. If the aphids get out of control, the whole plant will be weakened and can die.

Crops they like: Almost anything, but especially Brassicas such as broccoli, Brussels sprouts, cabbage, and cauliflower. Also known for attacking nasturtiums.

What to do—culture: Pull off and compost individual leaves with large aphid populations. Pull out entire plants that are badly infected. Clean your garden well, and work the soil in between

BEAN LEAF BEETLES, MEXICAN BEAN BEETLES

These shiny green beetles have copper-brown wings and are about ¼ or ½ in. long.

Telltale signs: Bean leaf beetles feed from the underside of leaves, resulting in round holes in the leaves. Mexican bean beetles strip plants of vegetation and flowers; stems and leaves will appear skeletonized.

Crops they like: Bush beans, pole beans, other related legumes.

What to do—culture: Rotate crops each season. Plant flowers to attract beneficial insects as predators. Remove all plant residues at the end of the season.

What to do—direct action: Handpicking beetles can be very effective.

CABBAGE LOOPERS, IMPORTED CABBAGEWORMS

These are two of several caterpillars that love to chew holes in the leaves of your Brassicas. Loopers are about 1½ in. long and greenish in color; cabbageworms are about 1¼ in. long and paler green, with a yellow stripe down their back.

Telltale signs: Look for holes in the leaves of your crops, and for *frass* (small greenish mounds of fecal matter). You'll often see the moths of these

plantings to kill eggs. Encourage aphid predators by including flowers in your garden and landscape.

What to do—direct action: Make a spray of 1½ cups of rubbing alcohol, 2½ cups of water, and 1 tablespoon of natural liquid dish soap. Spray the underside of aphid-infested leaves in the early morning or evening (the soap can be mildly toxic to the leaves if sprayed during the sunniest parts of the day). If you can stomach it, use your fingers to crush the aphids while you're spraying.

ABOVE TOP: Aphids reproduce rapidly and can overwhelm plants in a matter of days. ABOVE: Black aphids on the underside of a nasturtium leaf. RIGHT: Cabbage loopers and imported cabbage worms eat many round holes in all types of Brassica plants. Shown here: red cabbage.

caterpillars flying around the garden (the white ones produce cabbageworms; dark brown ones with silver markings in the center of their wings produce loopers).

Crops they like: Bok choy, broccoli, cabbage, cauliflower, kale, kohlrabi, radish, turnips.

What to do—culture: Encourage beneficial insects by including flowers in your garden and landscape.

What to do—direct action: If your garden is small, you can handpick the worms off of each plant and crush them. Do this twice a week, and be sure to check all the leaves. Another approach is to use Bt, a bacterium that attacks the intestinal tract of the caterpillars; it's available online and at many nurseries. Mix it in a hand sprayer as directed on the package, and spray once a week. Spinosad is another organic, bacterially based insecticide that is very effective against these pests.

ABOVE: Colorado potato beetle.

COLORADO POTATO BEETLES

These ravenous ½ in. yellow beetles with thin black stripes can devour entire plants and are active eaters as both larvae and adults. They overwinter in the soil and hatch once soil temperature hits 50°F.

Telltale signs: Plants may be completely stripped of vegetation. Look for black *frass* on damaged plants.

Crops they like: Eggplant, peppers, potatoes, tomatoes.

What to do—culture: Rotate your solanaceous crops each season. (Solanaceous crops are those in the Nightshade family—the scientific name for the family is *Solanaceae*. This plant family includes: eggplant, peppers, potatoes, and tomatoes, as well as some poisonous wild plants and other non-vegetable crops such as tobacco.) Heavy mulch on garden beds can help prevent larvae from climbing onto your crops. Mix susceptible crops with plants the pests do not like, such as beans, cilantro, garlic, and marigolds. Plant flowers to attract beneficial insects as predators.

What to do—direct action: Spray Bt if necessary.

CORN BORERS

These caterpillars are well-known pests in regions east of the Rocky Mountains. Fortunately, they are principally attracted to corn and will not spread to unrelated crops.

Telltale signs: Damage appears as "shot holes," numerous tiny ragged holes, in the leaves of the plant.

Crops they like: Corn.

What to do—culture: Keep the garden well weeded, and till the soil between plantings to destroy eggs. Include flowers in your garden and landscape to attract caterpillar predators.

What to do—direct action: Spray Bt if necessary.

CUCUMBER BEETLES: BANDED, STRIPED, AND SPOTTED

These related species of beetles are easy to identify by their coloration and markings. The striped beetle is about ¼ in. long, yellow with thick black stripes running from the head to the bottom. The similar-sized spotted beetle is green with a series of black spots. Banded beetles will appear green or yellow, with black bands running sideways across the wingspan.

Telltale signs: The larvae go after newly planted seeds and young transplants, sometimes killing seeds before seedlings even emerge from the soil. Larger plants may be completely stripped of vegetation, with holes in leaves and/or fruit. Bites may introduce squash mosaic virus or bacterial wilt to your plants.

Crops they like: Primarily cucumbers and summer and winter squash, but also corn, tomatoes, and a variety of other crops.

What to do—culture: Rotate crops each season. Heavy mulch on garden beds can help prevent larvae from climbing onto your crops. Plant flowers to attract beneficial insects as predators. Remove all plant residues at the end of the season.

ABOVE: Cutworms crawl through the soil and cut down plants by biting stems at soil level.

What to do—direct action: Pyrethrum and neem-based organic sprays are effective on cucumber beetles.

CUTWORMS

"Cutworms" is a catchall term for caterpillars that crawl along the soil's surface and eat through the stems of young transplants and seedlings. They can be gray, green, black, brown, white, or red; they're usually about 1½ in. long.

Telltale signs: Look for transplants and seedlings that have been chopped off at the soil's surface. The plant will often be lying untouched next to the severed stem.

Crops they like: Cutworms will attack almost any young seedling in the garden.

What to do—culture: Keep the garden well weeded, and till the soil between plantings to destroy eggs. Include flowers in your garden and landscape to attract caterpillar predators. You can make collars for your plants to protect the stem from the worms: Use cardboard tubes from toilet paper rolls, or cut old round plastic plant pots to make 3 in. high rings, and push them 1 in. into the ground around plants.

What to do—direct action: Not necessary if you take the above steps.

FLEA BEETLES

There are a number of types of flea beetles, but they all behave similarly in the garden. They're small (most are under $\frac{1}{10}$ in.), hard bodied, and range from black to blue to green. They're very active and can jump like crazy, so most of the time all you'll see of them is a haze around susceptible crops.

Telltale signs: Leaves of crops under attack will be riddled with tiny holes. A healthy plant can weather an attack if it isn't too bad, but most

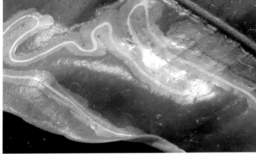

of the time you'll need to give the plant some assistance.

Crops they like: Different types of flea beetles attack different crops. The most common targets are beets, eggplant, peppers, potatoes, radishes, spinach, tomatoes, turnips, and all the Brassicas.

What to do—culture: Disturb the soil shallowly around plants to destroy eggs. Flea beetles feed during hot, dry periods of the day, so occasionally misting the plants will slow them down. Interplanting beneficial flowers in the garden will help deter them.

What to do—direct action: Flea beetles are very

ABOVE TOP: Flea beetles eat thousands of tiny holes in the leaves of plants. Shown here: a tomato leaf. ABOVE: Leaf miner damage to a citrus leaf *(photo by David Haviland, UCCE).*

difficult to control with sprays. If the above methods don't stop them, build a floating row cover (see chapter 12: Essential Garden Skills) to keep them off of susceptible crops.

JAPANESE BEETLES

These shiny green beetles have copper-brown wings and are about ¼ to ½ in. long. They are often seen in large clusters, attacking plants in groups.

Telltale signs: Plants may be completely stripped of vegetation and flowers. Stems and leaves will appear skeletonized.

Crops they like: Just about everything.

What to do—culture: Rotate crops each season. Heavy mulch on garden beds may help prevent larvae from climbing onto your crops. Plant flowers to attract beneficial insects as predators. Remove all plant residues at the end of the season.

What to do—direct action: Handpicking beetles can be very effective.

LEAF MINERS

Leaf miners are green, wormlike maggots, the larval stage of a small fly. They burrow inside individual leaves and proceed to eat tunnels through them.

Telltale signs: Watch for yellowing leaves and squiggling lines on the leaf surface. Eggs appear as small white clusters on the underside of leaves.

Crops they like: Beets, cabbage, chard, peppers, potatoes, spinach.

What to do—culture: Destroy any eggs you see on the underside of leaves. Work the soil between plantings to destroy eggs. As with any fly larvae, using floating row covers to block out the flies is an excellent option (see chapter 12: Essential Garden Skills).

What to do—direct action: Sprays are usually ineffective on leaf miners once they've burrowed into the leaf. Go with cultural control!

PARASITIC NEMATODES

Nematodes are microscopic roundworms that cruise around in the soil and feed on the roots of many garden vegetables. There are a number of different types; root knot nematodes are the most common.

Telltale signs: Plants may be stunted, wilt (even when the soil is adequately moist), turn yellow, and possibly die. Roots will be knobby and deformed.

Crops they like: Almost any garden vegetable is susceptible to different types of nematodes.

What to do—culture: Nematodes can be one of the most difficult garden pests to control, as most organic pesticides aren't highly effective on them. Rotate your crops. Interplant French and African marigolds to discourage them. If you have a nematode infestation, growing and turning in a cover crop of rye will reduce their population.

What to do—direct action: Check the Resources section for retailers of organic nematicides.

ROOT APHIDS

These are aphids that attack the roots of your plants as opposed to the leaves. They look just like the aphids described above, but you won't notice they're around until you see your crops looking wilted even when the soil is moist. Pull up the plant and check the roots for the aphids.

RIGHT: Root maggots have eaten all of the roots from this broccoli plant, leaving it unable to absorb water or nutrients from the soil.

Crops they like: Lettuce is the most common, but they can also go for beans, carrots, corn, and parsley.

What to do: Pull and compost infested plants. Work the soil deeply, and allow it to dry out between plantings. Rotate the space to a new crop for the next planting, especially for lettuce.

ROOT MAGGOTS, CARROT RUST FLY

There are a number of different types of root maggots, and all are the larval form of an insect similar to houseflies. The fly lays its eggs around the base of the host plant. The eggs hatch, and the approximately 1/3 in. long grayish-white grubs crawl down to the roots and start eating. Carrot rust fly is a different genus from other root maggots, but you control it using the same methods.

Telltale signs: Watch for plants wilting even

when the soil is adequately moist. Pulling up an infected plant will reveal the larvae crawling around in the roots. You may notice tunneling on root crops such as radishes. Carrots under attack from carrot rust fly larvae will have brownish-tinted tunnels on their outer surface.

Crops they like: Onions, leeks, and Brassicas are the most common hosts. Carrot rust flies go for carrots, celeriac, celery, dill, fennel, and parsley.

What to do—culture: Exclusion is the best way to keep root maggots and carrot rust flies off your crops. A 1 in. deep mulching of sawdust 6 in. in diameter will prevent the flies from laying their eggs. Also, a floating row cover will exclude flies completely from crops (see chapter 12: Essential Garden Skills).

What to do—direct action: Once root maggots have found their way to your crops' roots, there's not much you can do except pull out the affected plants and work the soil to expose the maggots to the air.

SLUGS, SNAILS

These slimy pests aren't really insects—they're mollusks ranging from ½ in. to several inches long—but their creepy-crawly nature encouraged us to lump them in the insect section. A slug has a soft body, two sets of tentacles on its head, and a foot that runs the length of its body. Snails have the same body structure and are encased in a characteristic spiral shell.

Telltale signs: Look for jagged holes in the foliage of older plants; younger transplants and newly emerged seedlings may be completely consumed except for the stem. Dried slime trails on the plant's leaves are a good indicator.

Crops they like: Slugs particularly love Brassicas, chard, lettuce, peas, spinach, and carrots but will eat almost anything.

What to do—culture: Keeping the garden clear of fallen leaves and debris minimizes slug habitat. Avoid the use of mulch in the spring and fall for the same reason.

What to do—direct action: A number of organic slug baits have recently come out on the market. Look for one that has the Organic Materials Review Institute (OMRI) seal on the label at nurseries, or order it online. All you need to do is sprinkle it around your plants once or twice a week. But as with any pesticide (even organic ones!), use it only as necessary, to prevent the development of resistance. We've found a few weekly applications in the spring and fall go a long way toward keeping slugs under control. Another option is dusting around your plants with diatomaceous earth. This fossilized shell material can be hard to find but is available at some nurseries. It should be reapplied after rain showers. Also, use caution to avoid breathing the dust.

ABOVE: A series of small, smooth-edged holes in your crops may be the work of slugs or snails. Shown here: bok choy.

SPIDER MITES

Spider mites are among the most common garden pests, but fortunately they are also among the easiest to identify. Members of the arachnid family, they are related to the spiders from which they take their name. They are very small and look like a cluster of tiny dots, often on the underside of leaves.

Telltale signs: Leaves or affected fruits will have a stippling of dots as a result of the mites sucking juices from the plant tissue. Severely damaged leaves may turn yellow and fall off the plant. Spider mites are given away by the webbing, similar to tiny spider webs, that they leave on the plants.

Crops they like: Almost any vegetable.

What to do—culture: Keep the garden well watered, since spider mites thrive in dry, dusty conditions. Include flowers in your garden and landscape to attract predatory insects.

What to do—direct action: Spray the plants with a hard spray of water or an insecticidal soap spray made of 1½ cups of rubbing alcohol, 2½ cups of water, and 1 tablespoon of natural liquid dish soap. Spray the infested areas in the early morning or evening (the soap can be mildly toxic to the leaves if sprayed during the sunniest parts of the day). If possible, use your fingers to crush the mites while you're spraying.

SQUASH BUGS

These dark-brown bugs are about ⅝ in. long and have flat backs, long legs, and antennae. They use their piercing mouthparts not only to suck sap out of your vegetables, but also to inject a toxic digestive juice that kills plant tissue.

Telltale signs: Look for wilted leaves that eventually blacken and die. You may see golden or reddish-brown eggs on the underside of leaves along the center vein.

Crops they like: Cucumbers, pumpkins, summer and winter squash.

What to do—culture: Keep the garden clear of dead leaves and stems of host plants. Rotate your crops. Marigolds, nasturtiums, and radishes interplanted in the garden help repel squash bugs. Floating row cover excludes the bugs from young plants (remove the cover before plants flower).

What to do—direct action: A spray made of 1 tablespoon of natural dish soap mixed with a quart of water will kill squash bugs.

SQUASH VINE BORERS

These caterpillars are well-known pests in regions east of the Rocky Mountains. Fortunately, each type is attracted to a particular plant family and will not spread to unrelated crops. Unfortunately, they can severely damage and kill otherwise healthy plants.

Telltale signs: Squash borers can be hard to detect until damage has already been done. They enter the plant near the base and eat the inside of the stem, until the plant can no longer absorb water and nutrients from the soil. The stem will appear mushy and may have piles of yellow or green "frass" surrounding it.

Crops they like: Beans, potatoes, squash.

What to do—culture: Keep the garden well weeded, and till the soil between plantings to destroy eggs. Include flowers in your garden and landscape to attract caterpillar predators. Try broadcasting diatomaceous earth around the base of each plant when you plant it to prevent squash vine borers from reaching the plant (reapply after rain), or cover the whole plant at planting time with a floating row cover to exclude the moth parents of the caterpillars (see chapter 12: Essential Garden Skills for more information).

What to do—direct action: Once squash vine borers have burrowed into the stem, they're very difficult to control, so preventive action is best!

STINKBUGS

These small bugs are typically brown, yellow, green, or a combination of these colors. They are less than 1 in. long and have an easily recognizable, angular, shieldlike shape. They use their piercing mouthparts to suck sap out of vegetables and inject a toxic digestive juice that can rot fruit and stop fruit development. The bugs get their name from a noticeable smell they give off as a defense mechanism.

Telltale signs: Look for stunted, undeveloped fruit with white-yellow spots and streaks.

Crops they like: Tomatoes, beans, summer and winter squash, most fruiting crops.

What to do—culture: Plant a variety of flowers to attract beneficial insects to the garden. Cover plants with floating row cover to exclude

ABOVE: **A common stinkbug variety known as Brown marmorated** *(photo © iStockPhoto).*

the bugs once flowers have been pollinated and fruit has started to develop.

What to do—direct action: Handpick and destroy bugs when possible.

TOMATO HORNWORMS

This large (up to 4 in. long) green caterpillar has diagonal white stripes along its sides and a small horn on the front of its head (like the unicorn of insects). Tomato hornworms have a black tail; tobacco hornworms have a red one. The adult form (a moth) is dark gray or brown and is easily camouflaged on trees and shrubs.

Telltale signs: Damage to leaves usually begins at the edges; entire leaf margins and full leaves may be consumed.

Crops they like: Eggplant, peppers, potatoes, tomatoes.

What to do—culture: Rotate your crops. Plant marigolds to help repel them, and beneficial-attracting flowers to invite predatory wasps. Floating row covers keep the moths from laying eggs on young plants (remove the covers before plants flower).

What to do—direct action: Caterpillars can be sprayed with organic controls like Bt or spinosad, but only as a last resort.

ANIMAL PESTS

CATS

Wandering neighborhood cats (or your own) will occasionally use the open soil in a newly planted garden as a litter box. This will usually stop as the plants size up and fill in the garden.

Telltale signs: Cat feces and paw prints.

What to do: To discourage cats, you can cover your newly planted garden with black poly netting or polyester row cover.

CROWS, OTHER BIRDS

Generally speaking, birds are a minimal problem for most gardeners. If birds do frequent your vegetable beds, they're likely to go for newly planted seeds, ripening fruit (from trees and berry bushes), and sweet corn. They are principally attracted to fruiting crops, and the sweeter the crop, the higher the chance of a bird attack. Crows will occasionally land in your garden and wreak havoc by playing roughly with new transplants, but this is usually a one-time, random occurrence.

Telltale signs: Look for uprooted vegetable transplants, disturbed seed rows, small holes pecked in ripe tomatoes and other fruit, and general mayhem.

What to do: Scarecrows don't do much to keep birds at bay, but a frequent human presence in the garden will discourage them. Use lightweight netting to protect fruit and newly seeded areas. A floating row cover will also protect sensitive crops from birds.

DEER

If these four-legged creatures live in your area, they'll definitely find their way into your garden and eat your crops. For those of us in strictly urban environments, deer are generally not a problem; deer pressure increases as you move from city centers toward suburban and rural environments.

Telltale signs: Look for jagged bites out of your plants. Check for small, rounded fecal matter and large, two-toed tracks in the garden.

What to do: A 6–8 ft. high fence around your garden perimeter will exclude deer and is the best solution in areas with large deer populations. If that's too expensive or problematic, hot-pepper sprays will make crops unpalatable to deer. Try mixing ½ tablespoon of Tabasco sauce with a quart of water and spraying it on your plants. Commercial scent repellents can also be effective in discouraging deer; check the Resources section for retailers.

DOGS

Dogs?! Yes, our furry friends can sometimes become pests in our vegetable gardens, due to their affinity for running around the yard with wild abandon. Fortunately, they're pretty easy to keep under control.

Telltale signs: Look for paw prints, disturbed seedlings, larger plants that are knocked over, and other general chaos.

What to do: Depending on the size of the dog in question, a short to medium (2–5 ft. high) fence will keep dogs at bay.

ABOVE: Ripe strawberries are safe under a layer of bird netting.

MOLES, VOLES

Moles and voles are often confused and/or taken for the same critter by frustrated gardeners. Moles are larger, burrowing mammals that have no interest in eating your garden plants. They actually eat insects, but they can become a problem when they dig large burrows right through your garden bed. Mouselike voles, on the other hand (think "Voles eat Vegetables"), are known to eat just about any plant in sight and will actually consume your garden crops, as well as dig tunnels through the area.

Telltale signs: Moles make large burrows and fewer, larger mounds of soil that disturb your beds. The mounds will appear in random spots. Voles produce many, smaller mounds all over and will actually consume the roots and bases of your crops.

What to do: Water the area around the garden with a castor oil mixture, as castor oil's smell is thought to repel both voles and moles. Add 2 tablespoons of castor oil and 1 drop of dishwashing liquid to 1 gal. of warm water, and stir well to prevent settling. Water the affected area with this solution until saturated. If possible, apply the mixture in dry weather. Reapply as needed (every two or three weeks to keep pests at bay, or after heavy rain). For voles, set rat traps baited with peanut butter at burrow entrances. However, to avoid dangers to children and non-target species, place any trap in a *bait station*— simply a small cardboard box with a hole cut at either end. If mole or vole problems are anticipated, try sealing the bottom of your wood-framed raised bed with a floor of hardware cloth during construction.

RACCOONS

These critters are prevalent all over the country. They have a reputation as garden marauders but are typically not much of a problem unless you're growing sweet corn. Occasionally, a frenzied raccoon may tear up a new patch of transplants or seedlings.

Telltale signs: Look for their tracks in the garden. If you grow corn, look for plants bent over with eaten ears.

What to do: Sprinkle baby powder or ground chili powder on ears of corn to discourage feeding. Draping corn plants with plastic netting can also help.

RATS, MICE

These rodents are usually active at night, so you won't see them during the day unless you've got a bad infestation. They live in underground burrows or in any sheltered crevice they can find. Rats tend to be a big problem in cities and are less so in suburban areas.

Telltale signs: Rats and mice will dig up and eat newly planted seeds (especially from large seeded crops like beans, peas, and corn), snack

ABOVE: Bites out of your ripe fruit may be a sign of rats or mice in the garden. Shown here: a tomato.

on young transplants, and steal bites out of fruiting crops and root crops (beets, potatoes, pumpkins, summer and winter squash, tomatoes, and turnips).

What to do: Rats and mice are very intelligent animals, and you may need to resort to a variety of techniques to deal with them. Begin by keeping your garden clear of food sources such as dropped tomatoes and overripe fruit. Also be mindful of attractants such as unsecured garbage cans and poorly managed compost piles. For direct action, rotating the following control methods is a good idea:

1. Snap traps baited with peanut butter work well for a low-pressure situation.
2. As an alternative to poison, try setting out a bowl of equal parts cornmeal and cement.
3. Commercial rat poison, while toxic, is sometimes the most effective way to get rid of rats. Poison should *not* be placed directly in the garden: Make sure to use a bait station, to keep kids and pets away and prevent poison from spilling from the trap. (See the entry on moles and voles.)
4. If you can't get a bad rat problem under control on your own, contact an exterminator.

Rats habitually travel along straight, sheltered corridors, so setting traps or poison along these routes will increase your chances of success.

WOODCHUCKS, GROUNDHOGS

One of the most notorious of all garden pests, the woodchuck (also called groundhog) has driven many a gardener to drink. These crafty mammals set up extensive underground burrows and dig into nearby gardens. Groundhogs hibernate all winter in their burrow, mate in the spring, and .raise a litter of three to five through the summer.

When not raising young, only one groundhog will live in each burrow.

Telltale signs: Groundhogs will eat most any garden vegetable. The burrow is often set up in an open grassy site and has one main entrance with a mound of excavated soil around its perimeter. There will be several more hidden entrances in the area to provide quick escape routes when the animal gets in trouble. Look for large bites taken from randomly selected fruiting crops, leafy greens, and root crops.

What to do: If you suspect that groundhogs are in your area, build a fence around the perimeter of the garden. Fencing should be 3–4 ft. high, since groundhogs can climb over short fences, and buried at least 12 in. deep, to prevent them from burrowing under. If possible, bend the bottom of the buried portion at a 90° angle pointing away from the garden area. It is possible to live-trap groundhogs, but relocation of wildlife can cause numerous problems (angry neighbors, damage to natural areas, stress to the animal) and is not advised.

DISEASES

Your best defense against any vegetable crop disease is to maintain healthy soil and healthy plants. If you've added sufficient compost to your soil and you fertilize properly, your plants are already ahead of the game in terms of disease control. Other crucial preventive actions include rotating your crops; spacing your plants properly to promote air circulation; and using drip or sprinkler irrigation only in the morning, to minimize leaf wetness. That being said, pest and disease problems will likely be worst in a newly built garden, since the soil may not have bred a large population of beneficial soil fungi and microorganisms yet. Don't let diseases discourage you: Do your best to control them, keep adding good compost, and try again next year.

Here are some particulars:

ALTERNARIA, EARLY BLIGHT

Alternaria is a fungus that causes foliar damage in vegetable crops. Different species of the fungus affect different crops. Look for small black dots on leaves that turn into brown lesions with concentric circles, and that eventually cause yellowing and and the death of entire leaves.

Crops it likes: Brassicas and tomatoes. Early blight, caused by *Alternaria solani* and *Alternaria tomatophila*, is one of the main problems for tomato growers in the Northeast and Midwest.

What to do: Cultural controls are your best option for controlling Alternaria. Maintain healthy soil and use organic fertilizers to promote healthy

plant growth. Rotate crops each year, use drip irrigation to help minimize leaf wetness, use mulch to prevent spores from splashing from the soil onto the plant, and provide adequate spacing between plants to maximize air circulation. Organic copper-based fungicides and compost tea will help control Alternaria, especially if used preventively.

ANTHRACNOSE

This fungal disease can attack a wide range of plants, and the damage can affect leaves, stems, and fruit. Fruit may develop brown, waterlogged spots that eventually turn black. Leaves and stems may develop yellow and brown spots with ragged holes.

Crops it likes: Tomatoes, melons, squash.

What to do—culture: Make sure to space plants properly to ensure proper air circulation. Rotate crops. Avoid sprinkler irrigation. Choose resistant varieties when possible.

What to do—direct action: Remove affected leaves and fruits from plants. Remove entire plant if disease continues to spread. Remove all plant debris at the end of the season.

BLACK ROT

Black rot is a fungal disease that likes high humidity and wet leaves. It creates characteristic black markings on the fruit of winter squash, and can also appear as brown, mushy spotting on leaves and brown cankers that exude black mush on plant stems (also called gummy stem blight).

Crops it likes: Cucumbers, pumpkins, winter squash.

What to do: Remove affected leaves from plants (or entire plants if necessary), and burn them or put them in your yard-waste bin. This will slow the spread of the disease. Keep your garden clear of dropped foliage. Using crop rotation and working the soil in between plantings will help you beat the disease in the future. Minimizing leaf wetness by using drip irrigation also helps reduce the threat of this disease.

CLUBROOT

Clubroot is a disease that causes deformation of Brassica roots. The roots are eventually unable to absorb water and nutrients, so the plant yellows and wilts, and growth is severely stunted. Clubroot is usually identifiable only by pulling out the plant and checking the roots for distorted galls. (A gall is an abnormal roundish or bumpy outgrowth, usually caused by a fungus, bacteria, virus, or parasite.)

Crops it likes: Broccoli, Brussels sprouts, cabbage, cauliflower.

What to do: Remove affected plants and burn them or put them in your yard-waste bin. Avoid planting Brassicas in the area for 7 years.

DAMPING OFF

"Damping off" refers to several different fungal diseases that attack the stems of young seedlings. If you see seedlings fall over and die soon after emerging, and the stem appears black or brownish and rotting, suspect damping off.

Crops it likes: Any seedling.

What to do: Water as minimally as possible; allowing the soil to dry at the surface between waterings will help kill the fungus. Cultivate the soil around affected plants, and sterilize tools with a 1:10 bleach solution afterward. Adding fresh compost every year helps maintain high levels of beneficial microorganisms that are antagonistic to damping off fungi. Avoid working in the garden when the soil is wet. If you're growing your own seedlings in contain-

ers, train a fan on them on its lowest setting to promote air circulation. Be sure to wash containers between seedings, and use a high-quality germination mix. To take direct action against damping off, spray chamomile tea on the plants. Also, try a one-time dusting of cinnamon around seedlings.

ABOVE TOP: A healthy cabbage root on the left vs. one infected with clubroot on the right *(photo courtesy of LS Plant Breeding).* ABOVE: Wet conditions can lead to damping off, a fungus that rots the plant stem near soil level.

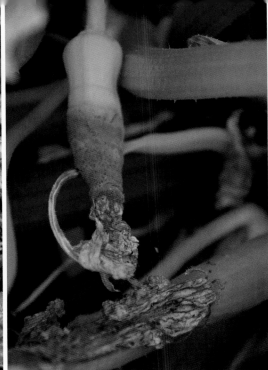

DOWNY MILDEW

Downy mildew is caused by a funguslike mold. It first shows up as light-green lesions on plant leaves. These eventually develop into characteristic brownish papery spots. Downy mildew stunts growth and decreases productivity, and eventually encourages the growth of parasitic bacteria and fungi.

Crops it likes: Beets, chard, and spinach are its main targets. It can also affect broccoli, cucumbers, lettuce, and summer and winter squash.

What to do: Rotate your crops. Remove affected leaves from plants and burn them or put them in your yard-waste bin. Pull entire plants if all the leaves are mildewed. Clean up dropped foliage, and work the soil in between plantings. If you irrigate with a sprinkler, do it in the morning so plant leaves can dry during the day. For direct action against downy mildew, spray affected crops with a mixture of ¼ cup of milk and about a quart of water.

GRAY MOLD

Gray mold is a fungal disease that proliferates in cool, damp conditions in the spring and fall. Look for gray, fuzzy growth that sends a small cloud of spores into the air when touched. Affected leaves and stems eventually brown out, get mushy, and die.

Crops it likes: Mainly tomatoes, green beans, and the fruit of strawberries, raspberries, and blueberries.

What to do: Rotate your crops. Prune tomatoes and fruit properly to improve air circulation. If

ABOVE: Downy mildew on rainbow chard.

ABOVE RIGHT: Gray mold can show up and quickly rot many different crops. Shown here: summer squash.

you irrigate with a sprinkler, do it in the morning so leaves can dry during the day. Remove affected leaves, stems, and buds from plants and burn them or put them in your yard-waste bin. If the infestation is bad, remove the whole plant and do the same. To take direct action, try spraying an organic copper-based fungicide.

LATE BLIGHT

Late blight is caused by the fungal-like pathogen *Phytopthora infestans*, and can cause serious problems for tomatoes and potatoes. Watch for brown lesions on the stems and leaves of these plants. Leaf lesions spread rapidly and cause the whole leaf to die. Other fungi in the *Phytopthora* genus can be responsible for root and stem rot (see other entries in this section for more information).

Crops it likes: Tomatoes, potatoes.

What to do: Culture, culture, culture! Healthy soil, minimizing leaf wetness with drip irrigation, and good air circulation help keep this disease under control. If it shows up, remove plants as soon as possible and clean up any dropped fruit, leaves, or foliage. Burn or professionally compost the debris. Work the soil to help break down remaining roots (this will help prevent the disease from showing up next year). Organic copper-based fungicides and compost tea can keep the disease from infecting plants, but they must be used preventively.

POWDERY MILDEW

Powdery mildew is caused by a fungus, and differs from downy mildew in that it can proliferate in hot, dry conditions. It's recognizable by a white powdery growth of spores on leaf surfaces, followed by yellowing and dying of leaves.

Crops it likes: Cucumbers, peas, summer and winter squash.

What to do: Rotate your crops. Choose varieties that are resistant to powdery mildew. Maintain adequate spacing between plants. Remove affected leaves from plants and compost them; pull entire plants if all the leaves are mildewed. Clean up dropped foliage, and work the soil in between plantings. To take direct action against powdery mildew, spray affected crops with a mixture of ¼ cup of milk and 1 quart of water.

ROOT ROT

Root rot is a general term to describe root diseases caused by fungi. Some people refer to damping off as root rot. If your plants appear stressed and generally unhealthy and the soil is heavy and wet, suspect root rot.

Crops it likes: Not crop specific. Often shows up in container gardens with improper drainage, and in poorly drained soils.

What to do: Maintain high-quality organic soil

ABOVE: Powdery mildew coats plants in a white or gray dust. Shown here: summer squash.

using methods described in chapter 4: Preparing Your Soil. Work soil deeply in between plantings. Check to see that containers are properly drained.

RUST

Rust is a term for a broad family of fungal diseases. Relatively easy to identify, the plants will actually appear rusty, and will be covered with orange specks and bumps.

Crops it likes: Fortunately, rusts are relatively specific to certain plant families, so it may not spread across the entire garden. Some species will attack chives, garlic, onions, or leeks, and others will attack beans or squash plants.

What to do: When possible, cut off rust-covered stems and leaves. In more serious cases, spray the plant with neem oil once every seven days until signs of rust are gone.

SCAB

Scab is a bacterial disease that causes corky, cracked lesions on the surface of potatoes.

Crops it likes: Beets, carrots, parsnips, radishes, and turnips can be carriers in addition to potatoes, so they should be avoided in the same area when rotating crops.

What to do: The best defense against scab is to choose potato varieties that are resistant to it. Avoid planting carrier crops in affected soil for 4 years.

STEM ROT

This is a general term that can refer to any number of fungal or bacterial diseases that cause a plant stem to become infected (often the same fungi that cause black rot and white mold). Look for lesions, rot, and general nastiness on your plants' stems.

Crops it likes: Can affect any number of young vegetable plants.

What to do: As always, cultural control is best: Maintain healthy soil, minimize leaf wetness, adequately space plants to ensure good air circulation.

WHITE MOLD

White mold is another fungal disease that loves cool, wet conditions. Infection starts as mushy, water-soaked lesions and progresses to a white

ABOVE: Verticillium wilt can make plants look droopy, as if they are underwatered. Shown here: eggplant.

fuzzy growth on stems and leaves. In lettuce, the entire plant wilts but the leaves remain attached to the plant.

Crops it likes: Beans, carrots, eggplant, lettuce, peppers, tomatoes, and Brassicas.

What to do: Maintain adequate spacing between plants. Prune tomatoes to maintain good ventilation. Avoid overwatering. Keep the garden well weeded. Remove affected plants and burn them or put them in your yard-waste bin.

WILTS: FUSARIUM AND VERTICILLIUM

These wilts are fungal diseases that first appear as a general yellowing/browning of leaves on a plant, followed by a wilted, dying appearance. The plant eventually dies.

Crops it likes: Verticillium wilt is a classic eggplant disease. It occasionally also affects tomatoes, peppers, and potatoes. Fusarium wilt affects tomatoes, peppers, and potatoes, as well as basil.

What to do: Rotate your crops! If you see signs of these wilts, don't plant susceptible crops in the same space for 8–10 years. If the infection is minor, you may get away with moving crops a short distance (to the next bed over, for example). But if the infection is severe and recurs each year, you may have to forgo growing affected crops in your garden for the full 10-year period (try growing them in containers in potting soil instead).

REFERENCE TABLES

SUCCESSION PLANTING

You can determine your last planting date for a given crop by adding or subtracting weeks from your first frost date. For example, if your first frost date is October 15, your date for transplanting your last cabbage is approximately July 15 (12 weeks or 3 months before your last frost date). Once you've done your calculations, fill in the right-hand column of this table for quick reference.

SUCCESSION PLANTING

CROPS	SUCCESSION SCHEDULE	RECOMMENDED LAST PLANTING DATE	MY LAST PLANTING DATE
ANNUAL VEGETABLES			
Arugula	every 2 weeks	4 weeks before 1st frost (direct-seed)	_____
Bean, bush	every 3 weeks	10 weeks before 1st frost (direct-seed)	_____
Bean, pole	1 planting only	N/A	_____
Bean, broad or fava	1 planting only	N/A	_____
Beet	every 3 weeks	12 weeks before 1st frost (direct-seed)	_____
Bok choy	every 2 weeks	6 weeks before 1st frost (direct-seed)	_____
Broccoli	every 2 weeks in spring and fall	12 weeks before 1st frost (transplant)	_____

OPPOSITE: Annual and perennial flowers will attract beneficial insects and beautify your garden.

SUCCESSION PLANTING (continued)

CROPS	SUCCESSION SCHEDULE	RECOMMENDED LAST PLANTING DATE	MY LAST PLANTING DATE
Brussels sprouts	1 planting only	N/A	_____
Cabbage	every 2 weeks in spring and fall	12 weeks before 1st frost (transplant)	_____
Carrot	every 3 weeks	12 weeks before 1st frost (direct-seed)	_____
Cauliflower	every 2 weeks in spring and fall	12 weeks before 1st frost (transplant)	_____
Celeriac	1 planting only	N/A	_____
Celery	1 planting only	N/A	_____
Chard	1 planting each in spring and fall	8 weeks before 1st frost (transplant)	_____
Collards	1 planting each in spring and fall	8 weeks before 1st frost (transplant)	_____
Corn	every 2 weeks	14 weeks before 1st frost (direct-seed)	_____
Cucumber, sprawling	1 planting only	N/A	_____
Cucumber, trellised	1 planting only	N/A	_____
Eggplant	1 planting only	N/A	_____
Fennel, annual	every 2 weeks	10 weeks before 1st frost (transplant)	_____
Garlic	1 planting only	N/A	_____
Kale	1 planting each in spring and fall	8 weeks before 1st frost (transplant)	_____
Kohlrabi	every 2 weeks in spring and fall	8 weeks before 1st frost (direct-seed or transplant)	_____
Leeks	1 planting	N/A	_____
Lettuce	every 2 weeks	6 weeks before 1st frost (direct-seed or transplant)	_____
Melons	1 planting	N/A	_____
Onions	1 planting only	N/A	_____
Peas, shell	every 3 weeks in spring	early summer (direct-seed)	_____
Peas, snap	1 planting only	N/A	_____
Peppers, hot and sweet	1 planting only	N/A	_____
Potato	1 planting only	N/A	_____
Pumpkin	1 planting only	N/A	_____

SUCCESSION PLANTING (continued)

CROPS	SUCCESSION SCHEDULE	RECOMMENDED LAST PLANTING DATE	MY LAST PLANTING DATE
Radish	every 2 weeks in spring and fall	4 weeks before 1st frost (direct-seed)	_____
Rutabaga	1 planting in fall	12 weeks before 1st frost (direct-seed)	_____
Scallion	every 2 weeks	6 weeks before 1st frost (direct-seed)	_____
Spinach	every 2 weeks in spring and fall	6 weeks before 1st frost (direct-seed)	_____
Squash, summer	every 4–5 weeks	14 weeks before 1st frost (transplant)	_____
Squash, winter	1 planting only	N/A	_____
Tomato	1 planting only	N/A	_____
Turnip	every 2 weeks in spring and fall	8 weeks before 1st frost (direct-seed)	_____
ANNUAL HERBS			
Basil	every 4 weeks	12 weeks before 1st frost (transplant)	_____
Cilantro	every 2 weeks	6 weeks before 1st frost (direct-seed)	_____
Dill	1 planting only	N/A	_____
Parsley	1 planting only	N/A	_____

PLANTING DATES

Determine your planting date for a given crop by adding or subtracting weeks from your last frost date. For example, if your last frost date is May 15, your date for transplanting your first cabbage is approximately May 1 (2 weeks before your last frost date). Calculate your planting dates, and fill in the relevant columns in the chart, below. NOTE: The planting dates are general guidelines and will work well for most gardeners. However, you may be able to fine-tune the dates for your particular climate, so don't hesitate to talk with other gardeners in your area to learn when they plant their crops.

PLANTING DATES

PLANT	SOWING INDOORS (IF GROWING YOUR OWN TRANS-PLANTS)	MY DATE IS:	TRANSPLANT-ING OUTSIDE	MY DATE IS:	DIRECT-SEEDING OUTSIDE	MY DATE IS:
ANNUAL VEGETABLES						
Arugula	6 wks. before last frost	———	2 wks. before last frost	———	4 wks. before last frost	———
Bean, bush	on last frost date	———	2 wks. after last frost	———	2 wks. after last frost	———
Bean, pole	on last frost date	———	2 wks. after last frost	———	2 wks. after last frost	———
Bean, broad or fava	not recommended	———	not recommended	———	10 wks. before last frost	———
Beet	not recommended	———	not recommended	———	on last frost date	———
Bok choy	2 wks. before last frost	———	2 wks. after last frost	———	2 wks. after last frost	———
Broccoli	4 wks. before last frost	———	on last frost date	———	2 wks. after last frost	———
Brussels sprouts	2 wks. before last frost	———	2 wks. after last frost	———	2 wks. after last frost	———
Cabbage	6 wks. before last frost	———	2 wks. before last frost	———	2 wks. before last frost	———
Cauliflower	4 wks. before last frost	———	on last frost date	———	2 wks. before last frost	———
Carrot	not recom-mended	———	not recommended	———	on last frost date	———
Celeriac	8 wks. before last frost	———	2 wks. after last frost	———	2 wks. before last frost	———

PLANTING DATES (continued)

PLANT	SOWING INDOORS (IF GROWING YOUR OWN TRANS-PLANTS)	MY DATE IS:	TRANSPLANT-ING OUTSIDE	MY DATE IS:	DIRECT-SEEDING OUTSIDE	MY DATE IS:
Celery	8 wks. before last frost	———	2 wks. after last frost	———	2 wks. before last frost	———
Chard	4 wks. before last frost	———	on last frost date	———	on last frost date	———
Corn	2 wks. before last frost	———	2 wks. after last frost	———	2 wks. after last frost	———
Collards	6 wks. before last frost	———	2 wks. before last frost	———	4 wks. before last frost	———
Cucumber, sprawling	on last frost date	———	4 wks. after last frost	———	3–4 wks. after last frost	———
Cucumber, trellised	on last frost date	———	4 wks. after last frost	———	3–4 wks. after last frost	———
Eggplant	4 wks. before last frost	———	4 wks. after last frost	———	not recom-mended	———
Fennel, annual	6 wks. before last frost	———	2 wks. before last frost	———	on last frost date	———
Garlic	N/A	———	N/A	———	4–6 wks.before first frost of fall	———
Kale	6 wks. before last frost	———	2 wks. before last frost	———	4 wks. before last frost	———
Kohlrabi	6 wks. before last frost	———	2 wks. before last frost	———	2 wks. before last frost	———
Leek	8 wks. before last frost	———	on last frost date	———	4 wks. before last frost	———
Lettuce, head	6 wks. before last frost	———	2 wks. before last frost	———	4 wks. before last frost	———
Melons	2 wks. before last frost	———	2 wks. after last frost	———	2 wks. after last frost	———
Onion	10 wks. before last frost	———	2 wks. before last frost	———	6 wks. before last frost	———
Peas, shell	8 wks. before last frost	———	4 wks. before last frost	———	as early as soil can be worked	———
Peas, snap	8 wks. before last frost	———	4 wks. before last frost	———	as early as soil can be worked	———
Peppers, hot and sweet	8 wks. before last frost	———	2 wks. after last frost	———	not recommended	———

PLANT	SOWING INDOORS (IF GROWING YOUR OWN TRANS-PLANTS)	MY DATE IS:	TRANSPLANT-ING OUTSIDE	MY DATE IS:	DIRECT-SEEDING OUTSIDE	MY DATE IS:
Potato	N/A	_____	N/A	_____	4 wks. before last frost	_____
Radish	not recommended	_____	not recommended	_____	4 wks. before last frost	_____
Rutabaga	N/A	_____	N/A	_____	4 mos. before first frost	_____
Scallion	up to 10 wks. before last frost	_____	up to 6 wks. before last frost	_____	up to 6 wks. before last frost	_____
Spinach	8 wks. before last frost	_____	4 wks. before last frost	_____	as early as soil can be worked	_____
Squash, summer	2 wks. before last frost	_____	2 wks. after last frost	_____	2 wks. after last frost	_____
Squash, winter	2 wks. before last frost	_____	2 wks. after last frost	_____	3 wks. after last frost	_____
Tomato	6 wks. before last frost	_____	2 wks. after last frost	_____	not recommended	_____
Turnip	not recommended	_____	not recommended	_____	4 wks. before last frost	_____
PERENNIAL VEGETABLES						
Artichoke	N/A	_____	2 wks. after last frost	_____	N/A	_____
Asparagus	N/A	_____	spring	_____	N/A	_____
Rhubarb	N/A	_____	spring or fall	_____	N/A	_____
ANNUAL HERBS						
Basil	4 wks. before last frost	_____	3 wks. after last frost	_____	3 wks. after last frost	_____
Cilantro	not recommended	_____	not recommended	_____	on last frost date	_____
Dill	not recommended	_____	not recommended	_____	2 wks. before last frost	_____
Parsley	8 wks. before last frost	_____	2 wks. before last frost	_____	2 wks. before last frost	_____

PLANTING DATES (continued)

PLANT	SOWING INDOORS (IF GROWING YOUR OWN TRANS-PLANTS)	MY DATE IS:	TRANSPLANT-ING OUTSIDE	MY DATE IS:	DIRECT-SEEDING OUTSIDE	MY DATE IS:
PERENNIAL HERBS						
Bay	N/A	_____	spring or fall	_____	N/A	_____
Chives	N/A	_____	spring or fall	_____	N/A	_____
Fennel, perennial	N/A	_____	spring or fall	_____	N/A	_____
Lavender	N/A	_____	spring or fall	_____	N/A	_____
Mint	N/A	_____	spring or fall	_____	N/A	_____
Oregano	N/A	_____	spring or fall	_____	N/A	_____
Rosemary	N/A	_____	spring or fall	_____	N/A	_____
Sage	N/A	_____	spring or fall	_____	N/A	_____
Thyme	N/A	_____	spring or fall	_____	N/A	_____
FLOWERS						
Alyssum	N/A	_____	N/A	_____	on last frost date	_____
Bachelor's button	4 wks. before last frost	_____	on last frost date	_____	on last frost date	_____
Borage	4 wks. before last frost	_____	on last frost date	_____	on last frost date	_____
Calendula	8 wks. before last frost	_____	2 wks. before last frost	_____	2 wks. before last frost	_____
Cosmos	4 wks. before last frost	_____	on last frost date	_____	on last frost date	_____
Carnation	6 wks. before last frost	_____	on last frost date	_____	on last frost date	_____
Marigold	4 wks. before last frost	_____	on last frost date	_____	on last frost date	_____
Nasturtium	4 wks. before last frost	_____	on last frost date	_____	on last frost date	_____
Pansy, viola	4–6 wks. before last frost	_____	on last frost date or 6 wks. before first frost	_____	on last frost date	_____
Sunflower	4 wks. before last frost	_____	on last frost date	_____	on last frost date	_____

CROP SIZING, SPACING, AND SCHEDULING

To prevent your garden from becoming a crowded, unproductive snarl, you need to know the growth habits of each of your crops before you plan your garden layout. Use this chart to determine each crop's height, desired spacing, and length of time it will be in the ground in a given season.

CROP SIZE, SPACING, AND SCHEDULING

CROPS	GROWTH FORM	SPACING	SCHEDULING
ANNUAL VEGETABLES			
Arugula	short	5–8 plants per inch of row	short season
Bean, bush	short	4 in.	short season
Bean, pole	tall	6 in.	long season
Bean, broad or fava	medium	6 in.	half season
Beet	short	4 in.	half season
Bok choy	short	6–12 in.	short season
Broccoli	medium	12 in.	half season
Brussels sprouts	medium	18 in.	long season
Cabbage	medium	12 in.	half season
Carrot	short	1 in.	half season
Cauliflower	medium	12 in.	half season
Celeriac	short	12 in.	long season
Celery	medium	12 in.	long season
Chard	medium	12 in.	half season
Collards	medium	12 in.	half season
Corn	tall	12 in.	long season
Cucumber, sprawling	sprawling	2 ft.	long season
Cucumber, trellised	tall	18 in.	long season
Eggplant	medium	12 in.	long season
Fennel, annual	short	6 in.	half season
Garlic	short	6 in.	long season (Oct.–June)
Kale	medium	12 in.	half season
Kohlrabi	short	4 in.	half season

CROPS	GROWTH FORM	SPACING	SCHEDULING
Leek	short	6 in.	long season
Lettuce	short	8 in.	short season
Melons	sprawling	3–4 ft.	long season
Onion	short	6 in.	long season
Peas, shell	medium	2 in.	half season
Peas, snap	tall	2 in.	half season
Peppers, hot and sweet	medium	12 in.	long season
Potato	short	12 in.	long season
Pumpkin	sprawling	2–3 ft.	long season
Radish	short	1 in.	short season
Rutabaga	short	4 in.	half season
Scallions	short	3 in.	short season
Spinach	short	4 in.	short season
Squash, summer	sprawling	2 ft.	half season
Squash, winter	sprawling	3–4 ft.	long season
Tomato	tall	18 in.	long season
Turnip	short	4 in.	short season
PERENNIAL VEGETABLES			
Artichoke	tall	4 ft.	perennial
Asparagus	tall	18 in.	perennial
Rhubarb	medium	3–4 ft.	perennial
ANNUAL HERBS			
Basil	short	6 in.	half season
Cilantro	short	1 in.	short season
Dill	medium	12 in.	half season
Parsley	short	8 in.	long season
PERENNIAL HERBS			
Bay	tall (in mild climates)	variable	perennial
Chives	short	8 in.	perennial
Fennel, perennial	tall	3 ft.	perennial
Lavender	medium	2–3 ft.	perennial

CROP SIZE, SPACING, AND SCHEDULING (continued)

CROPS	GROWTH FORM	SPACING	SCHEDULING
Mint	short, sprawling	18 in.	perennial
Oregano	short, sprawling	12 in.	perennial
Rosemary	medium	18–24 in.	perennial
Sage	medium	2–3 ft.	perennial
Thyme	short, sprawling	18–24 in.	perennial
FLOWERS			
Alyssum	short	variable	long season
Bachelor's button	medium	8 in.	short season
Borage	medium	18 in.	short season
Calendula	medium	variable	short season
Carnation	medium	12 in.	half season
Cosmos	medium–tall	18 in.	long season
Marigold	short	4–8 in.	half season
Nasturtium	sprawling	variable	short season
Pansy, viola	short	4 in.	long season
Sunflower	tall	12–18 in.	half season

FERTILIZATION

Providing your crops with the nutrients they need is crucial for good production. This chart details when to apply organic fertilizer for different vegetables.

FERTILIZATION

CROPS	FERTILIZE BEFORE PLANTING?	SUPPLEMENTAL FEEDING?
ANNUAL VEGETABLES		
Arugula	yes	no
Beans, bush	yes	no
Beans, pole	yes	no
Beans, broad	yes	no
Beets	yes	3 wks. after planting
Bok choy	yes	no
Broccoli	yes	3 & 6 wks. after planting
Brussels sprouts	yes	3 & 6 wks. after planting
Cabbage	yes	3 & 6 wks. after planting
Carrots	yes	no
Cauliflower	yes	3 & 6 wks. after planting
Celeriac	yes	3 & 6 wks. after planting
Celery	yes	3 & 6 wks. after planting
Chard	yes	no
Collards	yes	no
Corn	yes	3 & 6 wks. after planting
Cucumber, sprawling	yes	3 & 6 wks. after planting
Cucumber, trellised	yes	3 & 6 wks. after planting
Eggplant	yes	3 & 6 wks. after planting
Fennel, annual	yes	3 & 6 wks. after planting
Garlic	yes	in the spring
Kale	yes	no
Kohlrabi	yes	no
Leeks	yes	3 wks. after planting
Lettuce	yes	no

FERTILIZATION (continued)

CROPS	FERTILIZE BEFORE PLANTING?	SUPPLEMENTAL FEEDING?
Melons	yes	3 & 6 wks. after planting
Onions	yes	3 wks. after planting
Peas, shell	yes	no
Peas, snap	yes	no
Peppers, hot and sweet	yes	3 & 6 wks. after planting
Potatoes	yes	3 & 6 wks. after planting
Pumpkin	yes	3 & 6 wks. after planting
Radishes	yes	no
Rutabagas	yes	no
Scallions	yes	no
Spinach	yes	no
Squash, summer	yes	3 wks. after planting
Squash, winter	yes	3 & 6 wks. after planting
Tomatoes	yes	3 & 6 wks. after planting
Turnips	yes	no
ANNUAL HERBS		
Basil	yes	no
Cilantro	yes	no
Dill	yes	no
Parsley	yes	no
PERENNIALS		

All perennials discussed in this book should be fertilized at planting time and every spring but shouldn't require additional fertilization.

FLOWERS

All flowers discussed in this book should be fertilized at planting time but shouldn't require additional fertilization.

RESOURCES

SOIL TESTING

Many universities have soil-testing laboratories. If you prefer to use a lab in your region, search your regional universities' websites. Below are some we recommend.

Colorado State University
Soil, Water & Plant Testing Lab
Campus Delivery 1120
NESB Room A319
Fort Collins CO 80523-1120
phone: (970) 491-5061
fax: (970) 491-2930
www.soiltestinglab.colostate.edu

University of Connecticut
Soil Nutrient Analysis Laboratory
6 Sherman Place, U-5102
University of Connecticut
Storrs, CT 06269-5102
phone: (860) 486-4274
fax: (860) 486-4562
email: soiltest@uconn.edu
www.soiltest.uconn.edu/index.php

University of Massachusetts
Soil and Plant Tissue Testing Lab
West Experiment Station
682 North Pleasant Street
University of Massachusetts
Amherst, MA 01003
phone: (413) 545-2311
fax: (413) 545-1931
email: soiltest@psis.umass.edu
www.umass.edu/soiltest

HOME TEST KITS FOR ARSENIC

Industrial Test Systems, Inc.
1875 Langston Street
Rock Hill, SC 29730
phone: (800) 861-9712
www.sensafe.com/arsenictests

SEED SUPPLIERS

Baker Creek Heirloom Seeds
2278 Baker Creek Road
Mansfield, MO 65704
phone: (417) 924-8917
fax: (417) 924-8887
email: seeds@rareseeds.com
www.rareseeds.com

Fedco Seeds
PO Box 520
Waterville, ME 04903
phone: (207) 873-7333,
(207) 430-1106
www.fedcoseeds.com

High Mowing Organic Seeds
76 Quarry Road
Wolcott, VT 05680
phone: (802) 472-6174
fax: (802) 472-3201
www.highmowingseeds.com

Johnny's Selected Seeds
955 Benton Avenue
Winslow, ME 04901
phone: (877) 564-6697
www.johnnyseeds.com

Seed Savers Exchange
3094 North Winn Road
Decorah, Iowa 52101
phone: (563) 382-5990
fax (orders): (563) 382-6511
fax (general): (563) 382-5872
www.seedsavers.org

Territorial Seed Company
PO Box 158
Cottage Grove, OR 97424
phone (orders): (800) 626-0866
phone (customer service/gardening questions): (541) 942-9547, (800) 626-0866
fax (orders): (888) 657-3131
www.territorialseed.com

TOOLS, MATERIALS, ESSENTIAL SUPPLIES

Almost any local or big-box hardware store will carry almost all the tools you need, but we also like these mail-order and online sources:

Corona
22440 Temescal Canyon Road
Corona, CA 92883
phone: (800) 234-2547
www.coronatoolsusa.com

Felco Tools
The manufacturer of these fine tools is located in Switzerland, but you can buy them locally at nurseries or hardware stores, or online in the United States at www.felcostore.com.

For tools plus raised-bed kits, hoop house materials, floating row cover, etc.:

FarmTek
1440 Field of Dreams Way
Dyersville, IA 52040
phone: (800) 245-9881
phone: (800) 457-8887
www.farmtek.com/farm/supplies/home

Orcaboard Recycled Plastic Beds
available from Durable Plastic Design, LLC
17725 NE 65th Street, A-100
Redmond, WA 98052
phone: (425) 883-2570
fax: 425-885-0628
www.orcaboard.com

Peaceful Valley Farm Supply
PO Box 2209, 125 Clydesdale Court
Grass Valley, CA 95945
phone: (888) 784-1722
www.groworganic.com

For self-watering container inserts and other garden supplies:

Gardener's Supply Company
128 Intervale Road
Burlington, VT 05401
phone: (888) 833-1412
www.gardeners.com

IRRIGATION SUPPLIES

Drip irrigation supplies may be available at local and big-box hardware stores, or try these sources:

The Drip Store
(West Coast)
980 Park Center, Suite E
Vista, CA 92081
phone: (877) 597-1669
fax: (760) 597-1673
(East Coast)
160 Highway 70 West
Havelock, NC 28532
phone: (877) 858-4015
fax: (252) 463-3501
www.dripirrigation.com/drip_irrigation_categories/45

Dripworks
190 Sanhedrin Circle
Willits, CA 95490
phone: (800) 522-3747
www.dripworksusa.com

WOOD TREATMENTS

BioWash
available from Down to Earth Products
3541 Struble Road, Suite 100
Cincinnati, OH 45251-4947
phone (513) 245-2420
www.dtep-archive.com/ndoapp.htm

LifeTime
available from Valhalla Wood Preservatives Ltd.
Box 70, Site #2
RR #1
New Denver, BC, V0G 1S0, Canada
phone: (250) 368-2661
fax: (250) 358-2662
www.valhalco.com
(may also be available at some Ace Hardware stores)

PEST- AND DISEASE-MANAGEMENT SUPPLIES

Here are some online sources for beneficial nematodes, organic insecticides, and beneficial insects:

Arbico Organics
PO Box 8910
Tucson, AZ 85738
phone: (800) 827-2847
www.arbico-organics.com

Planet Natural
1612 Gold Avenue
Bozeman, MT 59715
phone: (406) 587-5891
fax: (406) 587-0223
www.planetnatural.com

GARDEN GIVING

Plant a Row for the Hungry is a program that encourages home gardeners to plant a little extra, to help feed America's hungry. For information, visit: www.gardenwriters.org/gwa .php?p=par/index.html.

If you're interested in donating produce from your garden to those in need, contact your local food bank to see what types of produce they accept.

MORE ABOUT US HARDINESS ZONES

The United States National Arboretum: www.usna.usda.gov /Hardzone/ushzmap.html

FURTHER READING

The following books, grouped by specialty, provide valuable additional information on every aspect of home gardening.

GENERAL VEGETABLE- MANAGEMENT RESOURCES

Four-Season Harvest: Organic Vegetables from Your Home Garden All Year Long by Eliot Coleman and Barbara Damrosch (White River Jct., VT: Chelsea Green, 1999)

Growing Great Garlic: The Definitive Guide for Organic Gardeners and Small Farmers by Ron Engeland (Okanogan, WA: Filaree, 1991)

The New Organic Grower: A Master's Manual of Tools and Techniques for the Home and Market Gardener by Eliot Coleman (White River Jct., VT: Chelsea Green, 1995)

The Winter Harvest Handbook: Year-Round Vegetable Production Using Deep-Organic Techniques and Unheated Greenhouses by Eliot Coleman (White River Jct., VT: Chelsea Green, 2009)

PERENNIAL HERBS

Ball Perennial Manual: Propagation and Production by Jim Nau (Greeneville, OH: Ball Publishing, 1996)

Your Backyard Herb Garden: A Gardener's Guide to Growing Over 50 Herbs Plus How to Use Them in Cooking, Crafts, Companion Planting and More by Miranda Smith (Emmaus, PA: Rodale, 1999)

COMPOSTING

Easy Composters You Can Build by Nick Noyes (North Adams, MA: Storey Publishing, 1995)

The Rodale Guide to Composting: Easy Methods for Every Gardener by Jerry Minnich and Marjorie Hunt (Emmaus, PA: Rodale, 1979)

Worms Eat My Garbage: How to Set Up and Maintain a Worm Composting System by Mary Appelhof (Kalamazoo, MI: Flower Press, 2006)

COVER CROPS

Cover Crop Gardening: Soil Enrichment with Green Manures. Storey's Country Wisdom Bulletin A-05, by Storey Publishing (North Adams, MA: Storey Publishing, 1983)

Managing Cover Crops Profitably by SARE Outreach and Andy Clark (College Park, MD: SARE Outreach, 2007)

IRRIGATION

Drip Irrigation for Every Landscape and All Climates by Robert Kourik (Occidental, CA: Metamorphic Press, 2009)

BERRIES AND FRUIT TREES

The Backyard Berry Book by Stella Otto (Maple City, MI: Otto-graphics, 1995)

The Backyard Orchardist by Stella Otto (Maple City, MI: Otto-graphics, 1995)

Designing and Maintaining Your Edible Landscape Naturally by Robert Kourik (East Meon, Hampshire, UK: Permanent Publications, 2005)

From Tree to Table: Growing Backyard Fruit Trees in the Pacific Maritime Climate by Barbara Edwards and Mary Olivella (Seattle: Skipstone, 2011)

The Pruning Book by Lee Reich (Newtown, CT: Taunton Press, 2010)

COOKING SEASONALLY, FOOD PRESERVATION

Ball Blue Book Guide to Preserving by Altrista Consumer Products (Cloquet, MN: Altrista Consumer Products, 2004)

From Asparagus to Zucchini: A Guide to Cooking Farm-Fresh Seasonal Produce by Madison Area Community Supported Agriculture Coalition (Madison, WI: MACSAC, 2004)

Putting Food By by Ruth Hertzberg, Janet Greene, and Beatrice Vaughan (NY: Plume, 2010)

Simply in Season by Mary Beth Lind and Cathleen Hockman-Wert (Harrisonburg, VA: Herald Press, 2009)

Urban Pantry: Tips & Recipes for a Thrifty, Sustainable & Seasonal Kitchen by Amy Pennington (Seattle: Skipstone, 2010)

PESTS AND DISEASES

American Horticultural Society Pests and Diseases: The Complete Guide to Preventing, Identifying and Treating Plant Problems by Pippa Greenwood, Andrew Halstead, A. R. Chase, and Daniel Gilrein (NY: DK Adult, 2000)

Bugs, Slugs, and Other Thugs: Controlling Garden Pests Organically by Rhonda Massingham Hart (North Adams, MA: Storey Publishing, 1991)

MISCELLANEOUS

Fences and Retaining Walls by William McElroy (Carlsbad, CA: Craftsman, 1990)

Walks, Walls & Patio Floors: Build with Brick, Stone, Pavers, Concrete, Tile and More by the Editors of Sunset Books (Birmingham, AL: Oxmoor House, 2008)

ACKNOWLEDGMENTS

This book would not have been possible without the tireless work of Devin McCrate.

Thanks to all of our friends and family who have supported us in making SUFCo a reality, especially Ryan McCrate; Suzanne and Jeff Halm; Emily and Ben Jenkins; Tom and Marilyn McCrate; Ann McCrate; Kerry McCrate; the Dahl family; Dave Hughes; Chad Hueter; Erika Kercher; Julie, Mike, Elliott, and Wyatt O'Brien; and Samantha Farbman.

A big thank-you to all the farmers out there who are teaching their skills to new growers, especially Paul Etheridge, Tim and Beth Knorr, Ben and Lisa Sippel, Roy and Hope Brubaker, and Peter and Anne Webber.

A huge shout-out to past and present SUFCo crew for inspiring us and keeping us in line: Thanks, Anna, Benn, Bru, Curran, Chelsea, John, Melissa, and Myra. And thanks to all past, present, and future Seattle Urban Farm Company clients; without you we wouldn't have anything to do.

INDEX

ABOUT THE AUTHORS

Brad Halm and Colin McCrate...a few years ago!

COLIN MCCRATE

Inspired by the writings of small-scale organic farmers such as Wendell Berry, Eliot Coleman, David Kline, and Gene Logsdon, Colin has been growing food since the late 1990s. He developed his unique set of backyard farming skills by working on organic production farms, teaching garden-based environmental education, and managing residential landscapes. He believes, in addition to the numerous, quantifiable benefits of local food production (better-tasting food, reduced carbon emissions, community building), that growing food is a worthy endeavor simply because it makes people happier. When he is not farming, Colin is usually talking about farming and/or drinking beer.

BRAD HALM

Brad got his start growing food in college in a small vegetable garden at The Homestead, an experiential living center at Denison University. His interest piqued, he went on to apprentice on organic farms at Stratford and Crown Point Ecology Centers in Ohio. A few seasons of farming brought him to the realization that growing food would be his life's vocation. After serving as the CSA manager at Village Acres Farm in Pennsylvania for several years, Brad moved to Seattle, where he has been helping people build and care for their urban farms ever since. On weekends, Brad keeps busy teaching classes on organic gardening and urban chicken care and learning Jethro Tull songs on the guitar.

SEATTLE URBAN FARM CO.

Colin and Brad are the owners of Seattle Urban Farm Company (SUFCo), a business that designs, builds, and maintains edible gardens. Founded in 2007, SUFCo has built hundreds of urban farms for homeowners, schools, restaurants, and other organizations. The company's work has won gold and silver awards at the prestigious Northwest Flower & Garden Show and has been profiled in several books including *Reclaiming Our Food* and *Carrot City*. SUFCo's innovative approach to agriculture has been featured in a wide range of media outlets including *GQ, Sunset, Newsweek, Outside* magazine, Grist.org, Slate.com, *Seattle* magazine, *The Seattle Times, Growing a Greener World,* and the Daily Candy.

HILARY DAHL

Hilary Dahl is a freelance photographer based out of Seattle. Her photography explores various built and natural environments and how they shape the human experience. She works with Seattle Urban Farm Company designing, installing, maintaining, and photographing edible landscapes. More of her photography can be found at hilarydahlphotography.com.

JOIN THE BACKYARD SUSTAINABILITY REVOLUTION WITH THESE OTHER TITLES FROM SKIPSTONE!

The Urban Farm Handbook: City-Slicker Resources for Growing, Raising, Sourcing, Trading, and Preparing What You Eat
Annette Cottrell, Joshua McNichols; Photography by Harley Soltes
An intensive primer for city-dwellers on how to opt out of the industrial food system, one step at a time.

From Tree to Table: Growing Backyard Fruit Trees in the Pacific Maritime Climate
Barbara Edwards, Mary Olivella
Plant and share fruit with this easy-to-use guide to growing in our sun-challenged region.

Edible Heirlooms: Heritage Vegetables for the Maritime Garden
Bill Thorness; Illustrations by Susie Thorness
The West Coast gardener's guide to growing and saving heirloom veggies.

Urban Pantry: Tips & Recipes for a Thrifty, Sustainable & Seasonal Kitchen
Amy Pennington; Photography by Della Chen
A modern, sustainable approach to stocking and cooking in an efficient kitchen.

Chefs on the Farm: Recipes and Inspiration from the Quillisascut Farm School of the Domestic Arts
Shannon Borg, Lora Lea Misterly, Karen Jurgensen; Photography by Harley Soltes
A visually rich tour of an organic farm, where award-winning chefs learn sustainable food practices.

SKIPSTONE

www.skipstonebooks.org
www.mountaineersbooks.org